FINALLY GETTING IT RIGHT

From Addictive Love to the Real Thing

HOWARD M. HALPERN, Ph.D.

BANTAM BOOKS

NEW YORK • TORONTO • LONDON • SYDNEY • AUCKLAND

FINALLY GETTING IT RIGHT:
From Addictive Love to the Real Thing
A Bantam Book / June 1994

Library of Congress Cataloging-in-Publication Data
Halpern, Howard Marvin, 1929–
    Finally getting it right : from addictive love to the real thing /
by Howard Halpern.
        p.   cm.
    ISBN 0-553-09003-8
    1. Relationship addiction.   2. Love.   I. Title.
RC552.R44H35   1994
816.86–dc20   93-47594
                                                            CIP

Published simultaneously in the United States and Canada

PRINTED IN THE UNITED STATES OF AMERICA
BVG   0   9   8   7   6   5   4   3   2   1

CONTENTS

INTRODUCTION

This book grew out of my psychotherapeutic work with people who tended to get into unfulfilling and frustrating romantic relationships. Often these men and women were tenaciously holding on to partners who were either unloving, unavailable, commitment-avoiding, immature, and emotionally impaired or outright mean and abusive. They consulted me because they had a sense of recognition and resonance with the ideas I had presented in my earlier book, *How to Break Your Addiction to a Person.* In therapy they struggled to understand and end their destructive patterns. After a while, it became apparent that ending their addictive relationship was only a part—sometimes the easiest part—of the process of forming a satisfying love relationship. All too often, they discovered that formidable psychological barriers still stood in the way of their attaining that goal. Together, we learned a great deal about the internal changes that have to take place if that goal is to be achieved.

Not everyone who consulted me, however, was in the throes of addictive relationship. To my surprise, some told me, "I read your book on how to *break* an addiction to someone because I thought maybe I'd find clues on how to *make* an addictive relationship. My problem is that I just can't seem to fall in love with anyone, or if I do, it is very brief and intense and then I seem to lose interest. When I read about those lovesick people in your book, I envied them! I would like to experience sustained feelings of love and to be able to make a commitment but it doesn't happen." I learned much from these people, too, so I have also addressed this book not only to those who tend to get obsessively involved with someone bad for them but also to those who have difficulty forming a lasting romantic relationship with anyone.

Whether you have tended to get caught up in frustrating and painful relationships that go nowhere or do not get into emotionally compelling involvements at all, *Finally Getting It Right* is aimed at helping you to explore why you deprive yourself of something so fundamentally desired and to make the changes necessary to find, nurture, and maintain a fulfilling love relationship.

1

You Can Get There From Here

There is more to making a good romantic relationship than getting out of a bad one, as important a step as that is. Kim was learning this, and she felt discouraged and demoralized. "I know I've come a long way," she said, "so how come I feel that I'm nowhere?"

I'd heard this question so often from my patients at a point in their lives and their psychotherapy where they had made considerable progress that I was not taken aback by it. I waited for Kim to continue.

"I've accomplished a lot," she said. "I was able to end that awful relationship with Kevin, and I'm certainly happy about that. I've mostly gotten over missing him and longing for him, and that feels like a wonderful achievement. I've even reached the point where I'm no longer attached to the Kevin kind of men who I used to go crazy over and who make me miserable. I have a clear idea of the kind of man who would be good for me—and I definitely feel I deserve someone like that."

"So?"

"The trouble is, *I can't feel attracted to the kind of guy I know*

1

would be right for me! There's just no chemistry, no excitement. I find them boring! I wonder if I wasn't better off with men who made me miserable, because at least they made me feel alive! Even that suffering I went through with Kevin and the others had more life to it than the wasteland I seem to be living in now. I'm afraid I'll never again feel the old intensity. I'm terrified that I'll never experience being in love again. And then what do I do? Just settle for someone I feel no passion for in order not to be alone?''

I could sympathize with what Kim was feeling, but I was not worried for her. I knew that this seemingly lifeless limbo in which she now found herself was a common, even predictable plateau on the journey from unhappy romantic addictions to a satisfying—and exciting—love relationship. While I could not guarantee Kim would achieve such a relationship, I had guided many others along the route she was traveling on, and I could see from how far she had come that it was likely that she would get to where she wanted to go. If you travel the route from destructive romantic addiction to fulfilling love, then you, like Kim, are likely to go through three specific, recognizable phases:

Phase One: Ending your current bad relationship (if you are still in it). Ask yourself if there is a realistic chance of making it a satisfying love relationship. If you know that it is not likely to substantially improve and yet you find yourself stuck ("I'm miserable and I know I should end it but I just can't leave"), then you will have to recognize that you are probably addicted to that person (or to being in an unhappy relationship), and to begin taking the steps necessary to break your addiction. Your journey will begin with that recognition and will lead you to face many questions: What do I get out of this painful addiction? What do I hope to get from this relationship? Why have I latched on to this particular person? How must I change my way of thinking and my longings so I can free myself from this unhappy, no-win involvement? Phase One can be very agonizing and often requires considerable courage. (Chapter 4 will deal more specifically with steps you can take to break romantic addictions.)

Phase Two: Ending your tendency to get involved with people who are bad for you. You might learn so much from the experience of ending your addictive relationship—from the pain, from understanding what it was about, from the relief of ending the misery, and from the increased self-confidence that came from being able to do it—that you are strengthened and immunized against ever again getting into a hurtful involvement. As Kim said once she got over the painful withdrawal symptoms that followed her breakup with Kevin, "I learned my lesson. From now on I want only relationships that feel good." If that is your experience, great! But it does not always go that way. I've seen many people successfully terminate a bad relationship only to get involved in a similar unhappy or self-demeaning bond with someone else. Nothing changed except the name of the latest source of their misery—the addiction was as irresistible as ever. To change the pattern itself you will have to get to know

how it works, where it comes from, and how to recognize and avoid getting involved with someone who is likely to be bad for you.

Phase Three: Getting attracted to and involved with someone who is good for you. Ending a bad relationship and even your tendency to get involved in such relationships may not be enough to move you toward a good relationship. Daniel, a twenty-nine-year-old science teacher, told me, disheartened, "I am now allergic to the kind of woman I used to be attracted to and who made my life a living hell, but now I am attracted to no one. I feel in limbo." And Laura, a thirty-four-year-old lawyer, said, "I'm finally nauseated by the kind of self-centered charmer who used to turn me on, and I'm thankful for that. I wasted enough tears and years. But I still find a man who could offer me a good and solid relationship about as exciting as tofu."

Excitement and passion are important ingredients of a fulfilling love relationship. A relationship based only on feelings of caring, friendship, and devotion can be warm and constructive. But, without passion, it will lack the intensity and aliveness that makes romantic love so special and powerful. There will often be an underlying deadness, a persistent sense of something missing that goes deeper than the expected lulls that occur at times as even a very passionate relationship becomes more routine. So when someone says, "He is nice but I just don't feel in love with him," we understand that she cannot force a feeling of being in love and that without it she may well decide that the relationship is not enough. But many people cannot fall in love with a particular person *precisely because* that person is good for them, or good to them, or available, or considerate, or loving.

When I work in psychotherapy with people who seem to have this problem, they often deny that they do. They tell me that all the people who are nice to them and want a committed relationship just happen to be boring, unattractive, and unappealing—a comment that seems to go against the law of averages and against all reason. Frequently, they become aware of how they disqualify those who would be good for them only when such a person becomes rejecting or interested in somebody else and suddenly seems terribly exciting!

If you suspect that you are unable to be attracted to someone simply because he or she might be good for you, you'll have to determine what that block is all about and what steps you can take so that you can find both romance and contentment in your next relationship.

PREDICTABLE PASSAGES

The three general phases of your journey to a fulfilling relationship can be divided into ten distinct passages you are likely to encounter. Knowing what these passages are will help you prepare for them and will enable you to mark your progress. Here is a summary of the passages. Can you identify the ones that you have navigated successfully and those where you are stuck?

1. You will end, probably with much difficulty, the addictive relationship that needed to be ended.

2. You will react to ending it with a period of pain, mourning, and longing to reconnect, but over time these feelings will lessen.

3. You will discover, with dismay, that you are still attracted to people who offer you similarly unfulfilling or destructive relationships.

4. You will come to understand how your history and your needs have programmed you to be drawn to such negative relationships.

5. You will decide to deliberately stop yourself from getting involved with people who offer you unfulfilling or destructive relationships, even though you are still attracted to them.

6. You will undergo an inner shift so that you will no longer be attracted to people who offer you such negative relationships—in fact, you may even be repelled by them.

7. You will deliberately make an effort to get to know people who are more appropriate and available for a fulfilling love relationship.

8. You will discover (or rediscover) that those people who would be good for you do not turn you on, excite you, or make you feel very involved with them.

9. You will come to see, in your history and in your needs, the reasons that you have not been attracted to people who are probably good candidates for a love relationship.

10. You will make further inner shifts that enable you to find a new basis for attraction and make you ready, willing, and able to be in a fulfilling love relationship.

When Kim complained she'd felt more alive when she had been with men who made her miserable, she was at Passage 8, a frustrating and discouraging point. As we proceed, we will see how Kim traversed the earlier passages that brought her to that point. We will examine how Kim and others then negotiated the tricky and often agonizing passages that led them from that love-less landscape to a good love relationship. We will see what we can glean from their experiences that will help you in your quest. But first we will look more closely at the goal: What is this "good love relationship" that you are seeking? How does it differ from where you have been? Is it really worth going through all these painful phases and passages in order to read it? To begin exploring this we will first jump ahead in time to a therapy session when it became happily clear that Kim had come to that long-sought final passage.

2

LOVE IS A MANY SPLENDORED THING

Kim sat down in the chair opposite mine as she had done so many times in the nearly three years since she began psychotherapy with me. She looked radiant and content, quite unlike the desperate, lost thirty-two-year-old who who had told me in a choked voice of her painful relationship with Kevin. Now there was energy in her words and even in the way she sat as she announced, "I'm so in love with David." Then, still with a touch of wonder, "And he's in love with me."

There was a long silence, bridged and made comfortable by her smile. "It's not like the other times," she said.

"I know."

"I finally got it right. I finally have a love relationship. And it's wonderful."

We were both smiling now, savoring her achievement. After two grueling and disastrous romantic entanglements (the one with Kevin and a previous one that had gone on for several years), after enumerable empty and disappointing brief encounters, after many demoralizing dry spells when it seemed to her that falling in love would be forever beyond her reach, after intensive psychotherapy that was often hard and frustrating—Kim had now attained one of life's incomparable treasures, a good love relationship.

While not everyone would agree with the high value Kim and I placed on her attaining a good love relationship, I believe that most people would. It seems pretty clear that those who do not have such a relationship usually want it and seek it in many different ways. Those who have just found it, like Kim and David, are joyful and delighted. Those who have had such a relationship and lost it grieve its ending. Those who are in a long-standing good relationship count themselves among the fortunate, and—whether they attribute it to luck, to their wisdom in choosing a partner, their ability to do what is needed to make love work, or to their partner's loving tolerance—they rarely take it for granted. When they see among their friends or relatives an angry, embittered, loveless couple or meet someone who is alone and ever searching for a love that eludes them, they may quietly squeeze each other's hand in appreciation and gratitude.

Recent societal developments have at times seemed to call into question the value of love relationships. Early feminist slogans such as "A woman needs a man like a fish needs a bicycle" attempted to counter the tendency of too many women to allow themselves to be so economically and emotionally dependent on men as to severely impair their autonomy and self-respect and sometimes lead them to accept abuse and exploitation. The women's movement has had an enormous positive impact; it has changed, hopefully forever, the way men and women see themselves and each other. But even the best of ideas, like the best of technology, can be misused. For some women, this healthy counterdependent stance became a rationale to avoid dealing with fears of intimacy, problems in relating, or unwillingness to risk getting rejected or making bad choices. For some who had been disappointed or hurt by romantic relationships, it could provide support for a "sour grapes" reaction ("Who needs it, it's more trouble and pain than it's worth") or even provide a reason for not sallying forth into that dangerous terrain again.

The beginning of the feminist awakening coincided with the

sexual revolution and the *Playboy* emphasis on a self-indulgent bachelor life. Men could have their sexual needs satisfied by desirable and interesting women without getting "tied down" and making commitments. There seemed no good reason to lock oneself into permanency and responsibility. For many men this position provided an excuse for not dealing with their difficulties in relating intimately and not looking at their fears that permitting their dependency needs to emerge would lead to their being engulfed, enslaved, or rejected. It also gave many men a rationale for not growing up and stretching themselves beyond their narrow self-interest.

Another development that gave love relationships a bum rap was the growing awareness, fostered by books and twelve-step programs, of the very real dangers of codependency. That we could become dependent on other people to the point of addiction was an important, even ground-breaking idea. However, it was misinterpreted by some to mean that wanting to have one's needs satisfied by the other person in a relationship or being concerned with that other person's needs was a sign of weakness and pathology. Many people became wary of any close and sustained involvement.

Despite all the red flags warning us of the dangers to our growth, independence, self-respect, and well-being, should we seek and enter into love relationships, most people still prize this quest, this goal, this achievement, this gift. Why? What does it hold for us? What is a love relationship, anyhow, and how does it differ from the feeling of being in love?

FALLING IN LOVE IS WONDERFUL

With David, Kim was having her first real love relationship, but it was certainly not the only time she had been in love. When she began psychotherapy with me, she knew it was in her best interest to leave her boyfriend Kevin but could not get herself to do it. She talked of incident after incident that made it clear that Kevin was usually unaffectionate and unreliable. What little caring he showed her was sporadic and superficial. He was often emotionally or actually unavailable and would become more inaccessible and even punishing if she asked for more shared time, closeness, or warmth. Her pre-Kevin world of varied interests and of intense satisfaction derived from her work as a magazine editor had diminished. She now looked at the world through a long tube with only Kevin at the other end. Her once curious and astute mind had narrowed to one question: How could she get Kevin to love her and want to be with her? When I asked her why she stayed with Kevin when the relationship made her so unhappy, her answer was immediate: "Because I love him."

I have heard this response from countless men and women who are in relationships that are causing them frustration, deprivation, anger, and pain. I have also heard it from people who are in relationships that add pleasure, happiness, and depth to their lives. If I asked Kim now why she stays with David, she might answer with the same words she used about Kevin: "Because I love him." But what a difference there would be in her tone, in her eyes, and even in the meaning of those words.

Being romantically in love is one of the most powerful experiences human beings can have. Although most people experience this emotional state at one time or another, it is special and unlike anything else. Psychologist Dorothy Tennov coined a word, *limerence*, to stand for that blissful state of walking on air and obsessively thinking about and longing to be with the loved one. When limerence is most intense, it is difficult to think about anything else or to see the loved one as anything but utterly wonderful. There is a longing for the other's love. Even in the most secure situation, there can be anxiety that the loved one's limerent feelings will change; less secure situations can lead to emotional torment.

This limerence, this feeling of romantic love, is found in poems and songs from around the world and from time immemorial. Some observers, it is true, see the state of being in love as stemming from immaturity, inadequacy, and even neurosis and as leading inevitably to problems. This view is expressed succinctly in the movie *Moonstruck* when Cher is telling her mother about her intention to marry. "Do you love him?" her mother asks. "No," Cher replies. "Good," her mother says. "When you love them, they drive you crazy."

My own view differs from this cynical one. I agree more with psychiatrist Ethel Person, who wrote:

> Romantic love remains one of the most worthwhile and transcendent human experiences, the fact that it serves as a magnet for psychopathology notwithstanding. Despite the general cautions of traditional wisdom and psychoanalytic theory, I am certain that romantic love is generally more enriching than it is depleting. It is a magnificent human condition.

Those who have been in love know that it is a glorious and heady feeling with enormous positive potential. It can increase our self-esteem, bring out the best in us, and make us feel that life is just wonderful. But we may have also discovered that it often leads us to be in relationships that diminish us and bring out the worst in us. By what sadistic alchemy does this heavenly feeling sometimes transform our lives into a living hell?

We can begin to explore this question by making a crucial distinction between two states of being that are often confused with each other: One is being in love; the other is being in a love relationship. The feeling of being in love (or in limerence) is usually a vital part of a love relationship but does not in itself make a love relationship or guarantee that a love relationship will come to exist. To paraphrase the old expression, "Limerence is not enough."

At one time, when people like Kim came to me in agony and told me that they are staying in an awful relationship because they were in love, I would challenge their use of the word to describe relationships that were distant, futile, destructive, demeaning, or outright abusive. "How can you call it love?" I would ask. "Love is not supposed to make you feel chronically miserable." But as I listened to them, there was no doubt that very often what they were subjectively feeling was indeed love. I could not challenge or dismiss an emotion that they experienced so intensely. So I began to approach the dilemma in a different way. Now, when someone tells me that he or she is involved in a frustrating, unfulfilling, or destructive relationship because he or she is in love, I say, "I believe you, and that's a powerful and wonderful feeling, *but the feeling of being in love does not mean that you are in a love relationship.*" I note that these are two different experiential states, which may at times happily overlap but often do not, because a love relationship has many characteristics that are not necessarily present every time there is a feeling of being in love. How can you differentiate between these two different basic human experiences?

CHARACTERISTICS OF A LOVE RELATIONSHIP

There are six areas in which you can see and almost measure the differences between the feelings of being in love and being in a love relationship.

1. A love relationship requires two people. The feeling of being in love requires only one. Nothing makes the distinction more clear than when someone "falls in love" with a movie star or rock star they have not even met. John Hinckley shot President Reagan because he was "in love" with Jodie Foster, a woman who didn't know of his existence. While this kind of "crush" is not common beyond adolescence, I recall Steven, an attorney, who was obsessed with Jennie, another attorney in his firm. Jennie was happily married and had no awareness of Steven's feelings, let alone similar feelings toward him. Steven found his obsession so painfully frustrating that eventually he had to leave the firm. I think also of Mia, who secretly felt so in love with her boss that she was unable to develop other relationships. Saddest of all, I know people who are in long relationships, even marriages, virtually by themselves.

Carla and Jack had been married for four years, but Carla was overcome with loneliness. "Everything I do seems bent on trying to get Jack to see who I am. I have no idea if he loves me." Jack told me, "I guess I must be in love with Carla. Otherwise, I wouldn't be there." But further discussion made it clear that he was out of touch with Carla's most basic concerns, fears, ambitions, and yearnings. He was also out of touch with his own need for and feelings about Carla.

2. A love relationship requires mutuality of feelings of caring and a commitment on the part of both people to try to make the relationship as satisfying and fulfilling as it can be. Feelings of being in love can keep someone attached to a person who they cannot or will not make a commitment to, or can keep someone attached to a person who will not make a commitment to them. Kim had grimly held on to feelings of being in love with Kevin despite evidence of his not caring much about her well-being and despite his not being able to commit himself to be with her much beyond the next few hours. I think also of Warren, a fashion photographer, who was in love with Diane, a model he met on the job. They had been seeing each other exclusively for three years, but she still reacted with anger, fear of suffocation, and withdrawal from him when he expressed wishes for closeness or affection or tried to make plans as a couple. Often, at such times, she would upset and enrage him by letting him know she had gone out for dinner with her previous boyfriend, "just to talk." There could be intense and passionate feelings between Kim and Kevin and between Warren and Diane, but the lack of mutual caring and commitment deprived them of enjoying the satisfactions of a love relationship. In fact, Kim, Warren, and many others have the bedeviling problem of being able to fall in love only with people who are not very loving to them or who cannot or will not make a commitment. This was the no-win scenario that Kim had to change before she could develop the kind of love relationship she now has with David.

3. A love relationship requires that both people be available to each other. Feelings of being in love may thrive on unavailability. This means that neither is married (as was Steven's beloved Jennie) or otherwise committed to someone else. Neither is so wrapped up in oneself (as was Kevin) or in work or other aspects of living as to be unable to give the relationship the time it needs for the development of intimacy and the growth of each partner. Neither is so dependent on drugs that alter or impair consciousness (such as alcohol, marijuana, or narcotics) as to be unable to be there with genuine and unsedated feelings, clear thoughts, and responsible actions. With drug dependency, one's accessibility as an authentic person is seriously compromised and real intimacy is near impossible. Likewise, if either person is addicted to some form of driven behavior, such as compulsive gambling or spending, it will be hard for that person to be available to fully share in building the relationship.

People vary greatly in how much time, closeness, and sharing they need in order to feel good about what they have with each other; some require a great deal of "togetherness," others much less. But for the nurturing of a love relationship, there must be a degree of accessibility that both partners find acceptable and gratifying.

In contrast, a feeling of being in love can exist toward someone who is committed elsewhere or is otherwise not emotionally available. In fact, for some people, the feeling of being in love can be intensified by the other person's elusiveness, inconstancy, and unavailability.

4. Those who have a good love relationship experience the joy and comfort of having a partner they can rely on to be there for them. They know they'll have the support that can ease life's trivial upsets and its Job-like tragedies. They know they'll receive smiles and applause for their small victories and their heroic triumphs. But those who have intense love feelings without being in a love relationship are deprived of the strength and security of a partner's constancy. When a columnist for Kim's magazine became ill and would not have her column ready for the next issue, Kim vented her worries to David in the "debriefing" they did with each other at the end of the work day and she felt lighter and less alone with them. When she received her promotion to editor, he responded with flowers and dinner at a fine restaurant. Contrast this with the fact that Kevin always seemed uninterested when Kim talked of her work and that when her father died suddenly and with devastating impact on Kim, Kevin went to the funeral service but not to the burial because he had to leave immediately for a week of skiing.

Unfortunately, there are many people whose feeling of being in love is amplified and intensified by not being able to rely on their partner. When they have good reason to distrust the other person, to be jealous, or to doubt the other person's caring, then they are driven to being even more obsessively involved in trying to make the other person be there for them in a way they can count on. They are tied to the other person with bonds of insecurity, and they mistake this tension for passion.

5. People in a love relationship often have many common goals, viewpoints, and interests, and these similarities enhance their closeness and joy in being with each other. But a feeling of love can exist toward someone whose personality, needs, outlook, and direction are so different from one's own that a love relationship is impossible. This sometimes happens when a powerful attraction blinds people to the fact that they have nothing in common. It often happens when "opposites attract," as when a highly emotional, impulsive, and flighty person, seeking more stability and boundaries, is attracted to someone compulsive, rigid, and reli-

able, who in turn, entranced by the other's spontaneity, is hoping to learn how to fly. As the song "Send in the Clowns" sadly says, "Me here alone on the ground, you in midair." When this difference is not extreme, it can actually add a delightful element to a love relationship and bring into the life of each partner some of the benefits that come with the personality of the other. This is particularly true if there is enough caring so that those differences that are not actually enjoyed will at least be tolerated. When the differences are too great, however, then prolonged interaction is likely to erode the feeling of being in love, no matter how romantic it once was. On the other hand, when the lovers find in each other qualities that they like best in themselves, they experience an affectionate bond of warm familiarity in that recognition.

6. A love relationship can help people to feel good about themselves, good about their partner, and good about life. It can make them more energetic and optimistic and can enhance their physical well-being. Certainly, a feeling of being in love can also initially make people feel wonderful, but when there is no love relationship, it will, sooner or later, make people feel bad about themselves, the other person, and life. It can make them feel drained, pessimistic, preoccupied, depressed, and demoralized. It can even make them subject to all manner of physical complaints and illnesses.

When Kim consulted me in a frenzy over her relationship with Kevin, her eating was out of control. Whenever Kevin would withdraw or disappear she would devour the contents of her refrigerator to its walls. Then she would become terrified that her increased weight would cause Kevin to reject her for good, so she would starve and purge herself. She began to get flutterings in her chest, which were diagnosed as cardiac arrhythmias or "palpitations." Kim's work also suffered; although her job was never in jeopardy, she lost her creativity and her efforts became uninspired. After Kim ended her relationship and went through a painful period of depression and loneliness, she began to widen her world again and to find the old pleasure and excitement in her work. When she began her richly fulfilling relationship with David, she was even more productive and original on the job, her weight stabilized, and those disconcerting flutterings in her chest mostly vanished.

The contentment that Kim found with David illustrates the fact that a good love relationship can give us a sense of inner peace, of being at home with ourselves and the world, of well-being and joy. These feelings will likely be strongest if we have in ourselves come a long way toward achieving them, but there is no doubt that being in a good love relationship will help us to develop them more fully.

I LOVE YOU AND YOU LOVE ME

There are many needs, longings, and desires that a love relationship can fulfill. These come from many levels of our history and still exist in us no matter what our age. The infant in us wants to be securely held and caressed and nurtured. The child in us wants to play and be adored and be admired for all we do and are. The adolescent in us wants to be told and shown that we are attractive, strong, desirable, and altogether wonderful. The adult we are wants all of this and wants a partner who is a special, devoted, romantic, and capable sharer of our life's journey. Sensual and sexual feelings from our child, adolescent, and adult selves yearn to be gratified in a context of caring and safety. But the overarching reason for love's universal appeal and pricelessness is our deep longing that there be someone in this world for whom we come first. Ethel Person puts it this way: "Being the most important person in someone else's life is one of the defining premises of passionate love." She reminds us that "aside from brief moments in infancy and childhood (when we may not even be aware of it), we hardly ever come first. But love restores that blissful state to us."

Clearly, being or wishing to be the first priority in another person's heart and life is a crucial element in the experience of feeling in love. If, however, we are to define not only love feelings but the state of being in a *love relationship*, we must expand the definition to read: *Being in a love relationship involves being the most important person in the life of that person who is the most important person in your life, so that there is a mutuality of affection, concern, commitment, and joy in the existence of the other.* This is for most people the top award, the Oscar, the Emmy, the Grammy, the Nobel Prize—the ultimate achievement in the interpersonal arena.

A Love Relationship Test

It may not be clear whether you and the person you are involved with have sufficient "mutuality of affection, concern, commitment, and joy in the existence of the other" to make for a love relationship. To gain more clarity, you will probably find it useful to respond to the Love Relationship Inventory that I compiled. It consists of thirty-five items concerning your feelings about the person with whom you are currently (or most recently, or most typically) *unhappily* involved. The inventory has two parts, represented by the two columns. For now just fill in the column marked "As Me." Respond to each statement by choosing, from the letters below, the one that most accurately expresses your feelings about that statement.

$$T = True$$
$$MT = Mostly\ true$$
$$MF = Mostly\ false$$
$$F = False$$

LOVE RELATIONSHIP INVENTORY

	AS ME	AS HIM/ HER	MY WISH
1. It makes me very happy to make him/her happy.	___	___	___
2. I am very physically attracted to him/her.	___	___	___

	AS ME	AS HIM/ HER	MY WISH
3. I want to spend the rest of my life with him/her.	1		
4. When we are away from each other for long, I miss him/her terribly.	1		
5. I am sure that I am in love with him/her.	1		
6. His/her welfare is as important to me as my own.	1		
7. My life would feel empty and barren if the relationship were to end.	1		
8. I am never happier than when I am with him/her and things are going well.	1		
9. There is no one else in the world I would love as much.	1		
10. I feel we are just right for each other.	MT		
11. Nobody else worthwhile could love me.	F		
12. I could never enjoy sex so much with anyone else.	F		
13. I think about him/her much of the time.	MT		
14. I look for opportunities to please him/her.	1		
15. I want to be there for him/her in sickness and health.	1		

	AS ME	AS HIM/HER	MY WISH
16. I accept him/her pretty much the way he/she is.	_____	_____	_____
17. I always look forward to being with him/her.	_____	_____	_____
18. I feel I know him/her so well.	_____	_____	_____
19. I feel he/she knows me so well.	_____	_____	_____
20. I can talk to him/her about almost everything.	_____	_____	_____
21. I feel safe with him/her.	_____	_____	_____
22. I look forward to making love to him/her.	_____	_____	_____
23. I feel head over heels in love with him/her.	_____	_____	_____
24. He/she is so reliable and dependable.	_____	_____	_____
25. I am willing to give at least as much as I receive.	_____	_____	_____
26. I can be very open and self-disclosing with him/her.	_____	_____	_____
27. I like the way I feel about myself when I am with him/her.	_____	_____	_____
28. He/She accepts me for who I am.	_____	_____	_____
29. I trust him/her.	_____	_____	_____
30. I want to be monogamous with him/her.	_____	_____	_____
31. I am willing to put up with some bad treatment as long as he/she loves me.	_____	_____	_____

	AS ME	AS HIM/ HER	MY WISH
32. I think I love him/her more than he/she loves me.	———	———	———
33. I think he/she loves me more than I love him/her.	———	———	———
34. Sometimes I feel hemmed in and suffocated in this relationship.	———	———	———
35. I wouldn't want to live without him/her.	———	———	———

What Is the Relationship Like?

Taking this inventory "As Me" will give you a picture of your basic feelings, hopes, and goals in your unhappy relationship. Look over your responses carefully. How do you feel about the picture that emerges? Do you like the you that is involved in that relationship? Do you wish there was something different about your responses?

While this picture can be useful, it really only depicts your feelings and not the total relationship. For this you will need the other half. So now, in the column headed "As Him/Her," respond to each item again, but this time as if you are the person you have been unhappily involved with. In other words, *make believe you are that person* and answer with your best *guess* as to how he or she would respond if asked to take this inventory of his or her feelings about you.

When you have completed the "As Him/Her" column, you can compare those responses you believe the other person would make about you and the relationship with your responses about him or her and the relationship. If you have answered forthrightly, you will have a portrait of the interaction that you can hang on the wall, so to speak, and stand back to observe. What do you see? Looking at these two sets of responses, ask yourself, "Are there enough mutual love feelings, common goals, and acts of caring to support a happy love relationship?" While no relationship can be the same for both partners or be characterized by an exact equality of feelings or sameness in goals, if there is too great an imbalance of feelings and goals, the emotional foundation of the relationship will be flawed, shaky, and dangerous.

When Kim filled out a version of the inventory, the contrast in the two columns, though expected, was nevertheless startling. For example, on the item "I look for opportunities to please him/her" Kim answered "True" for herself but "False" for Kevin. This same pattern occurred with several other items, including:

"His/her welfare is as important to me as my own."

"I wand to be there for him/her in sickness and health."

"I feel head over heels in love with him/her."

"I am willing to put up with some bad treatment as long as he/she loves me."

"I think about him/her much of the time."

Later, when Kim was in love with David, she took the test with him in mind. In describing her own feelings, she had given positive answers to many of the same items she had given these answers to in describing her feelings about Kevin. But her responses to these items as David, unlike those she had made for Kevin, were also positive. In other words, *there was a clear mutuality with David on these items and a lack of mutuality with Kevin.* Other items reflected similar differences in the two relationships. Kim could see that her feelings and goals in regard to Kevin had had so little similarity to his in regard to her that a satisfying love relationship had never been possible. With David, in contrast, the similarity of their feelings about each other and their goals for the relationship provided a fertile context for the growth of intimacy, commitment, and happiness. It is interesting, though not surprising, that when Kim gave David a copy of the Love Relationship Inventory to fill out, his responses were almost exactly as she guessed.

(Some items brought surprising responses. To the statement "I feel safe with him/her," Kim surprised herself by responding "Mostly True" in regard to Kevin. I asked her why she said she felt safe with Kevin when he treated her with such little regard. She said, "I know I was terribly unsafe with him in reality, but I think the indifferent and mean way he treated me was familiar from my childhood and that familiarity made it feel strangely safe to the little girl part of me.")

There are several other ways you can use this inventory. If there is a new love in your life you can, as Kim did with David, ask him or her to actually fill it out and compare it with how you responded. If you are both willing, you might find it useful to go over your responses together, discussing the similarities and differences, trying to understand each other's ways of feeling and being in the relationship, noting the areas where you feel pleased or disappointed in the other's responses, and discovering what foundation you have for a love relationship and what areas may need some work.

If you think you may have trouble being at all objective in guessing how someone you are romantically involved with would respond, then you might ask a friend who knows you and who has observed that relationship to take the inventory as if he or she is that other person. This will give you an "outside" perspective. For example, when Warren took the inventory as if he were his girlfriend, Diane, she came out as affectionate, caring, and committed. A friend of his, who had observed them together, felt he was way off the mark and responded as he believed Diane actually would, if she were being honest. A much less loving, less reciprocating, and more self-centered Diane emerged. The difference forced Warren to confront aspects of Diane his wishful thinking had kept him from acknowledging.

There is one other way you might find the inventory useful. *Make believe you are that person who you may not yet have met but with whom you hope one day to have a happy love relationship.* Respond to the inventory as yourself in regard to this still unknown but desired future partner. That should give you a good picture of what you really (or ideally) want to feel about him or her. Then answer as that unmet person would in describing his feelings about you. That should give you a good picture of the way you want to be seen and loved. Let these two sets of responses form a rough blueprint for what you are seeking.

STOP DOING WITHOUT IT

The difference between being in a love relationship and being in love but without a love relationship can be like the difference for one who is thirsty between swallowing a mouthful of cool water and a mouthful of desert sand. If you are settling for sand, you have to ask yourself why, and why you are not reaching for the cool water instead.

There are others whose lives, rather than flowering with love, have become dry deserts. These are people who are not in a love relationship and are not in love. Some had love affairs that were so disappointing or hurtful that they are reluctant to reach out again. It's as if they were suffering from a form of Post Traumatic Stress Syndrome. Others who are in this loveless state point to no great wounds. In fact, some simply have never been in a love relationship and wonder why. They are not sure if there is something wrong with their capacity to feel in love or to develop a love relationship or if they have just had bad luck.

Whether love is nonexistent in your life or you are in love but not in a love relationship, you can feel that you are in pretty arid terrain. Fortunately, there are some landmarks and charts you can use to guide yourself to a happier, more hospitable place. Let us begin by taking a look at some of the pitfalls and obstacles that may stand in your way.

3

LOVE ADDICTION
VS.
A LOVE RELATIONSHIP

In Kim's first consultation with me I asked her how she met Kevin. She recalled that she had been at her health club doing an exercise designed to tighten her rear end when a thin but muscular man walked by and said, unsmilingly, "It won't help." He kept walking. "I was instantly drawn to him," Kim said. She went after him, introduced herself, and found out his name was Kevin. The relationship progressed from unplanned meetings at the health club to planned dates, but what persisted at the core of the interaction was that Kevin continued to insult her and she continued to pursue him.

I always ask people who consult me about their relationships how they met their romantic partner because it is so often true that the way a relationship begins foretells how it will go. Milan Kundera, the Czech novelist, in *The Book of Laughter and Forgetting* says:

> Every love relationship is based on unwritten conventions rashly agreed upon by the lovers during the first weeks of their love. Without realizing it they are drawing up the fine

print of their contracts like the most hard nosed lawyers. Oh lovers! Be aware during these perilous few days! If you serve the other party breakfast in bed, you will be obliged to continue same in perpetuity or face charges of animosity and treason.

Kim's continuing efforts to pursue Kevin were not all in vain. She did manage to bring about moments of great intimacy, openness, and passion. Then, always to her surprise, he would suddenly pull back or would attack and criticize everything about her. Once, after he canceled a weekend trip they had planned and she found out he went away with another woman

instead, they had an enormous fight. She told him it really was over this time. He said that was okay because she just didn't turn him on anymore.

Kim was devastated and experienced withdrawal symptoms — weeping, sleeplessness, and nausea. She missed several days at work. A few weeks later, when she had begun to feel a little better, she returned to the health club. Just as she was doing the exercise to tighten her rear end, Kevin suddenly reappeared. Kim was overwhelmed by the coincidence, by how romantic it was that after their silly little tiff they should meet again just like that very first time. She was sure he felt the same way she did. He looked at her coldly and sneered, "It still won't help." Kim fled the gym crying, the wounds torn open again. It was at this point, at the urging of a friend, that Kim made her first appointment to see me for psychotherapy.

I wondered what there could be in Kim's history that led her not only to accept his rejection and abuse, but to keep coming back for more. And while Kim was my primary concern, I couldn't help but wonder what there could be in Kevin's history that led him to treat this good-natured and accomplished woman with such disdain. My speculations about Kevin took a very fanciful turn. Thirty years before, when I was a young graduate student, I had tested a seven-year-old boy named Kevin who was extremely aggressive and tough. He was a wiry little boy, surly and hard-edged. What particularly stayed in my mind was his response to an item on a projective test. I had asked him "What animal would you like to be?" He instantly answered, "A puppy." I asked him why. He responded, "Because puppies are cute and everyone would hold me and pet me." I gave him a piece of paper and told him to draw the puppy he would like to be. He drew a four-legged animal in side view, and then, beginning at the neck, started to draw little dashes coming out of the puppy's spine, saying, "This is his hair." Each dash got longer, so that by the time he got to the rear end of his animal they were quite long. Kevin looked at his drawing and said, "No, this isn't a puppy; it's a porcupine. It has these long needles to keep people away so he won't get hurt."

It was all there: His desire for warmth and stroking, his fear that he would be hurt if he let anyone close enough to give him that warmth, and his use of behavioral quills to keep others at a distance. And what was also implied was that already, in his young life, Kevin had had experiences with closeness that brought him sufficient pain to cause him to choose quills instead.

Could this be the same Kevin? He was the right age, his way of behaving with Kim was aggressively porcupinish, and Kim would tell of moments when a vulnerable, needy side of Kevin briefly emerged. She startled me once by saying, "Sometimes he's like a little puppy dog." I never found out if he was the same Kevin, and I probably never will. But I did find out a lot about why Kim was willing to be treated so badly in her desperation to win his love.

Kim and I explored together the factors in her background that made her vulnerable to Kevin. "Were there times early in your life, long before you started dating men, when you had to work hard to get someone to respond to your needs for affection and attention?" Kim felt that in different ways she had to work at getting nurturing and affectionate responses from each of her parents. She described her mother, a short and squat woman, as being built like a fire plug. "And she was just about as cold, hard, and unmoving," Kim added. "I didn't realize that when I was a child. I thought that's just the way mothers are. Then I saw the mothers of some of my friends were very different, so I began to think that she wasn't warm and loving like them because there was something wrong with me. I kept trying to figure out what it was."

Kim's father was tall, muscular, and moody. When in a good mood, he could bring sunshine into the home. She recalled his tossing her in the air when she was a small child. "And when I was about ten or eleven he would sometimes take me with him on his salesman's rounds just to keep him company. I loved that. He would talk to me in the car, and he seemed so proud when he introduced me to his customers." Unfortunately, these exciting occasions were rare compared to the times he was critical and disapproving. He would sometimes make fun of her looks.

Often he would retreat into surly silences, and Kim so dreaded these dark moods that she would try to forestall them by pleasing him, entertaining him, and being helpful. Sometimes it would work and she would feel appreciated. Sometimes she would try too hard and "mess up." She recalled an incident when she helped him with his clerical work by mailing circulars to his customers. "I was trying so hard to get his approval that I mailed more than he asked me to. I didn't realize I was using an additional list of deadbeats who owed him money. He was furious and called me stupid and incompetent. It still hurts."

Kim began to see more and more clearly the connection between her emotional enslavement to Kevin and the longings of the child she once was for the love and approval of her parents. "I've been doing this all my life. Even my first boyfriend in junior high school treated me like dirt and made out with my best friend at a party he took me to. I was crushed and I got much more sexually involved with him than I should have at that age because I would do anything to please him." She began to see that Kevin's magnetic pull had little to do with Kevin. She once said, "It has more to do with the desperate little girl in me trying to get love from a stone. It's the same need I've had all my life. That need has had other people's names on it at different times. This time it happens to have Kevin's name on it."

ROMANTIC ADDICTION

The similarity between people like Kim who are unable to stop themselves from being in a bad relationship and people who are unable to stop smoking, or drinking too much, or taking drugs is so great that it became obvious a while ago that these attachments to ungratifying and destructive relationships could best be understood as addictions. This notion of romantic addiction is now familiar to many. In fact, when I use the term with people who consult me professionally, some say impatiently, "I know all about that" or even, "Not that again." For many others, however, the idea that they are romantically addicted can strike with the power of lightning, illuminating and changing their way of seeing themselves and their relationships. But even those who feel that they know all there is to know about romantic addiction can expand and deepen their insight by reviewing the ever-developing concept. I have worked with love addicts for many years, but every day I come across new, unexpected twists and turns. If you are to get out of and stay out of such deadly connections, there is never too much you can know about romantic addiction. Knowledge is power, particularly when you apply it to understanding yourself. More importantly, when you are learning what you need to know *to stay out of an addictive relationship*, you are learning much of what you will need to know *to achieve a nonaddictive love relationship*.

The Language of Addiction

There is a remarkable similarity in the way people describe a substance addiction and an obsessive dependence on a particular person. If you listen closely to people (perhaps yourself) talking about a romantic dependency, you will hear the language of addiction. Look carefully at these statements. Could they not, with slight changes of wording, be uttered by a drug addict or alcoholic?

"Each time I get close to ending it, I panic."

"Life without her has no joy or excitement."

"Something in me doesn't want to give him up."

"I kept myself from calling her for almost two weeks and then I just had to—it was like needing a fix."

"I thought how could it hurt to see him just once, but it started my obsession all over again."

"I know she's poison for me, but I feel drawn to her like a magnet and I lose all control."

"I could have others, but there's something about her that turns me on like no one else."

And of course, "I can't live without him."

How can a person be addicted to something that is not a chemical substance? Studies and observations of people with substance addictions suggest that often an essential element is not in the substance but in the addict. What is that element in the love addict? The answer can be understood by looking at the explanations people give for staying in relationships that are obviously so bad for them.

"She fills a terrible emptiness inside me."

"I feel fully alive only when I'm with him."

"I feel incomplete without her. She makes me whole."

"Even though she's killing me, when I think of never seeing her again, I feel life would not be worth living."

"Without him I feel frightened and insecure. As much as he makes me miserable, when he holds me I feel safe."

"I feel depressed and miserable most of the time I'm with him, but there's something about feeling my skin against his skin that is so special, so electric."

"If I end it, I think I'll cry forever."

"I'm so used to his being there, to his habits, and to the things we do together that I'll be lost without him."

These statements indicate that the addictive element is something deep and primitive, something that has its origins very early in the life of each person. I call this element Attachment Hunger. We all share one universal human experience: Each of us lived through a period—infancy and early childhood—of complete dependence on another human being. We needed to be attached to someone, usually mother, to survive and to feel secure, worthwhile, complete, and happy. Our dependence on another person was once total.

Throughout our lives we all retain some remnants of that primary need for a basic attachment. It is too deeply imprinted in us ever to be completely wiped out of our repertoire of needs and longings. The way we usually try to gratify our attachment needs is through forming a romantic love relationship. There is nothing wrong or pathological about this very human endeavor. In fact, when the relationship is caring, compatible, and mutual, many of our inadequately met childhood needs can come forth safely. If they are not overwhelming or insatiable, they will probably receive a satisfying and healing response. When a couple has a reciprocal and loving reaction to one another's deepest attachment longings, their relationship gains in specialness, passion, and binding power.

But some people, like Kim, suffered such deficits in their early years, that their attachment yearnings dominate their thoughts and feelings. These common and normal desires become insistent and ravenous cravings. If this happens to us, these needs escalate into what I call *Attachment Hunger.* Attachment Hunger can drive us to pursue and remain involved with people who are not likely to satisfy our attachment needs. The deprivation and insecurity inherent in such bad choices intensifies our Attachment Hunger, and *when the Attachment Hunger becomes so powerful that it overrules our judgment about what is in our own best interest, we are suffering from a love addiction.* Whether we are twenty-five, thirty-five or sixty-five, when the Attachment Hunger takes over we are in the mind state of a very young child or infant. We believe our happiness and worth depend on this one particular person. We have lost control over that aspect of our lives.

The Signs of Addiction

How can you determine if you are addicted to someone? There are several diagnostic signs:

1. Even though your objective judgment (and perhaps the judgment of others) tells you that the relationship is bad for you and that you cannot realistically expect any improvement, you take no effective steps to end it.

2. You give yourself reasons for staying in it that do not hold water and are not really strong enough to balance the negatives.

3. You have feelings of emptiness, worthlessness, loneliness, and insecurity that you believe you can remedy only by staying connected with that particular person.

4. You feel dread when you think of ending the relationship and being without him or her. The dread becomes panic when you move toward ending it. One woman said, "Every time I'm about to call him and say it's over I get such an awful anxiety attack that I have trouble breathing. It's terrifying to think of life without him."

5. When you take steps to end the relationship you experience withdrawal symptoms, which may take the form of shakiness, crying spells, not being able to sleep, sleeping all the time, not being able to eat, eating all the time, chest pains, stomach and intestinal upset, and feelings of depression or grief.

6. After ending the relationship, you have the urge to reconnect. One man said, "I would find my fingers dialing her number of their own accord." A woman spoke of feeling compelled to walk down the streets where she might run into the man she had just broken up with.

THE IMPOSSIBLE TASK

The yearning to repair an old childhood deprivation is often the basis of romantic addictions. Like Kim, many men and women are seeking the love they did not get as children by repeatedly trying to extract it from an impossible or unyielding source. I think of Harry, who was sixty-two years old and owned a successful chain of dry cleaning stores. He had been married for fifteen years to a woman whose coldness and unresponsiveness had spurred him to pursue her relentlessly for three years before she begrudgingly gave in to his marriage proposals. Marriage and children did not bring forth any more warmth or affection from his wife, and after ten years of what he called "living on a glacier" Harry began a series of affairs that were intense but brief and emotionally meaningless. The marriage ended in divorce, and in the nearly two decades that followed there had been more women in his life than he could remember. He had given up on the possibility of a lasting and satisfying relationship but then met Ruth at a party and was smitten by her attractiveness and her aloof self-containment. "You seem proud," he told her, "and I like that." (Harry is not alone in fooling himself with a positive word like "proud," when words like "icy" or "arrogant" would be more apt and would better alert him to the dangers ahead.) He was aware that she did not seem very welcoming, but she did give him her phone number when he requested it, and they began to go out.

On their first date Ruth told him that she had given up on men and that she felt she never wanted to get involved again. He said, "That's the way I used to feel, till now." He continued to date her, always arriving with flowers and some small gift, which she received with a polite but removed "thank-you." As they saw each other more often, he found he was continually making statements that began "I'll bet I can make you . . ." and ended with words like "smile," "laugh," "happy," "enjoy sex," "trust me," or "marry me." But despite his efforts, he accomplished few of these tasks. Even her smiles did not come easily. He told me, "I stand on my head trying to please her, but the more I do for her, the more she treats me with contempt. I can see this, but I can't stop myself. Every word from her mouth is a criticism or a demand. . . . I believe the only thing that can save me is to walk out, or at least to know I could, but that's the one thing I cannot get myself to do, and she knows it."

The incident that brought Harry to consult with me occurred when, on one of the hottest nights of the summer, she would not "permit" him to stay in her air-conditioned bedroom because she felt "hemmed in" by his presence. Instead, she sent him to sleep on a cot in a windowless storage room. "I know there is something terribly wrong with me to accept that kind of treatment," Harry told me.

What could make this intelligent, handsome sixty-two-year-old man who had built a lucrative business through being decisive and aggressive be so helpless in the face of Ruth's demeaning and abusive attacks? I asked him whether in his childhood he had been treated in a similar way. His response was immediate. "My mother was like that. Not when I was very small. I can remember sitting on her lap and her reading to me and playing with me. Then when I was five or six my father left her for another woman and she changed. She went to work every day, and when she came home she would scream at me and blame me for everything. She even said it was my fault my father left, that he didn't want children. She was depressed and angry almost all the time. I tried so hard to be a good boy, to please her and make her smile, but she was always yelling that I was a bad boy."

The connection between Ruth and his mother was clear. Harry's Attachment Hunger, raging from early deprivation, did not simply crave the nurturing and affection of a loving woman. Instead, Harry needed to find women, like his wife and Ruth, who could have been chosen by central casting to play the role of his ungiving mother and then to try to be so good that these stand-in mothers would smile and love him. This longing was intensified because he had experienced his mother of his earliest years as playful and loving and he desperately wanted to make her come back. Recalling the years of his mother's bitterness and anger, Harry said, "But I knew there was a smiling mother in there somewhere because I had seen her. Everything depended on my being able to bring her out. It still does."

MEN AND WOMEN OF ALL AGES

Harry's story illustrates not only the role of Attachment Hunger in romantic addictions, but that it occurs in men as well as women. In fact, over half of those who called me for consultations after reading my book *How to Break Your Addiction to a Person* were men. I have an idea why this might be. Excessive Attachment Hunger derives largely from deficits in a parent's loving attentiveness during a child's earliest years. Since it is usually the mother who is the primary caretaker when the child is very young, deficits in nurturing can be particularly damaging if she has marked limitations in her ability to be loving, empathic, and attentive. Both women and men who grew up with excessive Attachment Hunger may seek romantic partners who

represent their depriving mother, but this tendency may be mag-
nified in men because most men form romantic relationships
with a person of the same gender as their mother. Harry, for
example, chose such women with unerring (though unconscious) accuracy.

Most people are startled to learn that so many men have consulted me with the problem of love addiction. There are probably
several reasons for their surprise. Men are often in a better eco-
nomic position than women and are favored by the statistics that
indicate there are more available women than men as you go up
the age ladder. Since men therefore seem to have more options,
it is easy to conclude that a man should not have a problem of
feeling dependent on any one women. This viewpoint overlooks
the magnetic power of Attachment Hunger to draw and hold
someone to a particular partner, even if others are available.

Since it is widely assumed that women have problems like
love addiction but men do not, countless articles are published
about women's problems with difficult men but not vice versa.
This reinforces the impression that love addiction is a women's
issue.

Perhaps the main reason men are not thought to suffer from
this obsession is that they are much more likely to keep their
situation carefully hidden. It simply is not macho for a man to
be addicted to a woman who is treating him badly. While a
woman who is being abysmally treated will often discuss her
plight with friends, men rarely do. It just doesn't make good
locker room conversation for a man to say that his girlfriend or
wife is treating him like dirt and that he is helpless to do anything about it because he feels desperately dependent on her.
(Harry's best friends thought Harry and Ruth were getting along
beautifully.) So men usually keep it to themselves until, perhaps,
they become so overwhelmed that they bring it to a therapist.
And even when people first come to see me, I have noted this
difference: Women are usually carrying my book in their hand,
unconcerned about who sees it; men, if they carry the book at
all, conceal it in a "plain brown wrapper," as if they are ashamed
of what it would reveal.

Harry's story also illustrates that this problem is not limited to young people. I have consulted with many men and women in their sixties and seventies who are attracted to terribly unhappy and destructive romantic relationships. There is a joke that illustrates this point. A seventy-year-old woman in a retirement community introduces herself to an elderly man who has just arrived there.

"You look pale," she says to him. "Have you been sick?"
"No," he answers, "I just got out of prison."
"Prison? Do you mind telling me what for?"
"I murdered my wife."
"Ah!" Her eyes light up. "You're single!"

Clearly, the tendency of many people, whether driven by desperation or addiction, to become obsessively involved with someone who is much more likely to make them miserable than add to their happiness is not limited to either gender or any age group. It is a widespread human problem, and if it is your problem, you know that it is a frustrating and self-destructive way to live. But unless you decide to overcome it, and act on that decision, you can be in this same place a year from now or ten years from now.

Or forever.

THE ROAD AHEAD

It can be terrifying to leave the parched and painful territory of addictive relationships. Even though you have found it agonizing and depleting to be in love without being in a love relationship, this suffering is familiar. It can be hard to leave it for the more relaxed and fulfilling warmth of a love relationship. To do so is to begin a voyage into the unknown, and even if you know that you have nothing to lose but your pain, that old pain can seem very appealing. It is, at least, the devil you know. Attempting to shift the object of your romantic feelings can be difficult and time-taking with no guarantee of the outcome. What

I can assure you, however, is that you are much more likely to find a gratifying love if you give up your involvement in the old, self-defeating relationships you have been clinging to and begin moving toward something immeasurably better. And it can be done.

4

ENDING YOUR LOVE ADDICTION

Soon after Kim first consulted me about the pain and despair she was feeling in her relationship with Kevin, I asked her if she would be willing to try a little experiment. "I would like you to make a living sculpture of your relationship with Kevin. Picture what a statue of the relationship would look like. Then place me in the pose of Kevin in that sculpture, and you pose as yourself."

"This sounds like a gimmick," Kim said.

"Sure it is, but we may learn something."

After thinking awhile Kim asked me to stand and placed me, as Kevin, with my back almost fully turned away from her. She instructed me to put one hand in my pocket and to trail the other hand out behind me. She said, "Put an expression on your face as if you can't wait to get out of here." Then Kim got down on her knees behind me and took my unpocketed hand in her own two hands. When I glanced back I saw her face had a desperate smile.

I said, "Kim, let's hold this pose for a while, and as we do I want you to think about several questions: How do you feel in this position? Have you ever been in this position in other romantic relationships? Were you ever in this position as a child? If so, who was the other person?"

After a while, I asked her to think about one more question: "What would it feel like to be in this position a year from now and five years from now?" We continued to hold the pose in unmoving silence. After four or five minutes she said, "My knees hurt. This is uncomfortable."

"Not for me," I said. "I could hold this pose all day."

Kim laughed and we both sat down to discuss what we had experienced. When I asked Kim how she felt, she said, "It wasn't just the pain in my knees and the cramping in my thighs. I felt sick to my core experiencing the truth of my relationship with Kevin and how I am demeaning myself. I wished I could get up off my knees and kick him out of my life and out of my head."

JUST SAY NO?

Being in a bad relationship can be, as Kim reexperienced in trying to maintain her pose in the sculpture, a distressingly uncomfortable position in which to spend the irreplaceable days of your life. And the longer you hold still for it, the more anguished it can get. Yet you may be choosing to remain in that same cramped position, even though the relationship is destroying your happiness, your self-esteem, your morale, and possibly even your immune system.

Knowing this, my first impulse is to exhort you to do what Nancy Reagan advised in relation to drug abuse—"Just say no." Who could argue with such advice? You will certainly have to say no to destructive and addictive relationships if you are to have a more fulfilling life. Ultimately, whether we are talking about cocaine or a cocktail, pot or a person, if you want to break your addiction, you will have to put your reason and your willpower at the service of your instinct for self-preservation and simply say no. But there is one problem with the "just say no" approach: saying no is much easier advice to give and to applaud than to put into practice. When you are in the throes of an addiction, your drive to get your fix is much stronger than your self-preservative instincts. The reason is that your Attachment Hunger is stronger than your willpower and judgment.

These two forces are waging a battle inside you, and to change your situation, you have to make yourself as consciously aware of this battle as possible. Up until now, your Attachment Hunger has been winning. It will go on winning until you find a way to reduce its power and to strengthen the power of your judgment. If you can do this, the balance will slowly tip so that the relative weight of the forces for self-destruction and self-preservation begin to equalize. At that point, willpower can take over and "just say no" will cease to be an impotent platitude and will become a real possibility.

Reducing the power of your Attachment Hunger will involve your acknowledging and accepting the needy child inside you, understanding what that child wants and fears, and learning to respond to him or her in a sympathetic and nurturing way. It will also mean learning to compassionately hold that child so that he or she feels safe, reassured, and amenable to reason. *Strengthening the power of your judgment* will involve your recognizing the terrible damage that the Attachment Hunger has been causing you, understanding your hidden reasons for choosing your self-destructive relationship, and dispelling the delusions you have used to enable yourself to stay in the relationship. (A key delusion to dispel is that because it feels so intense, it must be the real thing. The intensity may only signify that it is a real addiction.) It also involves viewing the future without that person realistically, and not with a desperate child's terror of abandonment and eternal loneliness. Strengthening your judgment entails widening your perspective so you can see your life as being, in truth, much bigger than this one relationship. And it entails finding ways to uncover, embrace, and direct your natural drive toward health, self-actualization, and fulfilling love.

ADDICTION-BREAKING TECHNIQUES
AND APPROACHES

Once we understand the necessity of putting the rational and caring adult part of you in charge of your life, it is essential to use *any and every nondestructive technique, approach, exercise, philosophy, or gimmick that you, I, or anyone else can devise to reduce the tyranny of your Attachment Hunger and strengthen the guiding power of your mature judgment.*

Techniques for Deciding

Many people who consult with me about their unhappy relationships do not know how to decide whether to call it quits. Others believe they have decided, but as I listen carefully I find that isn't really so. There are often qualifications and provisos, such as "But maybe I'm just being too sensitive to his ignoring me," "I know I said this six months ago, but if it doesn't start getting better in the next six months, then I will really end it," "If she just cuts down on her drinking, everything will be fine," "If I wait it out a little longer, maybe he will leave his wife." How can you really decide whether you want to end or continue your relationship?

For one thing, you can make what I call a *Benefit-Cost Analysis* of the relationship. In one column list all the ways the relationship contributes to your happiness, security, well-being, and self-esteem; in another column, list all the ways it contributes to your unhappiness and insecurity and is destructive to your well-being and self-esteem. Be ruthlessly honest in appraising the results of this balance sheet. Then, if the balance is clearly negative, ask yourself: Have I made real efforts to make the relationship better? Has it shown any *significant* improvement? Do I have any *evidence* to believe it will change for the better in any reasonable amount of time? If it stays this way, do I want it?

In calling this procedure a Benefit-Cost Analysis, I have used the cold and bloodless terms of accounting to help you to marshal your objectivity against the tendency of your Attachment

Hunger to distort your view. You will have to be vigilant to prevent your appraisal from being influenced by the fears, yearnings, and wishful thinking of your inner child.

Another useful and even indispensable technique is to keep a Relationship Log. This is a diary of the day-to-day incidents, events, and conversations, and above all, a record of your *feelings* in that relationship. When Kim was trying to decide what to do about Kevin, I asked her to keep such a log. It soon became clear to her that while there were entries about some wonderful times, several exciting and tender sexual encounters, and a few moments of shared openness and intimacy, the preponderance of entries were about incidents in which he treated her with disdain and disregard. The feelings she most frequently recorded were disappointment, hurt, depression, and anger at the way he treated her. For Kim, this log corroborated the Benefit-Cost Analysis she had made, which showed that the good feelings and experiences she was deriving were not worth the cost to her morale and well-being.

The Love Relationship Inventory discussed in Chapter 2 can also help you decide whether to end the relationship. If your feelings about that person and goals for the relationship are significantly at variance with your perception of that person's feelings toward you and his or her goals for the relationship, then unless there is realistic reason to believe that greater mutuality can develop, you have additional strong evidence in favor of ending it.

To get to a level even deeper than words, it can be helpful to use the "gimmick" that I had Kim try—making a sculpture of the relationship. Perhaps you can get a friend to stand in for the person who is the object of your addiction. In doing this exercise, bear in mind that you are the sculptor, the creator of this statue of the relationship, and the other person is your clay.

The first step is to think of the sculpture that best depicts how the relationship feels to you. Next, begin to create it by posing the other person and telling him or her what facial expression to assume. Then place yourself in the sculpture and assume the appropriate facial expression. The pose should be held silently for at least several minutes. While you're in the pose, ask yourself these questions:

- How do I feel in this position? How do I feel in my body and my emotions?
- Have I ever been in this or a similar position in another romantic relationship? In more than one?
- Was I ever in this position as a child? With whom?
- What title would I give to this sculpture?
- How would I feel if I was in this same position a year from now? Five years from now?
- If it will continue to be this way, do I want it or do I want to end it?

When Kim did this sculpture exercise, she realized not only that her relationships with Kevin and a previous boyfriend were uncomfortable and demeaning, but also that her position had a familiarity that went way back into her past. "I think I was in some ways always down on my knees, pleading for my father's attention. In fact, it was true with both my parents—my father was always walking away and I was trying to get him to stay, and my mother always seemed to have her back turned, never really looking at me to see who I am."

This sculpture exercise triggered connections between Kim's early experiences and her relationship with Kevin. She thought of the time she met Kevin and of how his telling her, "It won't help" as she worked away at an exercise machine had ignited her interest in him. Then she recalled the childhood incident when her father had been furious at her for using the wrong mailing list. She had sobbed, "I was only trying to help," and he had responded, "You're no help." Kim could feel how Kevin's words had set off her desperate longing to get her father's approval and love and had compelled her to automatically go after Kevin. As these pieces fell into place, Kim asked, "Will I be reenacting this sick drama forever?"

"That's up to you," I said. "You might. But you don't have to. You could decide to stop and get out of this position." At this point, Kim was not ready to get off her knees and say good-bye to Kevin, but she felt this exercise was important in tilting her toward that decision.

Warren decided to try the sculpting exercise directly with his girlfriend, Diane, instead of getting a stand-in for her. What came to his mind was a sculpture in which he would be behind Diane, his arms around her waist. She would be leaning a bit away from him, her hands behind his head, with a sexy, seductive expression on her face. They would be looking in the mirror, and both their gazes would be focused on her reflection. He placed them each in the pose he wanted, but even before he told her what expression to wear or who to look at in the mirror, she put a haughty, challenging look on her face and could not take her eyes off herself. Then she insisted on fixing her lipstick and she tried a variety of provocative poses. "It was amazing," Warren told me. "She had taken charge of the exercise and was totally unrelated to me, almost as if I didn't exist. The only thing that was exactly as I planned was that we were both looking at her, not at me or at us." Warren had to acknowledge that the Diane he created in his sculpture accurately reflected her and their relationship. It helped him move another small step toward deciding to end it.

Let us suppose that you have done a Benefit-Cost Analysis of the relationship, have kept a Relationship Log, have completed the Love Relationship Inventory, and have sculpted the basic interaction between you and this problematic person in your life. Let us further suppose that all these exercises indicate that you should be out of this relationship because you are too often unhappy and because there is little realistic possibility of it sufficiently improving. You may, even so, be unable to end it. If this happens, it is understandable. After all, there may be some powerful and deeply entrenched emotions at work, including being in love, sexual attraction, Attachment Hunger, and fear of pain and loneliness. But, while you may not be able to end the relationship today, *you can decide that it definitely must be ended and you can decide to work toward ending it as soon as possible.* Kim once told me, "I know for sure that I must stop seeing Kevin, totally and finally. I can't do it yet, but everything I do from now on will aim at loosening his hold on me and making myself strong enough to end it."

This kind of interim decision must not be used as a way of copping out of ending the relationship "as of right now." The decision is a commitment to stop making excuses for the other person, to put aside false hopes that the relationship will work out, and to cease all efforts to hold it together. In other words, it is a commitment to begin the process of disengaging that will lead you to end your involvement.

Dealing With Your Destructive Delusions

Once you have decided that you will break the addictive tie as soon as you are able, your task is to challenge every assault your Attachment Hunger makes on your resolve. One way that your resolve can be weakened is through the rationalizations and false beliefs that you will be tempted to use in order to delay taking that final step. Here are some typical ways people delude themselves in the service of their Attachment Hunger. Do any of them strike a chord?

Harry: "I am not sure if Ruth is really particularly mean and rejecting or if I am too sensitive. Maybe I'm asking for too much."

Laura: "I really shouldn't be upset about not being very high in Les's priorities. After all, I have a demanding career and not that much time myself."

Warren: "Diane can be self-centered and bitchy, but that's just the way she is—it's nothing personal against me. And she's so incredibly beautiful."

Kim: "He can be cold and cruel at times, but I think underneath all that Kevin really does love me. He just has a hard time showing it."

Daniel: "Maybe she isn't being promiscuous and I'm too suspicious. Maybe those times she didn't answer the phone all night her phone really was out of order. And maybe when my friend saw her holding hands with this guy in a restaurant he really was just a client."

Mia: "I know that I'm getting involved with a married man again, but this time it's different. Two people who make love as passionately as we do belong together. I can tell he loves me, and even though he says he'll never leave his wife, I believe he will."

Carla: "I'm terrified that if I leave Jack I'll be alone forever. Maybe there's no one else out there for me."

You probably can easily recognize the false thinking in these rationalizations put forth by others. Now you have to apply the same critical scrutiny to the reasons you give for continuing to sit on a painfully hot stove. I would suggest you write down all the reasons you stay in a relationship that is making you un-happy and then look at these reasons as if someone else had written them. Do they really read like the truth?

A certain amount of untruth may be part of falling in love, perhaps an essential part. We tend to idealize our beloved, to see mainly those aspects that delight and excite us, and to ignore or downplay the weaknesses and character flaws that we would not like. We can even, like a sorcerer, transform annoying habits and uncomely features into attributes we find cute, beguiling, and appealing. As Ethel Person writes in *Dreams of Love and Fateful Encounters*, "Loving may, in fact, feel so good because it is so creative." What is created is an illusion, an idealized image that forms a vital element in the loving bond. As the relationship con-tinues, the idealization is eroded by the realities that are exposed by time and by unavoidable conflicts but in enduring love, some of the idealized view remains.

These harmless and even constructive illusions are not, how-ever, the same as delusions.

Delusions are perceptions that are so counter to reality that they can distort and block out crucial negative facets of the be-loved's being and behavior. If a romantic relationship is causing you pain, you have to be alert to that often unclear boundary between illusion and delusion. You have to ask yourself whether you have crossed over from the natural idealization of being in love into the land of delusion.

Some delusions draw on cultural stereotypes. A man who is self-absorbed, uncaring, or emotionally unavailable may be idealized as "the strong, silent type." A woman who is dependent or flighty may be idealized as "ultrafeminine." Like other delusions these serve to obscure the truth. Harry labeled Ruth as "proud" to blind himself to her coldness and her inability to be affectionate or even nice. Kim labeled Kevin as "self-sufficient" to delude herself about his detachment and inability to love. In like manner, the sorcery of our idealization can convert someone *ungiving* into someone who is "self-contained," someone *unfeeling* into someone "cool," someone *mean* into someone "tough," someone *lazy* into someone "laid back," someone *possessive* into someone "loving," someone *picky* into someone "discriminating," someone *narcissistic* into someone who has an abundance of "self-esteem," someone who is *irresponsible* into someone who is a "nonconformist," someone *irritable* into someone "sensitive," someone *selfish* into someone who "knows what he wants," and so on.

It is essential for you to recognize that when your idealization is fueled by Attachment Hunger, it can become transformed from a romance and relationship enhancer into an ongoing *delusion* that can keep you trapped. It is important to admit the possibility that you may be deceiving yourself about this person you love—about the type of person he or she is, about how he or she really feels about you, about what he or she wants from the relationship and, above all, about the potential for things to change.

Often, people who go through the inevitable deidealization that occurs in relationships are convinced—particularly if the deidealization is rapid and revealing—that these negative facets only recently appeared. Sometimes this is true. But sometimes these undesirable qualities were there from the first. The idealization simply created a blinding halo. My friend and colleague Dr. Fred Hahn tells patients who believe that they are discovering negative things they had no idea about early in the relationship, "You did know then what you do know now." I have had many occasions to borrow this phrase, and I point out to people who consult me the clues that their idealization concealed.

There is a particular delusion that can come on with gripping intensity when you are getting closer to ending the tie—the frightening belief that this person you are about to leave is the *one and only* person who you could love so much, or who could love and accept you, or who you could enjoy sex with so much. Such a belief is almost always based on thinking that comes from the small child you once were and who still exists in you. For that child there truly was a "one and only" mommy or a "one and only" daddy. Having their love was bliss, having their care was comfort, and having their protection was security. When you have that "one and only" feeling now, your Attachment Hungry child is distorting reality.

The power of this false belief was unforgettably dramatized when Mia arrived for her session with me quite upset and distraught. "I just parked on the street downstairs, and after I got out of the car I decided to move it up a few feet. When I tried to restart it, it just wouldn't start. The starter didn't even make a sound. It will be dark when I leave, and I don't know what to do." She was near tears. I suggested that the car might not be fully in the parking gear and she should check that first. If that didn't work, there was a service station two blocks away that could help her. This turned out not to be very reassuring. She seemed paralyzed and was unable to either proceed with our session or go downstairs to check out the parking gear. She insisted on calling her boyfriend, the latest of the arrogant men she gravitated to, to ask him for advice. After I made some unsuccessful attempts to get her to look at why she wanted to do that, I agreed that she could use my phone to call him. She sounded almost hysterical as she told him what had happened. Then she listened, saying "I see, I see," and she got noticeably calmer. By the time she hung up she was completely composed. I was amazed by the transformation and was curious to know what sage counsel he had offered. Was there some particular information he had about this car? Was he driving over to help her? "He said I should check out whether it was fully in parking gear and, if that didn't do it, I should contact the nearest service station." We looked at each other, and then we both burst out laughing. All my previous suggestions that she overidealized him as a "one and only" font of strength and wisdom had not made a dent, but this time the magic she ascribed to him was so clear she could not deny it.

For Mia, or for you, there is not a "one and only" person in the world who you could love and feel passionate about, so if your best judgment is telling you that you have to break up with him or her there is every reason to believe that you will be opening the door to new possibilities of fulfillment.

Loosening the Grip of Guilt

For some, one of the most formidable feelings they encounter when they contemplate ending an unhappy relationship is guilt about the impact it will have on the other person. I have seen this guilt present an emotional obstacle even when the behavior of the other person has been atrocious. I have seen women who were being physically abused feel guilty about leaving a man who they felt was emotionally dependent on them ("He'll be lost without me"). I have seen men become paralyzed with guilt when they think about leaving a woman who subjected them to incessant criticism, unending demands, and a paucity of consideration or affection ("She counts on me for everything and will probably flip out if I leave her"). I have seen both men and women who, even though they often and vainly warned their partner, "Please hear me—if it goes on this way, I'm going to leave," still feel guilty when they finally do leave.

It is true that if you end an involvement with someone who doesn't want it to be over, they will be hurt. They will probably also be furious and accuse you of all kinds of things that are aimed at making you feel like a monster, a betrayer, a terrible person. It can be very hard for you to bear being the cause of so much pain and rage in someone you once loved and may still love. The longer and more involved the relationship has been, the greater the guilt is likely to be. Where it is a marriage and there are children in the picture, you are aware that many people that you care deeply about will feel hurt, rejected, and/or furious at you. You cannot simply dismiss your guilty feelings as neurotic and insubstantial. Your leaving may leave scars on those most vulnerable, and unless your rage at the person you are leaving is so enormous that you feel vindictively justified in causing them pain, you are not likely to dismiss their reactions with "who cares?" So how do you deal with this guilt if it is keeping you from acting on your decision?

The key to dealing with the guilt is to feel assured that you have made a responsible decision and to assume responsibility for it. There are steps you can take that can increase your sense of the appropriateness and even the inevitability of that decision:

- ◆ Make the decision with care, so that you're not acting impulsively out of an unwillingness to work through frustrations. You can use the decision-making techniques discussed earlier; for example, make a Benefit-Cost Analysis and keep a Relationship Log. Evaluate the possibilities that the relationship can improve, and explore your role in the difficulties. The longer and more involved the relationship, and the more people whose lives will be affected by a breakup, the more care this must be given.
- ◆ Weigh the consequences of *not* breaking the relationship; often these consequences can be worse for everyone than the consequences of breaking it.
- ◆ Consider the possibility that you may be overestimating the negative reactions of the person you are leaving; he or she may not be as devastated or enraged as you imagined.
- ◆ Consider the possibility that your guilt may not be coming solely from your feelings about leaving this particular person, but may also be coming from the child in you who was made to feel guilty about taking steps away from a parent or disappointing a parent. You may be unconsciously feeling more like a bad boy or a bad girl than a culpable adult.

- Resolve that if you do end the relationship you will do it in a way that is least harmful and destructive to the other person and to all concerned.

Facing That Moment

If you take these steps, then your awareness that you gave the decision thoughtful consideration may reduce the guilt enough so that it does not keep you from implementing your decision. I have found, however, that many people balk at facing what they often call "That Moment"—the actual moment of telling the other person that it is over. I know many who have come just to the brink of those fateful words and then pulled back in fear and guilt. Some have come to that brink countless times and are quite discouraged about their inability to take that one step more. One man's fear of facing that moment of telling his girl-friend he wanted to end it was so great that he had fantasies of her being killed in an auto accident so he would be out of the relationship without having to take action. And I know of a woman who constantly encouraged her boyfriend to talk with and dance with other women, hoping he'd get interested in someone else so he would be the one to end the relationship. If you are in that paralyzed place, I suggest that you sit down and write a description of the scene as you imagine it will be. Where does it take place? What exactly would you say? What might his or her reaction be? What reaction do you most dread? Rage? Threats? Violence? Accusations? Tears? Depression? Suicide?

One man I asked to do this imagined his girlfriend bursting into tears, turning around, and, before he could stop her, throwing herself out of the window of her tenth floor apartment. As he imagined it he could feel his sense of horror. When we talked about it later he realized that she wouldn't react that way, that it was just a fear of his with no basis in reality. I suggested that he let himself have the image again and again, making it as awful as he could. After a while, through repetition and through his knowledge that it really wouldn't happen that way, the frightening prospect began to lose some of its charge.

The woman who hoped her boyfriend would fall in love with someone else had another kind of image when I asked her to picture telling him it was over. She saw him collapse in a tearful heap, heard him repeat "How could you do this to me? You've destroyed me," over and over. At this image she cringed and felt terrible. Then the image gave way to one of her father, a frequently depressed man, sitting in his chair, looking sad, defeated, and hopeless. She realized that she expected her boyfriend to react like her father and could recognize that in reality her boyfriend had much more drive and resiliency.

I asked the man who fantasized that his girlfriend was killed in an accident to picture what frightened him about ending the relationship. He imagined his girlfriend taking a gun from a drawer and shooting him. He felt his terror and could hear himself beg her not to. Yet he realized that in reality his girlfriend was not a violent person, owned no gun, and even was afraid of guns. "The chances of that happening are zero," he said. He could see he had been paralyzed by unrealistic fears.

Let yourself feel the full horror of whatever awful reaction you anticipate. Write down the scenario and your feeling. Is your feeling fear? (Fear of what?) Guilt? Shame? Sadness? Loss? Then put what you have written aside for a while. When you come back to it an hour or a day later, try to evaluate how likely it is that the scenario would actually happen and, if it is likely, what you could do to deal with it. By repeatedly feeling the images of "That Moment," you can make them become less frightening, and that can free you to do what you know is best.

Coping With Infant Time

Once you have actually gotten through "That Moment" and have acted on your decision to end your addictive relationship, you will probably be rocked by withdrawal symptoms—pain, sadness, and a longing to reconnect. In withdrawal, you are emotionally reexperiencing the Attachment Hunger state of mind that you knew as an infant or toddler, when you were needy, vulnerable, limited in perspective, and lacking in willpower. And when you are in that state your experience of time is also that of a very young child. Without realizing it, you are on what I call Infant Time, and that is a very different dimension than adult time.

If you have waited for a phone call from someone who you love but whose love you feel unsure of, you know that if the call was late, every ticking second seemed like an eternity. You may be able to recall how your anxiety mounted, your apprehensive imaginings ran amok, and your body felt tense and agitated. Perhaps you sensed your heart beating faster. This is what happens to infants when they cry out for someone to come and nobody responds immediately. It may only be a minute or two while mom or dad is getting out of bed or warming up a bottle, but for infants who have no concept of "a minute or two," who know nothing about clocks or calendars or tomorrow, this tormented moment is all there is. They wail and thrash about because they feel helplessly alone forever.

We can assume that such infant and early childhood experiences happened to you because they happen to everyone to some degree. Maybe there were times when the baby-sitter arrived and you realized your parents were going out. They may have tried to reassure you, to tell you they would only be gone for a few hours. A few hours? What did that mean to you? Your parents were lost to you. Everlastingly gone.

You may have experienced deprivations and uncertainties in your earliest years that were much more damaging than being left with a baby-sitter. The attention you received may have been insufficient, inconsistent, or destructive. If one of your parents was frequently ill, depressed, alcoholic or otherwise limited in his or her capacity to love and care for you, you may have experienced too many interminable moments of distress. If you yourself, as a small child, were often sick or physically impaired or fearful, you may well have experienced an eternity of helplessness and loneliness. Today, when you are in a love relationship that presents you with a similar scenario of unreliable, insufficient or toxic loving—or if you are in the throes of ending such a relationship—you may relive the Infant Time foreverness of that pain you felt when you were young and dependent.

I remember hearing the panicked little boy in Harry's words and in his voice when he telephoned me the weekend after he had ended his relationship with Ruth. I could hear the vulnerable child whose mother had turned on him and cast him into never-ending blackness. "I can't stand it. I got through Friday night by going out drinking with some friends and bombing myself into oblivion. But now, even though I know it's only two in the afternoon on Saturday, I feel like it has been a century without her. How can I possibly get through the rest of the day or tonight if time is going to drag like that? And then there's tomorrow, a whole day, with nothing planned and no Ruth."

When I tried to indicate that the weekend was really a very brief period and that he would soon feel better, he said, "Maybe it's brief for you, but for me it feels like forever. When I feel like this, I have no belief that there will be a better time. I can't even imagine it. I just see pain and loneliness forever."

I explained to Harry the distortions of Infant Time and reminded him that he had felt similarly sure of eternal aloneness when other romantic relationships had ended. He was able to recall that this was so, and that recognition helped him to get some adult time perspective.

A few weeks later, Harry came to my office feeling very upbeat and at peace with himself. "I'm so glad to have Ruth out of my life," he said. "It's like a weight has lifted from my brain and my heart and I feel good about myself again. I'm *looking forward* to better times ahead."

On hearing this, I said, "Harry, I don't mean to be a killjoy, but just in case you slide back into a state of longing and lose your time perspective, I'd like you to try something a patient of mine invented for herself years ago. Write out some memos from the Harry you are now to the lost little kid you may become if Attachment Hunger hits you. If you have the time, you could sit in the waiting room at the end of this session and write the memos while you are feeling so good and are well rooted in adult time."

Harry wrote one memo and made two copies, one for the bulletin board he kept in his bedroom, the other for his wallet. It read:

Dear Harry-boy [which was what his father used to call him]:

I am writing this to you because I know something you don't know. You think that when you are miserable and lonely and miss Ruth so terribly that you will always feel this way. You believe that the dark view you have right now and the awful pain you are feeling is the way things will always be. But you are on Infant Time and you are seeing it all wrong. It makes you feel like returning to Ruth because you believe there will be no one else. But Ruth was a rejecting and angry woman, like your mother became after your father left. She made your life a misery of criticism and commands. Soon this attack of longing will pass and you will feel again what I feel at this moment of writing to you — happy, independent, and looking forward to tomorrow. So keep reading this memo till it sinks in or call a friend or write down all your feelings. I assure you that you will soon feel better.

When Harry did have other "attacks" he made himself read the memos and found that they gave him a foothold to begin his climb out of the abyss of Infant Time.

If you suffer from Infant Time losses of perspective, I suggest that you, too, prepare such memos when you are feeling content and can see a future with new possibilities. Then, during the periods you are most likely to lose perspective — after you come home from work, in the middle of the night, on weekends, or whenever — read these messages to yourself, preferably slowly and aloud.

Overcoming Addiction Amnesia

The agonized longings that follow the end of an addictive relationship often act as a very peculiar and selective eraser that rubs out all memories of what was bad about the relationship and what was difficult about the person. I call this phenomenon Addiction Amnesia, and it leaves you remembering only the good things, the wonderful moments, the times of closeness, comfort, and passion, no matter how rare. Once you have forgotten all the negatives, and recall only the positives, you will understandably feel "Why did I ever end it? It was really great—certainly better than the loneliness and emptiness I feel now. I must call him (or her) and reconnect before it's too late."

It is crucial that you be alert to this phenomenon of Addiction Amnesia and prepare yourself for it. The Relationship Log that I have urged you to keep can be a useful tool. It can function as your written memory, your proof of what did or did not take place, your record of feelings and incidents that your Addiction Amnesia has blocked you from recalling. Just as Kim used the diary of her relationship with Kevin to see in black and white why she had to leave him, she used it through many long and lonely nights of intense withdrawal suffering to remind her why she should not go back. She kept the log at her bedside and began to read it at the first signs that she was forgetting how bad the relationship often was.

If you have not kept a Relationship Log, make a list of all the negative things that you can remember about the relationship.

Do it at a time when you are feeling strong and not in the throes of Attachment Hunger. In his book *One Hundred Years of Solitude*, Gabriel Garcia Marquez recounts an episode in the history of his fictional town Macondo in which a plague of slowly spreading memory loss hits all the townspeople. One by one, day by day, they begin to forget things, until they are soon forgetting what objects are called and what their functions are. Some try to stem the inexorable march of this amnesia by putting name tags on objects. But before long, the meanings of the words on the tags are also forgotten. Your memory loss, however, is quite reversible and such "tagging" of the negatives in the relationship you have just ended can be an excellent antidote to your personal plague of Addiction Amnesia.

Your memory can also be greatly aided by preparing your friends to serve as auxiliary memories. When Warren broke off with Diane he told his friend Matt, "Just in case I ever get the urge to call her again, I'll call you and you remind me why I shouldn't call her." But then, one night, during a bout of missing her and being ravaged by fantasies that she probably was already with someone else, he called Diane instead of calling Matt. She was not in, and he left a romantic message on her answering machine and only then called Matt and told him what he had done. Matt reminded him of the many unkind and self-centered things Diane had said and done, of how she always found a way to hurt him whenever they got close, of how miserably unhappy he often was. "As Matt spoke to me," Warren told me later, "I felt my mind clear up and my feelings of desperate longing for her begin to evaporate. I left her another message, telling her that my first call came out of an attack of missing her but that I really did not want her to call back. I felt relieved."

In preparing your friends to be your memory, explain to them about Addiction Amnesia so they will not be surprised that you have forgotten your reasons for ending the relationship. They will then be able to clearly remind you, with concrete incidents, and to be firm with your attempts to disregard these incidents and rewrite history.

Multiple Attachments

When we recognize that we have been driven by our Attachment Hunger to narrow so much of ourselves and our lives to an obsession with one particular person, we realize how precariously dependent and limited we have become. There is probably, for each of us, some irreducible amount of Attachment Hunger, an inevitable legacy of our abject childhood needfulness. But why must we try to get all our Attachment Hunger gratified by one person in one relationship? Would it not be better to spread our attachment need around so that we get different aspects of it met in different ways—through friendships and family, through work, hobbies, pets, courses, or commitments?

Obviously, the answer to this last question is yes, but the paradox is that the more you get addictively involved in a romantic relationship, the more these other attachments, which could bring balance and comfort, tend to be loosened, discarded, and forgotten. This one relationship draws all your attachment needs like a powerful magnet, so it takes considerable effort for you to say to yourself, "No, my life has to have more to it than this, and then to work to make that enlargement happen.

At first, giving the time and involvement to wider interests may have little appeal to you; your view of what is important and what you need has become so narrowly tied to this one person, to how he or she is treating you and whether he or she loves you that you have little incentive or energy for anything else. But if you are to avoid being inexorably drawn into the black hole of your addictive tie, you must reach out a hand to the world that exists beyond it. So push yourself to get involved in friendships that are not centered around talking about your addictive relationship, to develop new skills, to take the course you always said you would take, to pursue new interests, and to learn more about yourself and what your larger desires and needs are. Certainly, it would be best if you did not consider these pursuits as "consolation prizes" or mere distractions, but could experience them as paths to satisfy different aspects of your complexity. But even if at first you can only see them as busywork, they are worth doing as an act of faith that says you are bigger than you have been letting yourself be.

Addiction-Breaking Groups

One special source of guidance and support that combines some of the best aspects of friendship and of forming multiple attachments is the self-help support groups aimed at breaking addictions. There are many such groups. Some, like AlAnon or ACOA (Adult Children of Alcoholics), are focused on coping with attachments to people addicted to a substance. Others, such as CODA (Codependents Anonymous), are composed of people who become addicted romantically to someone who may or may not be a substance abuser. These groups are helpful in many ways. You can discover that you are not alone and that there are surprisingly common patterns in these addictive relationships. You can see in others the self-defeating behavior that you have avoided recognizing in yourself and, hopefully, can then apply these observations to your own situation. You can enjoy the empathy and camaraderie of group members who share common painful experiences. And you can see alternative ways to look at your addictive relationship and your life. Many support groups adhere to a variation of the twelve-step programs that have been so successful with substance addictions and that provide a practical and spiritual framework for breaking addictions.

To find out about groups in your area, look in your area phone book or inquire at a local mental health center, church, community center, or YMCA or YWCA since it is at such places that these groups usually meet. If there is no Codependents Anonymous group, try AlAnon. Even if the object of your addiction is not himself or herself a substance abuser, the issue of needing to end your dependence on that person is much the same as if he or she were, and you will find useful observations and support.

Uses of Psychotherapy

A while after Kim stopped seeing Kevin, and before she met David, she was seriously considering calling Kevin up to get the relationship started again. In one psychotherapy visit she said, "Maybe if I don't expect too much, it can be okay."

"Lowering expectations can make a difference," I said, "when a person's expectations are too great. But that's not true for you. The things you wanted from Kevin—that he be caring, considerate, and reasonably reliable—are pretty basic requirements for what is supposed to be a love relationship."

"Maybe I didn't really give it a chance."

"Yes, you did, and you have abundant evidence that Kevin is unable to be there for you in a consistent way and probably never will be. In fact he repeatedly treated you badly."

"It wasn't that bad."

"Yes it was. And if you go back to him, you will be setting yourself up for more disappointment, frustration, and abuse."

"I don't understand you," Kim exploded. "Sometimes you are so sympathetic and in tune with what I feel and other times, like now, you can be so damn harsh and judgmental."

"I do feel a lot of sympathy with your feelings of love for Kevin and with your pain and loneliness as you go through withdrawing from him. I appreciate how hard it is to break your attachment and to stay away from him. But when you start to fool yourself and tell yourself that it wasn't so bad or that his behavior was all your fault just so that you can rationalize going back to him, then I have to call you on it. If you want to go back to him because you can't stand the withdrawal pains, that's up to you. Only you can decide how much you can take of that. But don't delude yourself that it will all be okay this time. Your past experience tells us that it will probably cost you dearly."

Kim left that session angry and frustrated saying, "I think you're wrong." But she didn't call him that day, or the day after, and her need to contact him diminished. As a psychotherapist with people caught in love addictions I usually follow the same approach I did with Kim. On the one hand, I feel deeply sympathetic with the painful human situation of being in a bad relationship and of being chained there by Attachment Hunger to the point of addiction. I resonate to the suffering of someone trying to leave such a relationship. I have easy and sincere patience with the often slow pace of taking action to end it. I encourage people not to give themselves a hard time or to feel like a failure if they have trouble ending the relationship or if their neediness brings them to reconnect time after time. I support each effort as a step in strengthening their sense of independence and their self-respect. On the other hand, I tend to speak out clearly and even vigorously when someone I am working with seems to be rationalizing, distorting reality, fooling himself or herself, and trying to fool me, all in order to give himself or herself license to continue being self-destructive. Alfred Adler, one of the founders of psychoanalysis, once said that at times psychoanalysis is the process of "spitting in the patient's soup." This is a very inelegant phrase, but it defines pretty well what I see myself doing when someone is feeding themselves a soup that is self-deluding and toxic.

Even if not all psychotherapists explicitly use this two-tier approach I've described, it is a valuable part of what psychotherapy offers someone struggling with addiction. Even more important, psychotherapy usually aims at helping a love addict see that his or her problem is not simply a situational one, but has its origins in his or her history, usually reflecting self-defeating behaviors learned years ago and repeated now in the vain hope of a different and better result. Effective psychotherapy aims to loosen the grip of the love addict's past on dysfunctional ways he or she selects and deals with current relationships.

When should you consider psychotherapy? Psychotherapy is appropriate when: (1) you are confused as to whether you should accept the relationship as it is, make further efforts to improve it, or get out; (2) you know that you should end it but remain painfully stuck; (3) you suspect that insecurity, fear of being alone, guilt, or Attachment Hunger is impairing your resolve to leave; (4) you recognize that you have a pattern of getting into and staying in bad relationships and have not been able to

change this pattern, even with the help of friends and support groups.

Does psychotherapy hold some hazards for the love addict? It can. Love addicts are usually people who have had a difficult time maintaining their judgment and their independence in the face of very strong Attachment Hunger. Psychotherapy requires that they meet regularly in an emotionally intimate way with someone who listens to them with empathy and concern. So it is not uncommon for people to develop some attachment to their therapist, especially during the withdrawal period when they have separated from the object of their addiction and their Attachment Hunger is suddenly unmoored. The dependency they then might feel on the therapist will be natural and even helpful as long as two conditions pertain: (1) they understand that the goal of their relationship with their therapist is to reach a point where they are not dependent on him or her and (2) the therapist is an ethical and competent professional who understands that even though some people may have to lean on him or her for a while, the therapist's aim is to help them understand the roots of their dependency and find their independence. Some therapists, like some parents, are better at this than others and find it easier to let go. If you are in psychotherapy and think it might be time to stop, listen with an open mind if your therapist suggests that this could be an attempt at self-sabotage or resistance to making changes. But if you examine your motives carefully and decide it is time to move on, you must honor your own judgment.

Ending psychotherapy can produce its own withdrawal symptoms, but if you are truly ready to go, that discomfort should be short-lived and outweighed by your gratification at moving forward with greater independence and self-direction. Usually this is a pleasure that you and your therapist will share.

Uses of Medication

Sometimes ending an addictive relationship can lead to so much anxiety and/or depression that the question arises whether tranquilizers or antidepressant medication can be useful. There are differing opinions about this. Some people in codependency work are leery about medication, fearing that it fosters a new kind of dependency or masks the person's problems. Certainly, there are these dangers. Furthermore, there are clear advantages to freeing yourself from a bad relationship without medication, as it is often in the arduous process of living through the self-discovery, the insights, and the psychological pain that the greatest strengthening and growth occur. Nevertheless, I have seen people whose fear and despair were so disabling that they could not act to end a bad relationship until these emotions were sufficiently reduced through medication.

If you find that your anxieties have been crippling your best efforts to break your attachment, I suggest that there is no need to be a hero. Consider consulting a psychiatrist who specializes in psychopharmacology. Tell him or her about the changes you want to make in your life and what emotions or symptoms have stood in the way. Make it clear that you want medication to help with a specific goal, not as a way of life. Bear in mind that there is no medication without side effects; find out all you can about a drug's side effects before deciding to use it. Also, bear in mind that these medications should not be used as a substitute for psychotherapy or support groups, because it is essential that you continue to work on your self-awareness and growth. Finally, with medication, as with psychotherapy, the aim is to get to a point where you will not need it anymore.

THE BASIC GOAL

The aim of all these approaches is liberation from the tyranny of your addiction. Some of the examples I have used, such as Kevin's mistreatment of Kim or Ruth's demeaning treatment of Harry, are so blatantly destructive that you can easily see the relationship should be terminated. And, of course, many people suffer even worse degradation and deprivation. But your unhappy situation need not be so extreme. The person you are addicted to may be decent and even admirable in many ways. But if you have done the decision-making work discussed here, have examined the relationship as objectively as you can, and have concluded there are significant frustrations and deprivations that are unlikely to change, you may still have found the relationship unacceptable or intolerable even though there have been no bruises or betrayals. And if what has ultimately been keeping you there is an addictive attachment, then by achieving your goal of breaking that addiction, you will gain the freedom to make more fulfilling choices. You will probably then go through a period of grieving, anxiety, and loneliness, but, as we will see, that is part of a process that will lead you to a better place.

5

A Period
of Consolidation
and Replenishment

You have gotten out of your addictive relationship. You have learned much about why you are drawn to people you will inevitably be miserable with, and you have firmed up your resolve not to waste another moment in frustrating and destructive relationships. Maybe it still takes willpower to say no, or maybe you have reached the point where you are turned off by, even "allergic" to, the type of person who once was so appealing.

But with all this considerable progress you might still not be ready to pursue, enjoy, and sustain a relationship with someone who you love and who enhances your feelings about yourself and your life. And that is perfectly okay. You have won a major victory. Now it's time to pause, reflect, and consolidate your gains.

The idea of a time to pause might go very much against the grain. Giving up your addictive love can leave you feeling that there is a huge void in the very center of your being, and just as "nature abhors a vacuum" you may find the feelings of emptiness and loneliness so intolerable that you will feel the need to

immediately pursue a new attachment. That can be very dangerous, because your perceptions and your judgment are likely to
be faulty and distorted when you are driven by such desperation.
You can easily overlook evidence that a given person may be bad
for you in the old way—or in some new but equally unwhole-
some way.

So take the pressure off yourself to get out there and find the
right person immediately. You have other tasks to accomplish
that will make your quest for a good relationship more likely to
be successful in the long run. This does not necessarily mean no
dating. In fact dating can help you consolidate your gains. Carrying your hard-won knowledge of what has been dangerously
attractive to you, you can look at each new person with your eyes
wide open: Who is this person? How does it feel to be with him
(her)? Do I want to get to know him (her) better? Now that I'm
free of my addiction, what else can attract me to someone?

These important questions can be best examined if you are
not propelled by a frantic urge to attach to someone new. It is
not only that rebounds too frequently are blind, but also that you
may be cutting short an important stage in your development.
(This does not mean that at this point you couldn't meet someone who is truly wonderful for you, and it would be folly to push
such a person away simply because you're taking time to consolidate your gains. But be alert to whether you are being driven by
a genuine feeling about this person or by a need to fill the vacuum.) So take the time to become at home with yourself in this
new place—a place that may seem strange, barren, and depressing because it is without the old drama, pain, and tension.

A TIME FOR MOURNING

One of the helpful tasks of this period will be mourning for
what was good in the last relationship. This starts with recognizing the fact that it is over and that you may never again see or
hear from or be intimate with that person who once seemed so
central to your existence. It can be useful, too, to mourn the
wasted months or years that you spent in that relationship and

perhaps in other dead-end relationships. The waste has been real (whatever the good things you may have derived from the relationship), and it is being honest with yourself to acknowledge that waste. You can use that recognition to increase your determination not to trash another life-minute that way.

How does one mourn a lost relationship and wasted years? It is mostly a matter of being open to your feelings of sadness and anger instead of pushing the pain away. This does not mean dwelling on these feelings endlessly, because being obsessed with thoughts about the relationship can become a way of keeping the connection alive. Mourning should not be a way of clinging but a way of letting go and saying good-bye. People I have worked with over the years have developed many ways to mourn. After finally severing her tie to Kevin, Kim at first tried to override her feelings of loss by telling herself how glad she was to be rid of him (which was true) and by immediately plunging into a social life. In some ways this worked well, providing distractions and interesting experiences. But she found herself at times unexpectedly breaking into tears, and she often awoke at three or four in the morning feeling frightened and hopeless. She realized that these unbidden tears and nocturnal attacks of desolation were telling her that she had to confront and deal with the fact that an emotionally powerful relationship had died. So she occasionally took the time just to sit and repeat, over and over, the words "no more Kevin," and let the accompanying feelings of grief wash over her. After many repetitions, stretching over many weeks, she found that "no more Kevin" had lost much of its power to evoke sadness. From time to time she would say, not as "sour grapes," but with genuineness, "no more Kevin—thank God."

Warren, the fashion photographer, who had finally broken his intense tie to the beautiful but self-serving and elusive Diane, claimed he felt nothing but rage toward her. This rage, along with other unfinished emotional business, was spilling over into his relationships with the new women he was pursuing as replacements for Diane. It was clear that even though he had not had contact with Diane for a while, he had not let go of her.

Borrowing Kim's method, I suggested he repeat the words "no more Diane" and get into the feelings these words evoked. Warren, ever creative, developed his own variation. Instead of just saying the words, he would look at pictures he had taken of her and write down short statements or questions that came to mind. One such list he made during his mourning period went like this:

> What will I do without you?
> What if I made a terrible mistake?
> It was not a mistake and I ended it and she's gone.
> You're so beautiful. I miss you so much.
> I can't believe we'll never make love again. Never, ever.
> I miss the fun times.
> If only you had tried a little harder.
> If only you wanted what I wanted.
> But she didn't and never will. Never, ever.
> I have to bury her.
> I picture her in a coffin. She is wearing her black transparent
>   negligee. Somebody is closing the coffin lid. Tightly.
> She is lowered into the ground.
> I throw dirt on her coffin.
> I cry and cry.
> Good-bye, Diane.
> I walk away. I fight looking back.

Warren did many such "mourning exercises," as he called them, and he found that he was thinking of her less and less. At times he would get what he called "Diane attacks," usually on weekends when he had made no plans. One night, in the midst of an acute episode of loss and loneliness, he sat down to write more statements, but this time they took a different and surprising turn.

> I feel like a helpless baby. Mommy, please come.
> Nobody loves me, not even you.
> Why are you always on the phone?

Why don't you ever play with me?
Why did you flirt with other men behind daddy's back?
Why didn't you protect me from that?
Didn't you love me?
Didn't you know how to take care of me?

This unplanned turn in his writing drove home to Warren that his mourning went far beyond his relationship with Diane. He was mourning for the relationship he had not had with his mother, for his mother not having been there enough, for what he had missed out on as a child and ways he had been short-changed. As he experienced the connection between his feelings for Diane and his childhood feelings, he was increasingly able not only to disconnect his longing for his mother's love from his longing for Diane's love, but also to let go of his longing for each of them.

Being Your Own Continuity

The mourning period involves your deepening recognition of the finality of what had been a central and intense romantic relationship. The loss of someone who, for whatever length of time, shared so many moments and experiences with you may well cause you to feel that your life is irreparably broken and discontinuous. And when that has happened several times, you can begin to feel like a shattered ceramic vase, with shards and fragments lying about. Penny, a forty-two-year-old woman who had been divorced after a ten-year marriage and had had several intense and lengthy relationships with romantic but commit-ment-phobic men, had just painfully ended the most recent of these affairs. "I can't stand the feeling that my life has been so chopped up," she said sadly. "I can hardly walk down a street or pass a restaurant or hear a song that doesn't bring to mind some beautiful moment with some man who was everything to me at the time. But none of them are there for me to say, 'Remember when we ate there?' 'Remember when we both cried at the end of *Terms of Endearment*?' 'Remember driving through the countryside listening to Linda Rondstat singing that?' There's no continuity to my life."

It is wonderful when people have long and lasting relationships and can look back over countless shared experiences, can laugh about them, can even argue about them all over again, and can look forward to more experiences together. And it can be demoralizing when there is no one with whom to share old memories or accumulate new ones. As Penny said, "I don't want to go for a drive with one more new guy and say, 'That's where I went to elementary school.' "

You may well be experiencing some version of that feeling at this point, so it is important to use this period of consolidation to see and be strengthened by a profoundly simple truth—*you are your own continuity.* That may seem self-evident, but if you let it fully in, it can heal over many of the cracks and discontinuities you feel in your life. In all the many experiences you've had, one person has always been present, and that is you. Etched in the neurons of your brain are the memories of every one of these experiences—some that can easily be brought to mind, others that can be unexpectedly triggered by a sudden sight, sound, or touch. You carry all these around. This is your story. These are the experiences that have gone into shaping you, who you are today, how you think and feel. You are the calendar of your years, the diary of your days, the time clock of your hours. You are, to a great extent, who you have been. Nobody can take that away. You will always be the person these experiences have formed.

So try to get to feel, know, and enjoy the continuity of your life. Don't push away memories that are painful because the relationship didn't work out. Focus instead on the fact that you were there and that it was you who felt certain things, did certain things, enjoyed some moments thoroughly and suffered through others. If you accept that your life has continuity and cohesiveness, even if people in that story are no longer in your life, you can decrease your sense of loss and bitterness about the relationships that didn't work out. If you recognize that you are the thread that connects the various beginnings and endings in your past, then you can realize that you will be the thread that will spin forward to connect the events of your future. And you can use all you have learned from seeing the continuity of your history to shape the future differently.

Carla, the woman who felt her husband Jack knew her so little after four years of marriage, separated from him when she felt that the loneliness of being without him couldn't be much worse than the loneliness of being with him. To her surprise, she felt like her whole life was shattered. "As little as I felt Jack knew me, I realize we spent a lot of time together and shared many activities, family events, and just the day-to-day living," she told me. "I feel like that whole period of my life didn't exist if he is no longer with me and like my current life doesn't have a foundation. Even though our tracks were separate, they were parallel, and now it's as if I'm a monorail."

To help her deal with this strange feeling of discontinuity, she began to look at the photos she had taken from the earliest days of their romance. Then she began writing down the memories the pictures brought back. At first it felt almost unbearably painful, but then she began to notice something—that so many of the memories of their laughing together were because of something funny she said and so many of the memories of their doing something together were of activities she initiated. Carla said, "I realized I am the owner of my sense of humor, I can initiate and plan interesting meetings, I am even the one who took the pictures. I own these abilities. I did these things before Jack, and they don't depend on my being with Jack. I am the me that runs through all this."

It can be difficult to hold on to the truth of your own continuity in a sustained and reliable way in the midst of the suffering that often accompanies the end of an important relationship. If you lose that perspective, it can be particularly helpful, as during the period of acute withdrawal from your addictive relationship, to turn to your friends, family, self-help groups, or psychotherapy. They can reflect your self and your history back to you, and thus help you to regain your sense of wholeness and ongoingness.

EASING YOUR LONELINESS

Loneliness is one of the few feelings nobody wants. People may choose to be alone and enjoy the sweet pleasure of their solitude, but that is not the painful feeling of loneliness. People may actively seek to experience other unpleasurable feelings — for example, to feel fear by reading horror tales or parachuting from airplanes, to feel sadness by going to tragic plays or tear-jerking movies, to feel anger and thus put themselves in situations that are enraging or to feel pain in mountain climbing and other pursuits. But nobody I know of enjoys the experience of being lonely.

Loneliness may in part reside in us as a primitive biological reaction — not unlike that of the steer who has been cut off from the herd and is bellowing to get back, or of the bear cub whose mother has been killed and who wanders around whimpering and lost. In the movie *Never Cry Wolf* there is an unforgettable scene where a young scientist who is studying the behavior of wolves is let off a small airplane onto a frozen arctic wasteland. His supplies and equipment are left with him, and then the plane taxis away on its ski landing gear. As it starts to take off, the young man looks around and sees icy barrenness stretching to every horizon. Panic sweeps over him. In terror, he runs after the plane, screaming for it to return, but it takes off without him, leaving him totally alone. The audience, certainly including me, could feel this nightmarish surge of loneliness.

The end of a romantic relationship — even a very unsatisfactory one, even one that you chose to end — leaves an empty space, and that empty space can fill up with loneliness. The task is to get through the pain without being dragged down into a prolonged despair, without taking self-destructive actions, without using alcohol or narcotics, and without forming attachments to people who are wrong for you.

A key to dealing constructively with your loneliness is to see that it is mostly coming from the lost and needy child in you. Once you see the Attachment Hunger origins of your loneliness, you can also recognize that your reality is being distorted through the eyes and emotions of that forsaken child. Your child self doesn't believe you can survive emotionally—or perhaps even physically—without ongoing attachment. But your adult self knows that you can survive and carry on alone quite well for as long as it's necessary. The child in you feels helpless to do anything to end the painful feelings, to soothe himself or to make new and better things happen; your adult self knows that there is much that you can do to change your feelings and your situation. The child in you is on Infant Time, believing this pain will go on forever, that a Saturday night alone is an eternity in the arctic; your adult self knows that the pain will end, perhaps with the next friendly voice, and that a Saturday night is just a few short hours that can be spent profitably or entertainingly. You may have to struggle to get your adult voice to rise above the child's howls, but once it does, and the perspective shifts, you can begin to reassure and comfort the child. You can tell the child that you know that loneliness hurts but that you are there for him so that he's not really alone, that there are all kinds of things that you and he can do to improve the situation, and that bad feelings, like all feelings, always change.

Your lonely inner child may also hold another mistaken belief—that there can never again be another person who will love him, or who he will love—perhaps at all, and certainly not as much—as the person he just lost. You can point out to this child that while there was only one mommy or one daddy, there are now many people who could give and receive his love. The inner child may at times feel, "nobody cares," but that is rarely true. And it certainly need never be true if you really and actively care for that little girl or boy in you who is feeling so forlorn. If *you* care, then even when there is not a romantic partner in your life, you are always with a person, yourself, who values you and is there for you. So, listen to the cries of loneliness from the child within, and then tell that child everything he or she needs to hear at a time like this.

One way of doing this is to write letters to that child from the most wise and loving part of yourself. Carla, who dealt with her feelings of her life being fragmented without Jack, by looking at photos of the two of them and getting a sense of her continuity with that woman in the pictures, also tried this technique. She wrote: "You are feeling that without Jack there, without his coming home each night, without his being there to watch TV with you or to sleep next to you or to make the coffee in the morning, there is nobody that loves you. First of all, you are forgetting that there were lots of time you were lonely when Jack was there in his absent way. Besides, I love you, I think you're terrific, and we will continue to do a lot together. And there are all our friends and relatives who love us both, little Carla and big Carla. Now, I know it's not the same as having that one special person, but I promise you that even if Jack and I never get together again, I will do my best to find someone we can love and feel safe with and who will love us and share our life. So there's really no need for you to feel so all alone and unloved." Carla told me, "When I start writing these things to the child in me at first I feel very silly and I'm glad nobody's watching. But I end up feeling much better."

Turning Your Loneliness Around

Besides comforting the forlorn inner child, there is much you can do to turn the lonely feelings into a positive force. This involves making specific and deliberate efforts to combat *the inertia of loneliness.* As we discussed, the feeling of loneliness can sometimes hurl us into self-destructive actions, aimed at anesthetizing us or distracting us from that loneliness. But it can also sink us into a paralysis, a helpless, hopeless passivity that keeps us from improving our lot. We may find it hard to make decisions. We may long to turn somewhere for solace and warmth but we don't know where. This inertia can drag us down and down, if we let it, until we either can't stand it anymore and fight back or we close the door to life and sit alone in the dark.

To begin to go from a passive to an active position, we have to see our loneliness not just as something undesirable, but also as an opportunity. The wise and caring parent part of us can help the inner child not only by holding, soothing, and reassuring it,

but also by taking it by the hand and saying, "Enough of just sitting there—let's go." For you to activate this more vital part of you, it can be useful to ask yourself, "What are all those things I always told myself I wanted to do when I had the time and opportunity?" Another way to phrase it is: "What are all the things I would like to do if I wasn't so lonely and depressed?" Actually make a list, as full and lengthy as you can. Then prioritize your list, and push yourself to begin on at least one or two of the items.

Warren, in a prolonged slump after breaking up with Diane, knew there were many things he always wanted to get around to, many interests he had stopped pursuing or never pursued. He couldn't get himself going until he posed the question to himself this way: "What are all the things I'd like to do if Diane had turned out to be more loving or if I really was in a good relationship?" He realized that if he weren't drained by his loneliness he would want to pursue the artistic and not just the fashion end of photography. He told me, "I first got into photography as an art form and won some photo contests as a teenager. Then life got too busy with making a living and getting involved with difficult women. I really could use this healing period to get myself back to my original interest, so I'll pretend that everything is beautiful and supportive in my love life to get me going, and then maybe, when I'm really into it and getting a charge out of it, I won't need that pretense."

Other people I know have put a whole host of activities and interests back on their agenda. They pursued new hobbies or returned to old ones. They took classes in things they always wanted to know more about. They got in touch with friends they had not seen for a while and with acquaintances they wanted to get to know better.

One particular type of activity has, for many people, an especially beneficial effect in combating loneliness. Recent research has shown that engaging in activities that help others has a definite antidepressant effect, not only by making us feel pleased that we are doing something worthwhile, but also by actually *releasing chemicals in our bodies that act as natural antidepressants*, lifting our spirits and giving us a happier outlook. This research suggests that the more this altruistic work is "hands on," the more it is directly interactive with the people we are helping, the more natural antidepressant is released. It can be in your own best interest to be altruistic, so consider scheduling some regular volunteer work as a way of combating your loneliness and depression. Many people who begin helping others for this reason continue doing so long after they have a new love relationship.

By activating multiple connections to people and activities, you can gratify much of the Attachment Hunger that has been floating about loosely and aimlessly since you ended your relationship. Taking these initiatives requires boldness, and it is not always easy to be bold when you are feeling the inertia of loneliness. But you can try to turn this defeated feeling into a feeling of nothing-to-lose that can then spur you to take effective action.

Anticipating Attacks of Loneliness

By now you know that there may be particular times of the day and particular events when you are most likely to be vulnerable to loneliness. For many people the most vulnerable time is the end of the day, when work is over and they come home to an "empty" apartment. For others it is that time before going to sleep. They resist turning off the light and the TV and leaving themselves in darkness and silence. For others it is when they awaken in the middle of the night and all seems desolate, bleak, and frightening. For others it is weekends without plans, vacations, or occasions they used to share with that person no longer in their life.

What can you do? If you anticipate these times, you can make plans for dealing with them, perhaps meeting someone for dinner instead of heading right home, or calling a friend you know you can talk to, perhaps about your feelings—or perhaps simply to be soothed by making contact. At other times, you may decide *not* to distract yourself from the loneliness, but to plunge very deeply into the feeling in order to explore it and get to know it. This approach can help you discover that it's a temporary and not necessarily formidable discomfort. For example, Harry, who had been treated so demeaningly by Ruth, suffered terrible episodes of loneliness in the middle of the night. He often woke about half-past three, and at that hour, his life seemed so hopelessly without warmth or connection that he would seriously contemplate suicide. He would watch TV or read and try to drive the despairing thoughts out of his mind. Sometimes this was helpful and he could return to sleep, but other times it was useless. I suggested that when he couldn't distract himself, he should get deeply into the painful feeling and write it all down, particularly the dark and pessimistic way his life seemed at these times. He found that writing his feelings put them more "out there" where he could look at them and often helped him get some relief. But more importantly, he told me, "The next day when I looked at what I had written it seemed both familiar and unfamiliar. I could recall the pain I was feeling when I wrote about being on an uninhabited planet where nobody will ever love me, but since I was not feeling the same way when I read it over, I realized that just because I sometimes felt something intensely didn't mean that's how things really were." Harry became more accepting of and less frightened by his middle of the night loneliness, and as he did, these episodes became less frequent and less intense.

ONE POTATO IS NOTHING TO BE ASHAMED OF

It is particularly important not to be put off by misguided feeling of *shame* about being alone. This feeling of shame can keep people from entering and enjoying a restaurant alone, participating in events intended for single people, feeling comfortable with couples and can even, as Kim discovered, crop up in relation to the smallest details of everyday life. Soon after she had stopped seeing Kevin, she was buying vegetables in a neighborhood store and had picked out a large potato for baking. She suddenly became terribly self-conscious. She was afraid that the checkout clerk would see her buying only one potato, conclude that she was alone, and see her as a failure and a loser. Swept with shame she bought a second potato she did not need. She told me, "The strange thing is, even when Kevin and I were seeing each other, we often didn't get together for dinner and many times I bought myself just one potato without thinking about it. But somehow, since I knew that I was no longer with Kevin, I felt the whole world knew—as if I was wearing a sign that said 'No man wants me.' "

Combating this feeling of shame requires that you recognize that you are a complete and worthwhile person all by yourself and that being "single" is a valid and okay place to be, even for those who dearly want to be in a good love relationship. Being alone is usually better and more fulfilling than being in an unsatisfying or destructive love relationship.

When I was writing my syndicated column "On Your Own," one of my readers, Tam Deachman of Vancouver, Canada, wrote to me that "I suspect many singles, whether they admit it or not, have low self-esteem. They have been conditioned to feel guilty about their condition, to feel that they are not quite whole or normal." Out of this concern, Deachman developed a set of positive statements that he calls "The Single Person's Declaration of Independence." Here are some portions of it:

> I am, for the foreseeable future, single and independent. . . . Do not feel sorry for me; for I am not at all sorry for myself. On the contrary, I enjoy a full spectrum of freedoms and options, and endeavor to use them with thoughtful responsibility toward others.
> I am free to form healthy relationships of any intensity or of any duration, without answering to anyone outside of that relationship; yet I am aware that love can be hurtful and must be cradled with sensitivity and respect.
> I am free to indulge in my own tastes. I can come and go as I please. I am free to choose my own friends, my home, and all my possessions. I am free to seek good health or to abuse my body. I need to conform to no one; yet I realize that bizarre nonconformity on my part may injure me or my reputation and embarrass or hurt friends, relatives, and associates.
> I am free to be me. Like you I am a totally unique individual. There is no one else, anywhere, quite like me. Sure, I may sometimes wish I were someone else. But all in all, I enjoy being me. I enjoy reacting spontaneously to the world around me without having to role play or otherwise allow for the reactions of a permanent partner. . . . I have made certain choices for now, and I willingly accept the responsibility those choices entail.

You might not feel quite this way. Nevertheless, when you are in danger of being inundated by feelings of loneliness, shame or failure because you have no partner in your life, reading this "Declaration of Independence" can be a useful antidote. It can help you to restore some of your lost perspective and self-esteem. This will make you feel better and more self-respecting about where you are now. From that more self-respecting place, you will then be more likely to create opportunities to meet new people and more likely to be responsive to people you meet. You will also come across as a more interesting and appealing person.

In sum, this interim period is a very critical time for strengthening your sense of who you are and what you want. The watchword I would suggest for this phase is this: Keep growing as if you'll be alone forever, but keep your eyes open for friendship and love as if you will meet someone wonderful today.

6

CHARTING YOUR PERSONAL JOURNEY

The humorist Robert Benchley once wrote an essay expressing his befuddlement about how to start building a bridge. Here I am, he mused, with all the building materials on my side of the river, and way over there is the other bank. Now what? How does the bridge get from here to there? More specifically, what do I do first?

In our intent to go from a bad love relationship (or no love relationship) to a satisfying one, we can often feel that we have all the materials—our insight into past self-defeating patterns, our awareness of what we must avoid, our strong desire to succeed—but we may still not be sure where to begin. More to the point, we may not know where we want to go. We may have a general idea of what we want—a loving relationship, commitment, marriage—but we may not clearly see what that involves for us or what kind of person we want and need for the relationship we desire. Without those insights, we may be attempting to build a bridge to nowhere.

Instead of just getting caught up in trying to meet, attract, and win someone in the world out there, we need to take the time and the care to look within us and to truly know what our deepest and most basic needs are. We may never have stopped to realize that we are, each of us, on a journey, a unique and profoundly personal journey that takes its direction and purpose from yearnings, wishes, and values at the core of our identity. If we are not in touch with the journey we need to take for our own unfolding, then how can we know what manner of companion would best accompany us? If we do not take our own development seriously, then how can we expect someone to take us seriously? If we don't know where we need to go, why should anyone want to go with us? Or if someone does go with us, might it not be with the expectation that we, rudderless and compassless, would easily sign on to his or her journey? And if this is the case, would that not lead to another bad and unhappy place?

It is probably unrealistic to try and determine where you want your journey to take you in the distant future, because your destination will shift as you develop and your life circumstances change. But it is essential wisdom to know where your personal growth and gratification lie in the next phase of your life. You will need to ask yourself some searching questions:

- What about myself do I value most and want to take with me on this journey?
- What do I want to leave behind?
- What do I enjoy in my life and want to pursue to a greater extent than I have?
- What parts of me feel underdeveloped or damaged and need to be strengthened or repaired?
- In this next phase of my life do I want to develop my spiritual side? My capacity to give love? My capacity to receive love?
- Do I need to stretch my self-confidence and my feelings of independence?
- Do I want to become more tuned in to my own inner rhythms and judgment and less dependent on the approval and acceptance of others?

- Do I want to become less self-absorbed and more open to others? Do I need to become less controlling?
- Do I need to enlarge my capacity for intimacy? For openness? For trust?
- And in practical terms, in the next phase of my journey, is it important for me to marry? To have a committed relationship without marriage? To have love without commitment? To create a family? To further my career? To be affluent? To give up certain addictions? To free up and develop my sexuality? To pursue certain interests or develop certain abilities?

A love relationship is in itself a wonderful and beckoning destination point. But unless you pause to realize that it is also just a part—however important—of a larger personal journey, you may look for a love relationship as if "one size fits all," without taking into consideration the unique size and shape of your own needs and goals; or as if anywhere the love relationship takes you is okay. Being aware of your needs and goals can help you to realize that you have much to say about where you want your life trip to go and that you can decide how fully or meagerly you will pursue that trip. Paradoxically the love relationship you seek will be immeasurably better if it enhances, nurtures, and supports those aspects of your journey that have nothing to do with a love relationship. Or, at the very least, it will be much more satisfying if it does not block or detour other important aspects of that journey.

It is important to take the time to ask yourself the questions I have just posed. Sit down and write out your responses. To focus your exploration, you might also find it helpful first to respond to the questionnaire on life goals below. In responding to the questionnaire, keep in mind that there are no correct answers. Just be searchingly honest with yourself. Joseph Campbell tells us that it is crucial for each of us to "follow our bliss." Let this exercise put you more in touch with what that wise advice means to you.

THE JOURNEY AHEAD

QUESTION:

What aspects of myself and what goals do I most deeply wish to develop and pursue in the years ahead?

SCORING: Place an "A" next to those aspects and goals that are very important to you.
Place a "B" next to those aspects and goals that are somewhat important to you.
Place a "C" next to those aspects and goals that are of little importance to you.

INNER DEVELOPMENT:

_____ Becoming more relaxed and less frantic.

_____ Becoming more self-confident.

_____ Becoming more in touch with my own needs.

_____ Developing my spiritual side.

_____ Increasing my feelings of worth and self-esteem.

_____ Increasing my capacity to be loving.

_____ Increasing my capacity to accept love.

_____ Becoming more free of the need for approval.

_____ Becoming less judgmental of myself and others.

_____ Becoming more playful.

_____ Becoming more generous spirited.

_____ Giving up an addiction (to a substance, person or behavior).

_____ Overcoming and/or accepting a personal handicap.

_____ Becoming more assertive.

_____ Becoming more competitive and aggressive.

_____ Becoming less fearful.

_____ Becoming more decisive.

_____ Becoming better able to express my anger.

_____ Becoming better able to control my anger.

RELATIONSHIPS:

_____ Becoming better able to state my needs and try to get them met.

_____ Becoming more open and self-disclosing.

_____ Refusing to be mistreated or misused.

_____ Avoiding behaving counter to my best interest in order to win love.

_____ Becoming more able to let someone take care of me.

_____ Becoming more able to let someone be good to me.

_____ Becoming more trusting.

_____ Becoming less trusting and more cautious.

_____ Becoming more independent from my family.

_____ Establishing greater closeness with my family.

_____ Becoming more responsible in my love relationships.

_____ Becoming more sensitive and giving in my love relation-ships.

_____ Increasing my ability to sustain a love relationship.

_____ Seeking involvement with a person who is giving and loving.

_____ Avoiding involvement with a person who is not giving and loving.

_____ Getting more joy and pleasure from sex.

INTERESTS:

_____ Having an exciting and adventurous life.

_____ Traveling frequently.

_____ Trying new things.

_____ Developing a particular talent.

_____ Keeping my body in good shape.

_____ Paying more attention to my appearance.

_____ Paying less attention to my appearance.

_____ Actively pursuing physical wellness.

_____ Developing a specific athletic ability.

_____ Exploring my own inner thoughts, feelings, and wishes.

_____ Making a contribution to society or the world.

_____ Deepening my commitment to a cause.

_____ Pursuing cultural and artistic interests.

_____ Deepening my religious involvement and development.

PRACTICAL MATTERS:

_____ Advancing my current career.

_____ Getting more training and education toward my work goals.

_____ Changing my career.

_____ Pursuing a career that will be more deeply satisfying.

_____ Becoming more competent and responsible.

_____ Becoming financially secure.

_____ Becoming affluent.

_____ Having a child (or children).

———— Having more free and unscheduled time.

———— Having a more stable life-style.

———— Moving from where I live.

———— Making a major geographical move.

HONORING YOUR PERSONAL JOURNEY

In that interim between Kevin and David, Kim, perhaps for the first time in her life, began to think about what she needed and wanted now that she was no longer propelled by her Attachment Hunger. She realized how important it was for her to firm up a shaky sense of self-worth, to feel more solid and grounded, and to be more direct and assertive with her friends and on her job. In her family relationships, she set as her goal no longer permitting herself to be emotionally stunted or manipulated by her cold and controlling mother. Kim could see that the men whose love she had been obsessed with winning, from her father to Kevin, had been worse than useless in helping her to develop those aspects of herself. Their disdain and rejection had seemed to confirm her most wretched feelings about her worth. The inconsistent ways they treated her had undermined her efforts to feel more substantial and firmly rooted. And all of this weakened her ability to deal effectively and competently with her mother. "I know that it is up to me to keep myself from being manipulated by my mother's icy anger and guilt trips," Kim told me. "It is not the job of the man in my life. But it's hard to stand up to her when there is no one to turn to for support. The only times that Kevin encouraged me to stand up to my mother was when my going along with her would interfere with his plans."

David, in contrast, gave Kim real support. He would say things like, "You're getting all upset and anxious about opposing your mother on this, but really she's being too darn demanding. She would like to make you feel that you're selfish but you're not. You're simply a grown-up woman with a right to make your own plans. So don't let her press your buttons." Kim, describing one such incident said "and then he gave me a big hug." She added, "It's not so much what David says—it's the feeling he's there on my side."

Kim clearly saw that getting free of her mother's control was an important goal in her developmental journey, and she could deeply appreciate the difference between a destructive and constructive traveling companion. When I asked Harry to think about his personal journey, he said, "I'm too old for the kind of relationship Ruth offers me. I was always too old to take that kind of abuse, but now it's clear I really need something different. I want my remaining years to be something that they've never been—mellow, fun filled, easy, and loving. . . . I don't want to struggle anymore to get someone to be nice to me. There will probably be some illnesses and infirmity ahead, and I don't want Ruth screaming at me for being an inconvenience. I'm basically a good man, and I want a companion to appreciate that and to value the love I would give her." It took Harry almost a year after this conversation to break with Ruth. But his awareness of how wrong Ruth was as a partner for his journey was a major step in his being able to let go of her and to open himself to someone much better suited.

At thirty-four, Laura was the youngest partner in a large New York law firm. As a matrimonial lawyer she was dynamic, hard working, and hard hitting. The men she went out with were similarly driven and successful. The few romantic relationships she had over the years were intense and passionate but not emotionally intimate. There never seemed to be enough time or serenity to develop much closeness, and she wasn't aware she wanted it. The same pattern held in her current relationship, with Les, the owner and chief executive officer of a chain of hotels. Laura had been seeing him once or twice a week for six months. Then she discovered he was also seeing two other women with at least equal frequency and involvement. She was devastated and enraged. Les said he was sorry she was so upset but he thought she understood that he was not "exclusive." He said he was surprised at her reaction because he always felt that she also wanted it that way. That is when Laura first consulted me. She was very

confused. "Sometimes I want to dump him. Sometimes I'm determined to win him and keep him. Sometimes I want to win
him just to get the satisfaction of then rejecting him." She daydreamed about creating a scene in his office. She even briefly
entertained the idea of hiring some thugs to beat him up. But
she continued to see Les and to share him with these two other
women (and, she believed, perhaps others) for more than a year,
hoping to get him to want her exclusively. She became obsessed
with this task.

Totally lost in all this was any basic self-exploration as to
whether she really wanted Les and, if so, why. Was it the challenge? Did she need to win the competition? Did she want a love
relationship with him? With anybody? How did she really feel
toward Les? She simply would not address her deepest wants
and needs. When I tried to get her to focus on this, she would
say, "Don't give me that garbage about seeing what personal
journey I am on. I'll know it when I get there. Right now all I
know is that I want Les."

As Laura lived with the increasing frustration of Les's inconsistent availability, his now obvious deceptions, and his pacifying
promises to spend more time with her, her health began to suffer. She developed painful and debilitating intestinal spasms.
She finally saw that she would have to end the relationship, but
Les beat her to it. Laura fell into a depressed mood that lasted
for months. But it was during this period that for the first time
she could hear my question about where she wanted her life to
take her. "I realize I don't have the slightest idea who I am," she
told me one day. "I've been superachieving since elementary
school as a way of blocking out my feelings and trying to make
myself totally self-reliant. It all worked very well until I collapsed
after I lost whatever I thought I had with Les. When he told me
he thought I didn't need much from him, I realized I'd often
heard that from other men. But I see now that it's not true."

Beneath her frenzied workaholism, Laura began to discover
deep longings for affection and closeness, longings made even
more intense by her depriving childhood home life and her self-
deprivation as an adult. When she accompanied a friend on a

weekend retreat, she also discovered a long buried meditative and spiritual side that she now yearned to pursue. Laura's discoveries about herself transformed her ideas about what she wanted from a relationship. "I used to say I need a man to accept my hard work and crazy hours. I still will need that, because I won't be able to change that so quickly, but now that I know what I want my journey to be, I also will need a man who can accept and support my neediness and my spiritual side. I need someone whose journey goes well with mine."

Peter, a forty-four-year-old biologist, who had gained international recognition for his medical research, had watched as one relationship after another deteriorated in much the same way. He told me, "My romantic relationships always start with great joy. We would be ecstatic that we found each other and would feel very in love. Then after a while she would increasingly feel that I was rejecting her in favor of my work. Several women have used almost the same words. 'I feel way down on your priority list.' Elly [his most recent girlfriend] screamed, 'I feel like a widow and we aren't even married.' And I would begin to feel that these women were needy and demanding little babies and had no sense of how important my work was to me. I screamed back at Elly, 'You're trying to strangle me. Get a life!' She walked out, and I was left with my usual mixture of relief, sadness, and confusion about why it always goes so wrong."

As Peter reviewed and examined his relationships, he noted that the women he chose were all somewhat naive and dependent, with few strong interests, viewpoints, or goals of their own. Often they were considerably younger than he was. "I can see that I am attracted to women who look up to me, who listen wide-eyed to my explaining things and teaching them about art or biology or music or politics or whatever. How I love that role! So for a while we are both blissfully happy. But this type of woman soon becomes very dependent on me and resents some of the other heavy demands on my time and interests. Then I begin to resent what feels like her nagging and making me feel guilty and smothered. Our bliss becomes a nightmare of misunderstandings and recriminations."

Peter came to realize that his work as a medical scientist is a central and vital part of his journey, and that if he is to have a satisfying love relationship, it has to be with someone who respects that. "I see that I have to give more time and attention to a relationship and I'll try to do that. But I have to choose a woman based on who I really am. It has to be a mature woman with a strong sense of herself and a purpose and direction of her own. The problem is I've never been attracted to such women. I guess I feel if they don't need me and look up to me they could easily leave me. I'm not sure I can easily change who I'm attracted to. But at least I'm determined not to keep getting involved with the same kind of dependent woman who I will disappoint and be disappointed by."

The kind of realization Peter had is not limited to people who do such important work as his. The compelling aspects of one's personal journey could be almost anything: amassing a fortune, raising children of a previous marriage, being a devout adherent of a particular religion, being devoted to a social or political cause, or being actively involved in a deeply satisfying hobby or avocation. What is important is to recognize and prioritize the various aspects of your journey and to evaluate how important it is to you to have someone supportive of or compatible with those aspects. You will need to determine which aspects of your journey you can modify in order to meet the requirements of a particular relationship—and to what extent you can modify them—and which aspects are simply not negotiable.

Kim, for example, became increasingly aware that having a child was a crucial element of the journey she foresaw for herself. She realized that creating a family with the self-centered and contemptuous men she had previously been drawn to would be disastrous. Several times she had gotten involved with men who clearly told her they did not want children. With each of these men, she would tell herself that perhaps children were really not that important to her or that perhaps he would change his mind. She did not take seriously her own wish for a child, or his wish not to have one, until it came to a crunch on this issue. One man she dated for two years had children from a previous marriage. He had told her, "You're not really hearing me—I don't want more children. There's nothing to negotiate because there's no way to have one half of a child."

Kim said, "I still hung on to him out of my Attachment Hunger, and I rationalized it because I had a friend who married a man who said absolutely no children and later he changed his mind. But that's a long shot, and if my having a child is as important to me as I believe it is, I have to find someone who wants to do that trip with me."

Some people, in contrast, conclude that for them having a child is a negotiable priority. Laura was able to say, after some honest self-examination, "I would like to have a child, but I realize that I would put a good and happy love relationship above that, so if I do find someone I love and who loves me and lets me be me and who didn't want a child, I could give up having one. I'd feel some regret, but the good relationship would override that."

A substantial portion of my psychotherapy practice has been with couples. As I have observed their struggles with feelings of frustration and disappointment in their relationships, I have come to realize two things. A certain amount of frustration and disappointment is inevitable; no matter who the other person is, no human being was assembled to our exact specifications. But, clearly, some couples would not have gotten together in the first place if one or both had known what his or her own journey was about, and what needs and goals were crucial. If they had, they would have looked for and found a partner who was much more compatible.

That said, as should be clear from this chapter, there is no simple formula for making a happy and gratifying choice. For one person, having a partner who is uninhibited and passionate sexually may be so important that if he chooses someone far less interested in sex than he or she is, then no matter how well they get along on other levels, there will be chronic conflict and disappointment. Another person may also wish for a more free and frequent sexual relationship but give such high priority to other factors—for example, communication, humor, shared interests—that for him or her there is an acceptable and satisfying trade-off.

In short, for every aspect that is part of your journey you have to know what your requirements are and, in choosing your traveling companion, know what trade-offs you are and are not willing to make. When you know what you need you have a much better chance of turning away from those who would not fulfill you and turning toward those who would. This simple idea probably works well for you in other areas of your life. If you want to visit museums and cathedrals on your vacation, then you don't go on safari; if you want bright lights and action, then you don't go to a remote and quiet tropical island. And if you want to buy a steak, you don't try to get it from a baker.

Take the journey that will satisfy your deepest and most important needs, and choose a travel companion who enhances rather than inhibits that journey.

7

How to Avoid a Good Love Relationship

It leaves you nowhere when you tell yourself, "The type of person who would be good for me just doesn't turn me on," as if that were an unchangeable fact, encoded in your genes or set in your stars. Just as there are reasons why you were drawn to someone bad for you, there are reasons why now, perhaps even after you are no longer hooked into bad relationships, you have not been able to be attracted to someone good for you, and why you may have disqualified people with whom you might have had a good and loving relationship.

Unfortunately, your reasons for this self-defeating avoidance are largely unconscious, camouflaged from your awareness by rationalization and other forms of self-delusion. There are, however, ways you can strip away that camouflage and make the hidden reasons accessible, and, when you do, your emerging awareness really can help you to feel excited about someone who is good for you. In Chapter 8, we'll look at your possible motives for shooting yourself in the foot. But first you need to learn to recognize your strategies for self-sabotage.

TOO NICE

About halfway through that long period between Kevin and David, a period of dating in which Kim was as distancing and porcupinish as Kevin ever was, an incident occurred that led Kim to a breakthrough in self-awareness. She had met Ralph at the wedding of a close friend. He was, in fact, the groom's best man, and she was attracted not only to his undeniable good looks but also to the articulate and humorous way he toasted the bride and groom and to his unself-conscious freedom in dancing with her and others. She was pleased when he called her and asked her out. On their first date, dinner at a quiet restaurant he had picked "so we can get to know each other," Kim found herself laughing a great deal and having a delightful time. But she also felt strangely uncomfortable and irritated. By the end of the evening she had made several remarks designed to keep him at a distance if not to push him away. She told me about these mixed feelings and explained her discomfort by saying, "Maybe I'm not ready yet." Although she accepted readily when he called for a second date, she could sense an underlying resentment toward him, a feeling that there was something "nerdy" in his obvious and open interest in her.

Kim felt tense and off center as she dressed for this second date. She made an effort to look especially attractive and yet felt annoyed at herself for doing so. Ralph arrived on time, not the hour or two late that was Kevin's style, and when she opened the door he was standing there with a warm smile and a bouquet of flowers. She took one look at the flowers and, before she could think about what she was doing, closed the door in his face! She stood with her back against the door as if keeping out something dangerous or repugnant. After about a minute she recovered and gasped, "Oh my God—what did I do?" She pulled the door open but Ralph was gone. He never called her again and she was too embarrassed to call him. (She learned weeks later from the friend at whose wedding she'd met him that he had been very shaken up by her behavior. He'd said, "I was very attracted to her, but anyone who would do something like that is too nuts for me.")

This incident became the subject of much exploration in Kim's therapy. Kim had come to recognize and understand the roots of her old attraction to men who treated her badly. As she put it, "I'm always hoping I can turn the frog into a prince but I end up croaking on a lily pad." Despite this awareness, Kim continued to deny that she was avoiding men who were good to her and for her. The only such men available, she insisted, were some undesirable losers. Kim tried to bolster her denial by painting a picture of Ralph as unappealingly needy and dependent. "Who brings flowers on a second date?" she remarked. I reminded her that she'd had a very favorable first impression of him and that she seemed to get uncomfortable during the first date only because he was interested in her and she was having a good time. She tried to deny that, too, but only half-heartedly. She knew it was the truth. "For the sake of our trying to understand what's going on," I said, "let's assume that you were threatened about the possibility of a relationship with someone potentially available for something good so you panicked and blew it out of the water. If we assume that's true, then why? What might be so threatening about it?"

We will look later at the intriguing answers that Kim and I discovered together. But for now I ask you to notice whether you tend to discount someone who easily and openly shows his or her interest in you as "too nice." Is that a weakness? Does it show an excess of neediness and dependence? In some instances, it might. Or, is "too nice" simply your rationalization for closing out a threatening possibility? Like Kim, you must ask yourself, "What might be so threatening about that? And just what do I do to avoid a relationship with someone good for me?"

Your self-defeating maneuvers are probably not as blatant and dramatic as Kim's literally and figuratively slamming the door on someone with promise. But they can be just as effective.

MAGNIFYING THE IMPERFECTIONS

It still amazes me when people who have overlooked and made excuses for the most offensive characteristics in someone they were unhappily addicted to magnify the slightest imperfections in someone with potential for a good relationship. They are often so repelled by these imperfections that they either write the person off or they make such a big deal about these that the person says, "Forget it."

Laura went through a period when she forced herself to go out with men who were much more emotionally available than Les and others had been, but she continued to find these more responsive men bland and dull. When she met Bob, however, she was instantly attracted to his combination of quiet reserve and warm interest in her and everything she said. "There's something very comfortable and solid about him. He's easy to be with. I'm sure when we go to bed it will be wonderful." And it was. They quickly developed a powerful and passionate sexual connection. "I think I'm in love," she told me. "I can't believe it. For the first time I think I'm falling in love with someone who loves me back and who makes me feel just great."

But a few weeks later Laura came in looking glum. "There's trouble in paradise," she announced. "I feel ashamed of what I am feeling but I can't help it. There are little things that Bob does that are turning me off. When he gets excited about something his voice goes up about an octave and he talks fast in a high-pitched tone that I simply can't stand. And also he sometimes dresses badly, like a dork, and I can hardly look at him. I know these things shouldn't mean anything compared to all the good stuff and the way he's being more and more affectionate, but these defects literally keep me up at night. I lie there with my eyes open feeling that I don't think I can go on, and that makes me feel awful and petty. And sad. But I'm afraid that if these things don't change, I will have to stop seeing him."

In his book *I'm Okay, You're Okay*, Tom Harris recounts a childhood incident. His friend's mother had announced that dessert would be a batch of homemade cookies. She then set the cookie jar on the table. Harris writes, "There followed a noisy scramble by the children to get into the jar with the littlest brother, age four, last, as usual. When he got to the jar he found only one cookie left and it had a small piece missing whereupon he grabbed it and threw it on the floor in a rage of despair, crying, 'My cookie is all broke.' " He comments, "It is the nature of the Child to mistake disappointment for disaster, to destroy the whole cookie because a piece is missing or because it isn't as big, as perfect or as tasty as someone else's cookie."

It struck me that something similarly childlike was going on in Laura. Because of a small imperfection, Laura was getting perilously close to smashing her promising relationship with Bob to smithereens. This raised many questions: Why is the voice of that picky child in her becoming so loud and overbearing at this particular time? Why this perfectionistic need to see the man she is involved with as being without a blemish? Why does she magnify these minor imperfections into unbearable deficiencies?

The most crucial question, in light of Laura's dismal romantic track record, was whether she was acting under some *inner unconscious compulsion to destroy a potentially good love relationship.*

For a while it was touch and go, and I wasn't sure Laura would be able to sustain a relationship with Bob while we explored these issues. Later, we will look at the course of this exploration and at how Laura resolved her internal conflicts. But if

you feel you may have a similar tendency, take the time to examine, as honestly as you can and preferably in writing, the following questions:

- What is there about this imperfection that makes it seem
  so crucial? Does it have a particular meaning for you? Does
  it remind you of something or someone?
- Are you so concerned with appearances and with how he
  or she will reflect on you that you let this imperfection
  override all the good things in your relationship?
- Do you have "pictures" of who you want that you formed
  a long time ago? Are you holding on to them too rigidly?
- Since you can always discover defects and shortcomings in
  anyone, is it possible that you are unconsciously driven to
  find, amplify, and obsess about these imperfections in order to give yourself a rationale to destroy a relationship that
  otherwise might develop happily?

I'M BORED OUT OF MY MIND

In the period following his breakup with the self-centered
and demanding Diane, Warren dated a succession of attractive
women, many of whom seemed sufficiently interesting, responsive, and emotionally available for the loving involvement he
claimed he wanted. With all of them, however, no matter how
promising the start, he soon told me, "I have to end it. She's very
nice but I am bored out of my mind."

The more involved and affectionate Warren's new woman
was, the more distracted and restless he seemed to become. After
a while his boredom would spread like a thick dark mist into his
sexual interest. "Maybe I just can't sustain a feeling of being
sexually excited about someone for long. Maybe nobody can and
I am expecting too much. After we've done everything and explored everything and it loses its novelty, the sex just doesn't
drive me wild the way it first did, the way I want it to." Later he
said, "I think I am looking for a woman I never get bored with
in bed and out of bed. You may think that's impossible, but let
me tell you that as infuriating as Diane was, I was never bored."

What is this boredom that Warren and others often complain of when they are in a nonaddicting relationship? There are certainly some individuals who many would agree are more boring than others—perhaps they have a limited range of interests, are cut off from their own feelings, or are dull and unengaging in their conversation. And there are some people who you might find boring because your style and interests are so extremely different from theirs. But often, these shortcomings are not the true basis for boredom.

I've often had the experience of meeting someone a patient had dismissed as boring and finding him or her quite interesting—sometimes much more interesting, in fact, than the "exciting" person who had been the object of the addiction.

As beauty is in the eyes of the beholder, boredom is often in the mind of the bored.

In the mind of each of us there is a place that is flat and barren and empty. Sometimes it is experienced as depression. Often it is experienced as boredom. For some people, it is a small place, a mere whistle stop. For others—including many who tend to get involved in tumultuous addictive relationships—it can be a desert that spreads across half a continent. If you recognize a sterile, colorless area within you, it can be helpful to acknowledge it and to know how it came to be there.

It likely came about through a deficiency in what child psychology researchers call a capacity for *self-soothing*. Since not all gratification can come from the outside, every infant and child must develop the ability to soothe some of the upset feelings precipitated by pain, needs, and even curiosity and desire for stimulation. Children adept at self-stimulation can entertain themselves, stretch their horizons, and take care of many of their own internal needs. Those less adept at it lean heavily on external caretaking and stimulation to calm their excitement and excite their calms. Independence grows from self-soothing and militates against the development of large barren areas within.

When a child is very young, this independence is nurtured by parenting that is neither underprotective nor overprotective. If parenting is underprotective, children can become overwhelmed by unmet needs and unsoothed pain and, as a result, can feel distraught and disorganized. They may attempt to escape these disturbing feelings by retreating into a detached and barren mind state. This state may then form the lunar landscape for future feelings of emptiness and boredom. If parenting is so overprotective that children are not allowed to experience any discomfort, satisfy their innate curiosity, or learn to amuse themselves, children can fail to learn emotional self-gratification. They may then be forever seeking external stimulation and giving others the responsibility to keep them from feeling empty and bored.

The tendency to conclude that if you are bored it means the other person is boring, instead of first owning, understanding, and dealing with your own inner place of boredom, can cause you to disqualify many a potentially good partner. If you accept responsibility for your boredom, you may discover that it is fed by your failing to invest yourself fully in your life and in getting to know and enjoy your partner. Permitting the deepest parts of yourself to connect with this other person's depth may turn out to be a much more satisfying antidote to boredom than the suffering and turmoil of romantic addiction.

If you find that you repeatedly get bored in relationships that are otherwise satisfying, consider the possibility that you might be giving your partner the impossible job of rescuing you from an inner boredom. Also consider the possibility that you are focusing on those inevitable unexciting moments in order to disqualify that person. Unless the people you have been choosing are clearly dull and hold little interest for you, it may be useful to ask yourself, "Do I make myself bored when there is the possibility of developing something really good? And if so, why?"

SCREENING OUT THE GOOD ONES

We have seen three ways you may unconsciously sabotage a potentially good love relationship: interpreting good traits negatively; magnifying imperfections; and labeling people as boring. You can also go one step further by avoiding such a relationship before it can even get started! You can do this by simply not seeing those who might be available for real romantic involvement.

Even after we've given up being attracted to those who make us unhappy, we may continue to blot out of our visual field all those with whom we might be happy.

Often we do not realize we have been screening people out until we stop doing it. As long as Laura was drawn to hard-driving and uncaring men she never noticed the many more sensitive and responsive men that she met at work or at social occasions. After breaking with Les, she went through a stage of insisting that there were simply "no men out there" who had the self-confidence she admired without the self-involvement that made them basically uncaring. Later, when she had dealt with some of her own fears of closeness and commitment, she asked me with wonder, "Where did all these nice guys come from?" She had opened her eyes to men who at one time she simply would not have seen. And once she opened her eyes to them they suddenly became, as if by magic, more responsive to her.

I am not underestimating the real difficulties in meeting appropriate and attractive people. But you may be compounding these difficulties enormously if you are making yourself perceptually blind. If you are convinced that the kind of person you want is so rare as to belong on the endangered species list, I urge you to consider the possibility that you may simply not be seeing some that are right in front of you. You may be looking right past them, through them, and around them. Perhaps you have so long had tunnel vision for your addictive type that you do not notice anyone else.

THE NARROW CHECKLIST

You may also be screening out the good ones by having a narrow and rigid checklist of traits and characteristics the other person must have before you allow yourself to feel interest.

We all have such checklists, whether they are explicit or not. After all, nobody is attracted to just anybody. And these checklists can be invaluable in focusing us toward those most appropriate for us. Checklist items often have to do with physical attributes, personality, character, intelligence, life-style, and values. Some of these items reflect our deepest needs and preferences. Some can be downright self-protective, such as items that rule out anyone who is abusive, irresponsible, substance addicted, or impossibly self-absorbed. But some items fix on petty traits that we put on our checklist when we were very young and have never taken the time or effort to reevaluate. For example, in junior high school or high school it may be crucial that the person we are attracted to look and act "cool." But later, when we are looking for a serious involvement, ruling out people because they are not "cool" can eliminate many interesting and appealing possibilities.

Physical traits are often among these preferences that became fixed early on and have gone unexamined. People may feel they can be sexually attracted only to someone with a particular hair color, eye color, height, or body type. Craig was over six feet, three inches tall, but he was consistently drawn to very short women, disqualifying some appropriate and lovely women he met because they exceeded his puzzling height requirement. "Do I have to tower over a woman to feel powerful and confident?" he wondered. That was one reason, but it was not the main reason. Craig found a family picture taken when he was about two or three. "In the photo my mother is about the same age as the women I go out with now. She's not only the same height of the women I'm most attracted to, but she has the same hair color, hair length, and even the same shape face. It's amazing."

But why should it be so amazing that the first people we were close to have left their stamp on our preferences, longings, and desires? Even if we are no longer aware of the early origins of the traits we find so compelling, the chances are we will always find these traits have a special attraction for us. This is only a problem under three circumstances: (1) The appeal of these traits is so great that it blinds us to very troublesome negatives about that person; (2) the attraction is to traits that are in themselves negatives; or (3) the traits fall within such a narrow range that we are severely limited in who we find appealing.

If you suspect that your checklist is unduly constricting the scope of your attractions, it is time to make that checklist explicit and conscious and to see if you want to revise it. Write down the sentence "The traits I find essential for me to be attracted to someone are—" and list the traits under four categories: physical attributes, personality, occupations, and interests and life-style. Then, for each trait, write the answers to these questions: Where did I form this preference? Is it still valid? Is it valid to the same degree it once was? Does it rule out too many people who might be good and appropriate for me? Do I want to give myself more latitude?

Does insight into the origins of your preferences enable you to broaden them? Not always, but it can definitely help. For example, Craig began to push himself to make dates with and get to know women with a wider range of physical attributes. Sometimes he still could not stir up enthusiasm toward these women, despite his acknowledging that, objectively speaking, they were appealing and despite his giving it a good try. But then he became involved with a woman who was tall and in other ways didn't fit his usual preference but who was attractive and had a warm personality. As the relationship progressed he was surprised to find that he was falling in love with her. One night, after a particularly amorous time together, they were looking tenderly at each other and he said, "You know something funny? You didn't used to be my type."

You won't be able to change your "type" to include everyone who might be nice and appropriate, but if your current range is too exclusive, you certainly can broaden it somewhat. It is important to recognize that there is no great virtue in having too specific a checklist. You may pride yourself on being very particular and discriminating, when in fact your narrow range may simply indicate a fixation at some childhood place. When you were eight or fifteen it didn't matter if your food preferences focused almost excusively on hamburgers and pizza. But if they still do at twenty-five or thirty-eight or forty-eight, then you might acknowledge that your tastes have failed to mature. The chances are, however, that you now enjoy red snapper and Caesar salad and perhaps even broccoli. Your tastes in partners can also mature if, instead of insisting on the romantic equivalent of hamburgers and pizza, you give yourself leeway to explore a wider, more adventurous romantic menu.

8

Ten Hidden Reasons for Avoiding a Good Love Relationship

Your best efforts to develop a love relationship with someone ready, willing, and able to have such a relationship are not likely to be successful if you are unconsciously programmed to fail in those efforts. This unwitting self-sabotage may be keeping you frustrated and stuck despite your ardent longing to move forward in this area of your life. Why would you do such a mean thing to yourself? And if your self-destructive script is unconscious, then how can you know you are doing it? Can you become aware of the workings of such a malevolent inner saboteur? And would such an awareness change anything?

To start with the last questions first: Yes, you can become aware of your self-defeating motivations and strategies if you open yourself up to the possibility that they exist and push yourself to look for them. And yes, such awarenesses can reduce the power of that internal enemy, or at least can direct your efforts to effectively counter its devious strategies. To help you become aware of your hidden reasons for avoiding or destroying good love relationships, we will look at what I have found to be the ten most common and potent motives for self-sabotage. These motives have a common goal—*to defend you against something that consciously or unconsciously frightens you.* Unfortunately, however, even though they are designed to protect you from psychological or actual danger, they can also deprive you of achieving the love relationship that you deeply desire. What perils could you be warding off that make you persist at such a self-depriving price?

1. FEAR OF INTIMACY

One of the most precious aspects of a good love relationship is that it fulfills our profound desire to be known and understood by another human being. But this desire is an ambivalent one. There is also a terror of being known, a fear that we lay ourselves vulnerable when we let someone in, a fear that taking our walls down in the tempting glow of intimacy makes us subject to being hurt, controlled, or betrayed by our loving invader.

Often this fear began long before our first adult romantic relationships. By repeatedly choosing hostile women like Diane, Warren was always having to be on guard, always afraid he might reveal something that they could use to criticize or hurt him. He had never had a relationship that permitted true intimacy. He could hardly picture what one would be like. As he began to wonder why not, he realized how little expression of feelings, wishes, or hopes there had been in his family. "Emotions were considered bad form. We usually dealt with each other at arm's length, and the few times I opened up did not go well." He recalled an incident of rare closeness with his mother when he was about seven years old. He was at the kitchen table drawing pictures while she prepared dinner. She seemed genuinely interested in what he was thinking and feeling so he felt encouraged to reveal, with much anxiety, that sometimes he hated his father for frequently being mean to him and to her. "The next day I overheard her telling him what I said. I was horrified that she would do that. My father tortured me for weeks by yelling at me for everything I did. He would say, 'I'll show you what mean is.' "

Another indelible incident occurred when Warren was in sixth grade. "I was not much of an athlete as a child, but one day in a baseball game in the school yard I hit the ball really deep and it went for a game-winning home run. That night, in my euphoria and exuberance I told my father, 'I'm going to be a baseball player when I grow up.' He responded, 'They won't let anyone into the majors who runs like a duck.' "

In high school Warren fell in love and discovered the pleasure of sharing secrets with his girlfriend as they sat for hours in his parked car. He told her of family conflicts and of the time when he was in camp at age nine and he and other boys in his bunk touched each other sexually. "I let her know that I had never told anyone else about these things. Later, she got interested in another guy in class and broke off with me. This guy had the next locker to me in gym, and I could tell from the derisive comments he made that she had told him all the things I told her. I felt humiliated and destroyed. I could feel myself closing off again." When Warren tried to move toward women whose warmth tempted him to voice his feelings and share his experiences, his fears and his walls went with him. Several women made remarks such as "We've spent a lot of time with each other but I hardly know you." Warren told me, "Being close to someone can be very risky business."

Laura also found intimacy risky and avoided it through her workaholism and by choosing aloof men like Les. But Laura also craved intimacy. She told me, "I have always daydreamed of having a man who would be my soulmate, someone I could share my every thought with. But I have to admit that when it comes right down to it, that possibility scares me." As we tried to understand why, she said, "The whole atmosphere at home, with my father being so angry, particularly when he had been drinking, and my mother acting as if she were the helpless but silent and stoic victim, made us all keep our feelings to ourselves. Often I wouldn't know what I felt because there was no place safe to feel it."

Laura remembered that as a child she had frightening nightmares about being chased by polar bears or tigers and would cry out for her mother. "My mother would come running more in panic that I might wake my father than to comfort me. She would tell me to stop crying, that it was just a dream. But she never asked what the dream was about or held me or stayed a moment longer than was necessary to quiet me. She just kind of managed me." Laura added, "I did take some comfort from just getting her attention, and I had to make do with that."

Laura also recalled that most of her early attempts to share intimacies ended badly. "In third grade I had a crush on this little boy, Arthur. For some reason I told my mother about it when she picked me up at school and she asked me all about him and took me very seriously. That felt wonderful. The next week was my ninth birthday party and she announced to all my friends that I was in love with Arthur. I ran from the table and stayed in my room for what seemed like hours."

Not everyone with fears of intimacy can recount traumatic incidents such as those recalled by Warren and Laura. Furthermore, many people who *can* remember similar upsetting experiences have grown up with no major problems about intimacy. The crucial question to ask yourself is whether the atmosphere in your home was generally receptive and responsive to a wide range of feelings, or whether it was so limited that you came to feel shame and guilt about any thoughts, feelings, and actions that didn't fit a narrow range of acceptability. Also explore whether later on, in romantic relationships, you had bad experiences that may have added to your earlier fears or that may themselves have caused you to become wary about intimacy. When this wariness exists, a potential love partner can seem like a Trojan horse who will plunder and pillage your equilibrium and self-esteem if you open your gates. Without realizing it you may be warding off this fate by keeping your gates closed—and by becoming ingenious at finding "good" reasons to do so.

2. FEAR OF LOSS OF SELF

You may have wishes, perhaps not conscious, to become extremely dependent on someone you love. You can then become afraid that you will be tempted to give up your independence in a kind of fusion with a person who is caring and available. This is a level of anxiety even deeper than the fears of being hurt by the self-exposure of intimacy.

Warren once expressed his fear this way: "I think I've always been drawn to impossible women for just that reason—they were *impossible* to remain close to. With Diane, the needy little boy in me would come out and make a fool of himself, but I knew that Diane would never hold me long enough for all that neediness to come out. So I was safe. An affectionate woman would make it too easy for the baby in me to take over."

Similarly, when Kim first started feeling that she and David were falling in love, she told me: "I know there is a longing to surrender and to lose myself in him. With Kevin I could indulge these feelings because his perpetual running away made them safe, but David does not run from closeness. I'm afraid I could lose all the independence I worked so hard to get." (Later, Kim discovered that when her desire to fuse was not intensified by her lover's elusiveness, she could manage it quite well. Further, she found that while David loved her and was there for her, he had no wish for her to lose herself in him and would not let it happen.) We are all to some degree caught up in this conflict between separateness and symbiosis. Unless we work on gaining confidence that we can maintain our independence even in the closest of relationships, we may unconsciously choose people who will not permit closeness.

3. FEAR OF BEING ABANDONED

"If nobody holds you, then nobody can drop you." This was Laura's response when I commented that she never permitted herself a relationship in which she was fully embraced. I have heard similar words from many people whose experiences and whose feelings about themselves make them fearful of getting deeply involved and then abondoned. This is particularly clear in those who repeatedly fall in love with people who are married or otherwise involved with someone else. In Chapter 2, I wrote about Steven, a lawyer who was so obsessed with Jennie, a married colleague at his law firm, that he finally left the firm to break his obsession. When he consulted me and we reviewed his history, he revealed that he had previously had two fairly long affairs with married women. In each case he was ardently in love and had been quite depressed when the affair ended. It wasn't until the therapy had proceeded for many months that he could see that he had stopped each of these relationships when there was some hint that the woman might leave her marriage. As we will see, the reasons for Steven's repeated involvements with married women were much more complex than just fear of abandonment, but fear certainly played a part. He told me, "I never expect to have a full relationship with these women, so as much as it hurts when it's over it's not as bad as it would be to lose someone who I believed would be there forever."

When Steve and I explored his vulnerability to loss, it was not difficult to see its origins. Steve said, "When I was six years old my mother threw my father out. I knew they had been arguing a lot but I was stunned when he told me, 'Mommy doesn't want me to live here anymore.' Then, after a very short time, another man started coming around and practically moved in. My mother was totally involved with and obsessed with this man. She hardly paid attention to me and my little sister. I felt that my sister and I were like Hansel and Gretel and that my mother had turned into the unloving stepmother who tries to lose the children in the woods. Sometimes I even felt she was the witch who was going to kill us. Over and over I would coerce my sister to enact scenes from Hansel and Gretel with me."

In addition to this loss of his father and mother, Steve had experienced earlier losses: first when his sister was born (a common loss, not necessarily damaging in itself), and then when his mother and father were so caught up in their marital fights and affairs that he felt that he didn't exist for them. Early loss occurs in many ways: A parent dies or goes away or becomes sick, depressed, self-absorbed, intensely preoccupied, or unavailable. The damage from this loss can be minimized by sensitive and loving responsiveness from others in the family. But whatever residue remains may leave a vulnerability to fears of abandonment that makes promising relationships feel hazardous.

Explore the role your own fears of abandonment may play in your relationships by answering these questions:

- When I am in a romantic relationship, do I become apprehensive that I will be left? Does this become a persistent worry or preoccupation?
- Did an important romantic relationship end in my being left? Was I so hurt by this that even though I very much want closeness and commitment I may be afraid to put myself fully on the line again?
- Have my fears of being left caused me to fall in love with people who are so needy and dependent they would never leave me, even if their neediness then becomes oppressive or they have other traits I do not like?
- Did I feel securely and unconditionally held and loved by the important people in my childhood? Were there ruptures or impairments to these feelings of security caused by family conflict? By separation or divorce? By a parent's illness, depression, or self-absorption?
- Is it possible that I choose people who I know can only be involved with me in a limited way because they are committed elsewhere or have emotional barriers to involvement? Are these choices accidental? Bad luck? Or an unconscious avoidance?
- Do I dare choose someone where there are real possibilities of having a good love relationship and therefore a risk of painful loss?

4. FEAR OF BEING REJECTED

One particularly paralyzing kind of abandonment anxiety is the fear of being rejected. Rejection implies not only loss but being found lacking, inadequate, or unappealing. Almost all of us have this fear to some degree. But certain people have it to such a degree that they avoid any potentially good relationship or destroy it so that its demise is under their control and therefore less devastating. Laura once said, "With men who are available and show that they are getting seriously interested, I get very nervous. I feel sure they will be turned off by getting to know me better, so I quit before I am fired. In fact, I quit before I am even hired."

Excessive fear of rejection implies shaky self-esteem. Something in your growing years contributed to feelings that you are not sufficiently worthy, interesting, or attractive to win and sustain the love of a person who is worthy, interesting, and attractive. Or perhaps previous romantic experiences in which you were rejected were so traumatic that you were left with scars you are afraid can be ripped open again. So you feel that you only have three choices available:

1. You can decide never to get deeply involved again. This is clearly the safest option, but it can lead you to feel undeveloped, deprived, and lonely.

2. You can avoid getting involved with people who you really value but who you believe could never really love a person like you. (This is a variation of Groucho Marx's famous dictum that he would never join a club that would have him as a member.) Instead, you get involved with people who you do not particularly value but who are very interested in you. Unless you come to love such a person (which does sometimes happen), your relationships will not be nearly as gratifying as they might be.

3. You can get very involved with or even addicted to people whose built-in inability to have a full love relationship is evident fairly early. This way you will suffer chronic or repeated rejection but that may feel less threatening than the prospect of getting fully involved in a relationship where your hopes are raised high and then devastatingly dashed.

If you seem to be caught in a pattern of accepting half a loaf, you have to ask yourself if you believe that the alternative is to reach for a whole loaf, only to have it snatched away.

5. FEAR OF WINNING

It is easy to understand that we may avoid a good relationship because we are afraid we have something to lose—our selfhood, our independence, our self-esteem. It is harder to understand that we may avoid a good relationship because of something we have to gain—a fulfilling love relationship. But this is often the case if we believe, even though unconsciously, that in attaining a love of our own *we would be winning some old rivalry that we feel we are forbidden to win.*

Warren always balked when I suggested that part of his reason for getting involved with impossible women was that he felt it was taboo and dangerous to have the devoted love of a caring woman. He could understand the other underlying reasons for his misguided choices—the challenge that self-centered women posed, how these women triggered old feelings of trying to win the love of his unaffectionate parents, and why he felt bored with women who did not pose the challenge. But he assured me that he really wanted a good love relationship and that nothing about achieving it frightened him. I agreed that he really did prize it, but I believed he had unconscious fears that this triumph would result in terrible consequences.

What led me to this belief? Largely my knowledge of Warren's family life. Warren's father was a self-righteous, critical, and at times, despotic man. He demanded total attention from his wife and total obedience from his children. He put Warren and his siblings down with sarcastic or belittling comments. Warren's mother, a beautiful, high-cheekboned woman, was respectful of her husband's wishes but not openly affectionate with him. At times when she was affectionate with Warren, his father commented that she was spoiling or coddling him.

The first time Warren thought that I might not be completely off the wall was when he started to date a woman he felt enthusiastic about and almost immediately began to have dreams of conflict with men. In one dream he had an auto accident in which his new car rammed an "older beat-up car." Warren recounted that "the other driver burst out of his car in a rage, waving a tire iron at me. I tried to apologize and I kept saying, 'I'm insured, I'm insured.' But he rushed at me and began to beat me with the tire iron. I tried to ward off the blows with my arms. I woke with my heart pounding."

Warren continued to have such dreams of conflict with men, including ones in which he defeated or even killed the other man. He was then able to recognize that he had often had dreams like these, that they had begun as childhood nightmares in which the frightening man was sometimes his father, and that they now usually occurred when a new relationship with a woman was exciting and seemed full of promise.

Months later, when Warren found himself falling in love with Pamela, a caring woman who was almost the opposite of Diane, he again began to have those embattled dreams. But he was now in a better position to understand them as remnants of old conflicts. They did not lead him to feel bored or cause him to turn off his loving feelings toward Pamela as they had, quite unconsciously, in past relationships. However, when he began to think that he might want to marry Pamela, he began to find all kinds of fault with her and his criticisms began to jeopardize the relationship. I reminded him of how his father would belligerently say, "I'm the only man around here, and don't you forget it." He still found it hard to believe that he would be accumulating reasons to disqualify Pamela because he was afraid to challenge his father's position by moving toward becoming a husband and head of his own household. I asked him, "If you marry Pamela and you invite your parents to your place for dinner, who will sit at the head of the table?" This threw him. He could not easily see himself sitting at the head of the table in his father's presence, but he could not tolerate picturing his father at the head of the table, either. He finally said, "I'll get a round table." We both laughed, and the insight Warren gained at that moment freed him to keep moving forward in his relationship with Pamela.

This dynamic arises out of the oedipal conflict which began in earliest childhood with our fear of challenging the same sex parent for the affection and "possession" of the opposite sex parent. It can induce both men and women, unwittingly, to mess up a potentially satisfying and lasting love relationship. Kim discovered that when she was pursuing unavailable and punishing men like Kevin she was not only symbolically trying to get the love of her difficult and emotionally elusive father but was also insuring that she would never have a man of her own. This guaranteed, again symbolically, that she would never challenge or defeat her mother by winning her father.

It can be hard for you to accept the possibility that you may be "programmed" to stop yourself from being a winner in love. It can be even more difficult to accept that this self-defeating programming results from an old fear of winning a tabooed childhood victory over the parent of the same sex. And what can really make you reject this possibility is that the childhood situation that provoked it may not be nearly as blatant as was Warren's with his clearly tyrannizing father or Kim's with her cold mother and emotionally elusive father. In most oedipal triangles, the competition with the same sex parent for the love of the other parent is much more subtle, often going on primarily in the mind of the child. At times the child can feel in fearful conflict with a parent who has nothing but goodwill and love toward him or her. It is as if the child were feeling, "If he (she) knew what I was thinking, he'd (she'd) kill me or banish me. Or maybe I'd have to kill or banish him (her), which is just as frightening." These feelings, if not defused, can remain in us as adults and become transferred symbolically to other romantic situations. It is as if we were saying to the parent of the same sex, "Don't worry, Dad (Mom), I'm not your rival. You have nothing to fear from me."

Since this conflict is so subtle and largely unconscious, how can you know if it is operating to undermine your relationships? There are several ways that you can explore it:

- First, and most important, do not dismiss the possibility out of hand. Instead, open yourself to the idea that it just may have relevance to you. This will help you to begin noticing thoughts and feelings that you may have been denying or overlooking.
- Begin to note if you feel anxious and fearful when your relationship seems to be progressing and you have been entertaining pleasant thoughts of a possible future with this person. Does it feel that somebody would be opposed to your being happy in this way? Do you feel apprehensive that something terrible will happen?
- Be alert to your dreams as you become more excited about

and involved with someone who seems right for you. Are there more dreams of conflict, danger, and even violence? Is there conflict with people of the same sex? Do you dream of being punished? Of having to fight for your life? If so, you have to ask yourself why you should be having such dreams at a time when something promising and good is happening.

- If your parents are still alive, notice what it feels like to tell each of them about this new relationship. Don't dismiss any feelings because they seem irrational. Take it a step further by imagining telling each parent that you intend to marry this person. Picture the reaction they are most likely to have. Then picture the reaction you would most dread their having.

- Think back to your childhood relationships with each of your parents and their relationship with each other. Explore early feelings of being drawn to and wanting a special relationship with your parent of the opposite sex. Do you remember such feelings and wishes? How did they make you feel in regard to your same sex parent?

- Try also to recall whether you ever felt that if you have something really good in your life, it would be taken from you. Would it be resented by the same sex parent? Would it put you in conflict with him or her? Would it feel like you were surpassing or defeating him or her?

- Finally, become aware of the main patterns of emotional interaction in your family and particularly how your oedipal triangle worked. The shape of this triangle can differ greatly from one nuclear family to another. For example, if you were raised in a family where your opposite sex parent was highly rivalrous and intimidating, your anxieties about winning will be different than if your opposite sex parent seemed self-effacing and easy to defeat or was a long-suffering martyr who could make your wishes to triumph reek with guilt. Any of these constellations from your past can make you feel apprehensive about attaining a good love relationship in the present.

There are other family constellations that, to the contrary, are likely to help children to reach adulthood without being unduly burdened by vestiges of the oedipal conflict. You are most likely to be someone who is ready, willing, and able to effectively develop a good love relationship if your home was one in which: (1) your parents' love for each other was unmistakable so that you did not feel that you could displace either of them; (2) your parents were actually and emotionally available to each other and to you; and (3) you felt unconditional love from each of them clearly enough to assure you that your feelings of rivalry would not lead to retaliation and conflict.

To the extent that this ideal picture did not exist, use the guidelines above to make yourself aware how that old triangle may still be interfering with your ability to find fulfilling love. If you do discover that you may be holding yourself back out of fears of winning, direct your attention to dispelling those childhood fears and to preventing them from negatively influencing the way you live your life today. You are entitled to a good love relationship with a man or woman of your own, even if you were not entitled to have a romantic relationship with daddy or mommy. The past belongs in the past, not in your current love life.

6. GUILT ABOUT LEAVING SOMEONE BEHIND

You can feel uneasy about having it good when you feel that somebody important in your life is having it bad. You can feel uncomfortable about moving forward when somebody important in your life is standing still or even moving backward. And you can feel guilty if you believe that your moving toward happiness is causing that person unhappiness.

One of Laura's discoveries in therapy was that every step she took toward a better life was accompanied by feelings that she was somehow hurting her parents. Her father's alcoholism made him not only an inconsistent and frequently frightening father, but also an intimidating, unreliable, and sometimes abusive husband. Her mother seemed to Laura to be trapped, miserable, and ineffectual in dealing with her husband. When Laura was in her teens she would frequently ask her mother, "How can you take it? Why don't you leave him?" Her mother would respond wearily, "That's easier said than done." Laura realized that her mother was unbudgeably entrenched in her role as martyr and she determined to save herself. At every opportunity she got out of the house. When she was invited to a friend's country house for the weekend, her mother would sigh and say "Aren't you lucky?" in a tone that seemed to mean "You can go off and have fun, and I'm stuck here in this unhappy place." When Laura was a junior in high school she told her parents of her wishes to go to college out of town. Her father said there wasn't enough money for it, but Laura got scholarships and loans, worked hard at summer jobs, and said she would work while in college. With some help from her parents, she managed to swing it. During her first visit home after starting college, she told her mother about some of the exciting things she was doing and her mother responded, "That must be nice." Laura told me, "There was nothing wrong with the words, but the way she said them—part envious, part wistful—felt like an accusation. She was implying that such exciting things never were or would be part of her dismal life."

Soon Laura learned to tell her mother only of the hard work, the difficulties, her occasional ailments, and all the bad things that happened. But her mother's barbed pronouncement, "That must be nice," was repeated at every positive event in Laura's life—her getting in to and graduating from law school, her becoming partner in a law firm, her buying a spacious apartment, her vacations in the Caribbean or Europe. And while Laura never let her mother's martyred envy deter her from succeeding or from living well, there was always a shadow of guilt that dulled the gloss of her experiences.

I suggested that to her motives for avoiding a good love relationship we had to add her guilt about having a better life than her mother. Laura protested, "But I never let it stop me from going to college or law school, or making partner or traveling or living well—so why should it interfere with my love life?" I said nothing and Laura was silent for a long time. Then she said, "Because that's the one thing I would find almost unbearable—to have a happy marriage when hers is so awful. It would really be leaving her sitting in her own muck, while I would be off making a good life with a good man." Laura began to cry. "We would be in two different worlds then. Right now, with all my achievements and comforts, when it comes to men, my mother and I are companions in misery."

For many people leaving someone "behind" in an unhappy, unfulfilled, or lonely place while they move on to a fuller and more joyful life creates both guilt and a fear of the loss involved in living "in two different worlds." Often that person left behind is a parent, but it is sometimes a sibling or even a good friend. Recall, for example, Daniel, the twenty-nine-year-old science teacher who seemed to have radar for honing in on playful, seductive women who invariably turned out to be promiscuous. He discovered that in addition to being attracted to these women because they energized him and made him feel less detached, he was unconsciously motivated not to succeed owing to guilt about his older brother who was partially paralyzed and had been confined to a wheelchair since age ten. And Mia, the young woman who had been in love with her boss and other unavailable men, discovered that part of her hidden motivation for avoiding a good love relationship had to do with not wanting to surpass Nan, a chronically ill and depressed friend who had been her dearest confidante since childhood.

Ask yourself, "If I made a happy and lasting love connection, is there anyone I feel I would be hurting, or separating myself from, or leaving behind?" If you discover that this stirs up feelings of discomfort or guilt, you need to consider what a terrible price you are paying just so the other person can have your company in misery. You also have to consider the possibility that this other person really does not want your company in misery and that the drama is going on largely in your own mind.

7. FEAR OF BEING A GROWN-UP

Little children can have crushes. Teenagers often have intense infatuations and fall head over heels in lust. People of all ages can feel passionate, fall in love, and become obsessed or romantically addicted. But only grown-ups can have a full love relationship. Some people don't have a full love relationship because they are not grown up enough. And some people avoid one (even though they may say they want one) because they really don't *want* to grow up.

After Mia became aware of her guilt and reluctance about leaving her unhappy friend Nan behind, she realized that she was also using her tie to Nan as a way of remaining a litle girl and avoiding what she saw as the fearful and unpalatable responsibilities of adulthood. She acknowledged that her tendency to get involved with older married men was her way of repeatedly putting herself in the position of the child in comparison to the "big people," such as her boss and his wife, who had children, lived in a comfortable house, took trips together, made important decisions, and were involved in their community. She, in contrast, remained in her studio apartment and often stayed home weekends obsessing sadly about what the grown-ups—her beloved boss and his wife—were doing. When she was not home alone, she might go out to a club or bar, dancing and drinking till late hours, or go to Nan's apartment where she would watch a video and eat ice cream. She had always seen these weekends as an unfortunate consequence of being in love with a married man. But suddenly she saw that she was choosing these weekends and this life because she wanted to remain a little girl. "It's bad enough living like a kid at thirty, but it's horrifying to see myself still being here at forty and beyond."

Warren also explored his tendency to move from one tumultuous affair to another as his way to remain the perpetual adolescent. He could see that the beautiful models he chose were usually very immature themselves and would not stimulate him to grow or to become more solid, thoughtful, or responsible. "I have had a series of childish playmates," he told me. "We play and fight like two kids in a sandbox until one of us says, 'I'm not going to be your friend anymore.' Then I go find another playmate." He added, "I'm not sure I want to change this even though it's beginning to feel meaningless. From what I've seen of my parents' marriage and the marriages of some of my friends, I don't see what's so great about being a responsible adult."

There are many reasons why people may not want a grown-up love relationship—such as Warren's negative views of marriage, or the delightful fun he often had with his playmates, or Mia's fear of leaving someone behind, or the apprehension that many men and women feel about responsibility, commitment, and playing "for real." It can be helpful to see if this aversion to growing up is operating for you. Imagine that you are involved with someone you love who is available, caring, and mature. Imagine that you are each committed to doing all you can to make the relationship fulfilling and intimate. Be candidly in touch with your feelings about this image. Do you notice the little girl or boy in you feeling resistant, feeling frightened, wanting to run away to Never Never Land? If so, in order to have the love relationship you say you want, you will first have to come to grips with your anxieties about being an adult.

8. FEAR OF GIVING UP THE "POOR ME" POSITION

Laura's recognition of her guilt about having it better than her long-suffering mother was a ground-breaking awareness. She worked hard to understand that the unhappy choices her mother had made were her mother's responsibility and that it was not her mission to try to keep her mother from feeling more unhappy by keeping herself from finding a fulfilling love. She could feel herself opening to new possibilities. And yet she was still troubled by anxiety and feelings of loss. I asked her to describe these feelings as fully as she could. "It's no longer that I'm leaving my mother behind," she said, "but that I am leaving a part of me behind. Maybe I am abandoning that unhappy little girl part of me or the part of me that had to battle to survive and to stay hopeful in that tense and joyless home." This came up again later when she told me about Bob, the warm and responsive man she'd begun seeing. "Despite all I have accomplished, I have a core of unhappiness and toughness that feels basic to who I am. Feelings of sadness and making do with very little affection or nurturing are so familiar that I have a hard time leaving them for something strange and new. Whenever I'm going along happily with Bob, I feel the old sad me pulling me back. It's not just my mother I'd be abandoning, but the Laura I once was and her whole loveless world."

The magnetic power of the person you once were and the feelings you once had can be intense. Those fortunate enough to have felt well loved retain feelings that can keep them hopeful and optimistic through later periods of terrible adversity. Those, like Laura, who felt poorly nurtured and became pessimistic and wary retain feelings that can act like a black hole sucking them back into their familiar unhappiness whenever they move toward a lighter, brighter, more fulfilling place.

Notice if the paragraphs above, particularly the statements by Laura, strike some resonant chord in you. Ask yourself, "When I feel the possibility of happiness, and particularly of a happy love relationship, do I begin to experience the discomfort of entering a new and alien territory and of leaving behind an inner emotional atmosphere that was not happy but remains comfortably familiar? How strong is the pull of those old unhappy feelings that I still carry around inside myself?"

It is important to see what you are up against and to realize that it will take courage to leave that unhappy place. You may even be reassured to know that you are not likely to leave your sad or cynical self behind completely. He or she will always be, to some degree, a part of you; you will always carry something of his or her gray landscape with you. But, by reducing the influence that part of you has over your decisions and actions, you'll be able to move toward more self-fulfillment. And that gray landscape will remain only as an occasional dark area in a colorful world.

9. SEXUAL ANXIETIES

Kim's parents made her feel that sex was bad, dirty, and disgusting. For the most part, these attitudes were conveyed by what was *not* said or done—by the near total absence of any discussion of matters remotely sexual and by the lack of any kind of physical affection or playfulness between her parents. Kim remembered her mother's obvious discomfort when, as a little girl, she asked about her aunt's pregnancy. She remembered the general feeling of distaste her mother conveyed in regard to anything about bodies and their functions. Sometimes these attitudes were conveyed more directly. When Kim had her first menstrual period, she told her mother about it with a mixture of fear that something was wrong and pride at becoming more grown-up. (Some friends—not her mother—had told her what to expect.) Her mother's first response was "Damn, as if I don't have enough to worry about." Then she added, "What a mess. You can get some pads from my bathroom." Kim said, "I never told my father, but I could tell she told him. When he was in his occasional good moods he used to horse around with me and sit me on his lap, but that stopped suddenly, with no explanations."

When Kim started dating, her mother admonished her that boys "only want one thing." She never left the house on a date without her mother saying a stern "be careful." That she might talk to either parent about her sexual feelings and concerns was unthinkable. Starting with her first sexual experiences of kissing and groping in the back seats of cars, Kim was tense and jittery. She felt that whatever sexual feelings were aroused were dirty. "There was the nicest boy I was dating in high school, and he tried hard to be gentle and considerate of my fears, but I gave him such a hard time he finally gave up on me. I was hurt but relieved. Then I started going out with Ben, a guy everyone knew was a selfish bastard and just used girls for his pleasure. He made it clear that he wouldn't stand for me being so uptight. He was rough and forceful, and I went along with him and began to get very turned on. I would feel dirty after, but I didn't care because then I felt I was crazy in love with him. The more Ben gave me a hard time, the more I wanted to please him sexually and the more abandoned I became sexually. I guess he was the first guy I became addicted to."

Kim came to understand that sexual release occurred with self-centered and emotionally unavailable men because she felt her sexuality was not in her control but was at the service of their wishes. "I would feel, it isn't me who is doing it, it's my addiction—except I didn't call it my addiction then. Even now, in addictive relationships I can enjoy sex because I can't help myself. So I can forgive myself all that shameful stuff." But when Kim became sexually involved with someone who really seemed to like her and wanted a relationship with her, her sexual feelings would turn off and she would literally dry up. "When I wasn't addicted, I had to own my sexual desires, and that brought up the old feelings that my sexual desires and actions were shameful and dirty." With these nice guys I was sure they would see me as disgusting if I really got passionate."

This pattern continued for many years. By the time Kim met David, however, she had lessened her fears of intimacy, had largely overcome her addiction to trying to win the love of her moody and unavailable father, and had markedly modified her feeling that her sexuality was shameful. These changes enabled her to delight in sex with a man whom she cared about and who cared about her. "It's becoming more and more free and wonderful, because with David I am not being driven by my addictive need to please him but I just enjoy myself and enjoy his enjoying me."

Many people with sexual anxieties are most able to feel passion in an addictive relationship, often one in which they are being badly treated. When they try to feel sexual in a more mutual and loving relationship, they often feel turned off or, at best, much less passionate than in the addictive involvement. One of the main reasons for this is that, as with Kim, the addiction gives them permission to act on their sexual desires. But there are often other reasons. Some of these reasons are related to the oedipal conflict discussed earlier, in that the object of their addiction often stands for the forbidden parent. What was impossible and withheld is symbolically right there, and the resulting excitement and release creates an overwhelming wave of passion. At the same time, the fact that the person is not available for a full love relationship insures against the terror of completely possessing the forbidden parent. It also insures against anxieties about the risks of sustained intimacy, potential loss of selfhood, leaving someone behind, and so forth. The absence of these anxieties also allows sexuality to emerge unencumbered. Kim summed this up by saying, *"His unavailability is my aphrodisiac."* (In actuality, for Kim, as for others, it is not just the unavailability of the object of her addiction that ignited her desire, but also the mistreatment, the abuse, the surrender of the child in her to a controlling parent.) To Kim's pronouncement we could add: "His availability for a love relationship is my terror and turnoff."

Feelings that sex is bad or taboo are not the only reasons for sexual anxieties. Many people harbor fears that they are sexually inadequate, and these fears sometimes cause them to cling to a bad relationship either because they feel sexually accepted or because they are so caught up in trying to prove their desirability that they lose sight of whether the relationship is good for them. Women's feelings of sexual inadequacy often revolve around how they feel their body looks. Men's feelings of inadequacy have to do with doubts about their performance. Both can be concerned about how appealing they are and how they measure up to others.

Laura, for example, despite her emphasis on being independent and on not being concerned about what men thought of her, would feel very sexually undesirable when she gained just two or three pounds over the weight she had decided was ideal. It was hard for her to feel passion when she felt "fat" and undesirable. This contributed to her penchant for uncommitted and vaguely defined relationships, because in such a relationship she could avoid the person when she was, to her mind, unappealing.

Part of the reason that Peter, the medical scientist, fell madly in love with younger women who looked up to him was, we found out, that he had doubts about his ability to satisfy and to hold a mature woman's sexual interest. He would stay too long with a woman he had little in common with rather than end it and have to put his sexuality on the line with someone new. For him, every new relationship had the potential for failure and rejection, and the more the new woman had attributes he highly regarded, the more devastating the potential rejection would be. Better to be in an unsatisfying relationship with an immature woman who idolized him, he felt: "I have less to lose."

It is important to examine whether sexual anxieties may be part of what is preventing you from developing a good love relationship. Do you carry around, perhaps not fully in your awareness, feelings that your sexual desires are dirty, sinful, or disgusting? Is it easier for you to feel turned on sexually when you are so driven by your addiction that your inhibitions are put aside? Do you feel that combining your sexual feelings with a good love relationship is a forbidden victory that you dare not permit yourself? Do you have doubts about your sexual appeal or adequacy that make you hold on to an established relationship, no matter how unhappy you are in it, rather than risk being found inadequate by someone new?

Because these anxieties can be so self-destructive, it is crucial that you understand the distorted notions they are based on and unbrainwash yourself from these notions. You have to work toward owning your sexuality as a source of pleasure and intimacy that you are entitled to and to feel that you have the right to enjoy the deep satisfaction that can occur within a good love relationship. If you can enjoy giving and getting sexual pleasure, then you are highly likely to be an adequate, appealing sexual partner for someone who appreciates who you are.

10. GIVING UP THE HIGH OF A BAD RELATIONSHIP

In the immediate post-Kevin period, Kim tried in vain to get interested in men who were not elusive and did not treat her badly. She found herself missing the elation, pain, and almost unbearable anxiety that had tormented her in her addictive relationships. She felt like her feelings were flattened and her landscape was arid. Kim had discovered an important truth about herself—that she had been using the intensity of her addictive relationships to ward off feelings of bleakness, deadness, and meaninglessness that threatened to engulf her. When she stopped pursuing the Kevins in her life and experienced some of the grayness that sat like a fog in the bottomland of her mind, she found that men who were truly interested in her and did not give her a hard time simply did not create enough turbulence in her life to chase away the fog. So one of the main reasons that Kim found it hard to feel involved with a man who was available and caring was that she had not yet discovered other, nonaddictive, ways to deal with her underlying depression and had not yet learned that a good love relationship can provide delightful highs.

Warren made some self-discoveries along similar lines when he began to realize that his involvement with Pamela was different than any of the countless relationships he had previously had. He was feeling increasingly in love with her and often found himself daydreaming about what a future with her would be like. At this point he became aware not only of his anxieties about "winning" in his rivalry with his father, (sitting at the head of the table), but also of a definite reluctance on his part to give up pursuing other women. This reluctance surprised him a little. He knew that he had had many love affairs and that he had enjoyed the seduction and conquest. But he saw his long list of lovers as mainly a consequence of his not having found the right one. Now, when he thought of someday marrying Pamela, he knew that he would want to make it a commitment to fidelity, so he was disturbed that he would feel dread at the thought "No one else ever." As Warren looked at his feelings more closely, he realized that he had been using the tumult of his involvements to distract himself from moods of dark pessimism that had been with him all his life. As a child he had dealt with the gloom in his family and in himself by always having an interest that took his focus off his despair. He would become obsessed with a particular pursuit—collecting baseball cards, building model airplanes, learning to play the clarinet, and playing basketball. Each pursuit would dominate his life for a period of time and then be dropped in favor of something new. He compulsively masturbated from the age of four and began actively pursuing sex when he was fourteen. There was always something, some activity or person, that was his diversion and mood elevator. And when it stopped having that antidepressant potency, he would move on. This pattern characterized his sexual and romantic life. He became terrified that if he committed himself to Pamela, he would sooner or later fall into the pit of boredom and deadness.

For many people, the intensity of a troubled relationship or the excitement of conquests carries an addictive high that can be as difficult for them to give up as is going "cold turkey" to a junkie. The excitement and distraction might come in as many forms as the array offered on a drug dealer's menu—the pursuit of the unavailable, repeated disappointments alternating with occasional ecstasy, or even from emotional or physical abuse. Or they might come from the pursuit of endless conquests, from the heart-pounding intrigue of avoiding getting caught, from the lies and deceits of living on the edge. The patterns are endless.

It is essential to recognize that *if these needs dominate in you, you will not be able to have a good love relationship, no matter how fervently you crave one. To change this, you will first have to understand what you are doing and why.* You have to reframe the issue for yourself. Instead of focusing on getting a particular person to love you or on proving yet again your ability to seduce and conquer, you have to see these maneuvers for what they are. And what they are are short-term palliatives for long-term impairments of self-esteem and long-standing fears, conflicts, obsessions, and depressed tendencies. As we will see in Chapters 9 and 10, there are better ways to soften, reduce, and transcend these areas of pain and deadness.

LEVELS OF MOTIVATION

It is pretty obvious by now that rarely is there one single motive, hidden or not, that causes people to avoid or throw a hand grenade into a good loving relationship. If there were only one motive, it would be relatively simple to find it, understand it, and reduce its sabotaging effect. But we are, for better or worse, more complicated than that. As we have seen with Kim, Warren, Laura, and others, there are often many internal causes for being self-defeating in love. Psychoanalysts would say our behavior is "multidetermined." Often, therefore, when we think we have found the motivational culprit and reduce its influence, we are disappointed to discover that this helps only partially in our being able to break an unsatisfying addictive tie and form a good loving relationship. We may still be stuck and may have to keep looking for the self-understanding that will free us.

Some of our motives for not trading in bad relationships for good ones are more accessible to our understanding than others. Like the many strata of sedimentary rock formed over countless eras of geological time, our motives lie at different layers of our consciousness and were formed in different eras in our lives. Let us look at these levels, starting with those closest to our conscious awareness and proceeding down to those that are deeper, earlier, and more primitive. Let us do it by seeing how these levels operate in Kim.

LEVEL 1
This is the topmost layer, the level of the rationales, rationalizations, and self-deceptions we use in order to stay with something bad and avoid something good. Kim would say:
- "It's not that Kevin doesn't love me—he's just afraid of commitment."
- "The guys who are nice to me and make it clear that they are interested strike me as wishy-washy, boring, and unmanly."

LEVEL 2
This is the level of the unfinished tasks related to getting parental love. It is fueled by the drive to repair old hurts, deprivations, and deficits. If Kim were to put these motives into words, she might say:

♦ "I need to make my cold and unaffectionate mother more warm and loving to me, and Kevin stands for my mother. I must succeed."

♦ "I need to make my moody, critical, and inconsistently loving father into someone who is fun and who adores me, and Kevin stands for my father. I must succeed."

♦ "Men who are warm, loving, and adoring and who are not moody and difficult do not excite me because they do not present me with the frustrating challenge of my lifelong goal."

LEVEL 3

This is the level of the desires and fears that arise out of the oedipal triangle of childhood. Kim might state her conflictful feelings this way:

♦ "If I have a good and happy relationship with a man who openly and consistently loves me, it would be as if my childhood fantasy of having daddy to myself has come true, and mommy will be angry. We will become deadly enemies. She might kill me or I might kill her. Or she might turn her back on me forever. It is too scary."

♦ "It's safer to choose men like Kevin where that is unlikely to happen. I must avoid men who would be caring and available and who would put me in danger."

LEVEL 4

This is the level of the first few years of life, before oedipal issues arise, when our world consists mainly of our parents and the warm security we feel at being their little girl or boy. The little child in Kim would say:

♦ "I need to be tied to mommy and daddy forever. If I grow up and have a mature and satisfying relationship with a real and loving man, I would no longer be taken care of as their little girl. I would be an adult, and I would be separate from them."

IF YOU REALLY LOVED ME YOU WOULD HOLD ME !!

LEVEL 5

This is similar to the previous level, but is a source of a deeper strata of feelings, feelings that go back to early infancy, maybe even to our forgotten intrauterine days. They reflect feelings of comfort and safety that arise in the warm and protective attachments of that period. The infant Kim might say:

♦ "I don't want to leave the comfort of the protective arms and the warm womb of what is so familiar to go out into a world that is unknown and seems perilous and terrifying. I want to make no changes and remain merged with my mother."

♦ "With men like Kevin, I may make brief sallies into the

adult world but I can count on them to dump me back into my safe infant place."
- ◆ "Men who offer me a grown-up relationship frighten me and must be avoided, resisted, and discarded."

LEVEL 5a

On the same level of early infancy and possible intrauterine experiences are also the feelings that originate in the primal experiences we had when our needs for loving attachment, affirmation, and emotional nurturance were poorly or inconsistently met. These deficits left us with a residue of feelings of emptiness, flatness, or depression that we try to dispel by the tension and turmoil of troubled love affairs. Kim was expressing feelings from this level when she said:

- ◆ "When I was in agony over Kevin at least I felt alive, I would feel, 'I hurt, therefore I am.' "
- ◆ "When I get involved with a man where there is no pain and strife, I get overcome by feelings of boredom and deadness."

Seeing that there are so many levels of motivation that could be blocking your attraction to someone right for you might make you feel that it is all too complicated and requires too much introspection. But don't despair. It is not necessary for you to uncover all the motivational layers in order to bring about change. Some motivations may be far more influential over your behavior than others, and at times even the most partial insight can be enough to weaken the destructive magnetism of those hidden goals.

When Kim first clearly recognized that her involvement with Kevin and men like him was driven by a desperate wish to get her father to be loving, she said she felt "doomed" to repeat this script endlessly. "It's too deeply engrained in me." I replied, "You may have been doomed before you saw the connection between your father's rejection and your being drawn to impossible men, but now you are in a position to decide to change the script." After a while, however, I had to admit that although the insight helped her break with Kevin, it did not seem to be leading her to form new and more satisfying relationships. I wondered if it was just a matter of time before she could use this insight—it often does take time for an insight to become usable—or if her progress was being blocked by influences still not understood. Then Kim became aware that she was playing out an internal childhood prohibition against winning her father away from her very grim and seemingly formidable mother. By not allowing herself to have a good love relationship now she was still avoiding the dangers of that competition. With this insight, an important missing piece seemed to fall into place. Kim was able to say, "I want something really good with a man, and I'm going to stop disqualifying perfectly okay guys because I'm programmed to end up with no one better than my mother had." This inner decision, based not on empty wishful thinking but on self-knowledge and a resolve to use that self-knowledge, was a crucial step in a series of steps that eventually led to her love relationship with David.

It's a matter of, as much as possible, catching on to yourself so that you do not continue unknowingly to trip yourself up. Just by being aware that there are unknown factors at work, you can reorient your focus away from a frantic search for the "right" person and toward self-understanding and inner change. Important as it may be to actively seek someone who is right for you, that endeavor can be futile unless you are also working on understanding and minimizing your tendency to undermine it. Just striving to uncover your hidden motives and to liberate yourself from their influence can, in itself, make you freer, more courageous, and more loving.

9

LOVING SOMEONE RIGHT FOR YOU

Let us suppose that you are no longer drawn to people who are bad for you, you have worked on expanding your capacity to love, you have gotten clearer on your goals and your journey, and you have started to think in terms of what kind of love companion you want for that journey. But at this point you hit a snag that seems to stop all forward movement. *The kind of person you have concluded would be a good love companion simply does not turn you on!* In fact, for some the very idea of finding a good "love companion" for one's journey may seem like a spiceless and un-romantic undertaking, like looking through the want ads for jobs that do not appeal to you because the fringe benefits are good. The very "practicality" of it can seem to drain the passion out of it.

But this need not be true. In fact, nothing can murder passion and romance more surely than trying to make a life with someone who is at odds with your needs and your journey. And despite your track record, it is certainly possible to become attracted to and passionate about someone who is also a good love

135

companion. It happens all the time. But if it has not happened for you despite the changes you've made to this point, there is an additional line of approach that can be helpful. This involves *clearly identifying what it is that has been irresistibly appealing about the kind of person who has been bad for you and looking for these traits in a nondestructive, nontoxic form in a person who could be good for you.* Let us see how this works.

BEING MEAN IS NOT BEING STRONG

When Kim reached that point of being repelled by the disdainful stance of the Kevins of the world, she went through a period of forcing herself to go out with their opposites, men who let her get away with too much or allowed her to treat them badly. To her amazement, she found an arrogance and cruelty in herself that she never had suspected. She would break dates with the men at the last minute. She would spot their vulnerable area and tease them about it. And she would lead them to believe she was interested and then suddenly tell them she would not see them again. "I must admit," Kim told me, "sometimes this is fun. There is power in it, and I can see how Kevin must have felt. But then I hate myself for it. I don't like this me. And it certainly isn't going to lead anywhere good. What's going on here?"

As we tried to understand what was going on, we could see how much buried rage had existed in Kim all her life, rage stemming from being at the mercy of her mother's coldness and father's cruel inconsistency. When she got older, she put herself in that same subservient position with men, and this added fuel to her rage. Partly she was allowing Kevin and others to act out her anger for her, identifying with them even though, in reality, she was the victim. Now, when she went out with men who let themselves be treated badly, her anger and cruelty no longer were hidden. It frightened and intrigued her at first, but she soon tired of acting it out and could see that men who could be treated this way would never appeal to her. At this point she became demoralized because in her mind the world was pretty much divided up into "the dumpers and the dumpees," with no in between.

No longer could she tolerate getting dumped on, and she had no respect for men she felt she could push around. Who else was there? I assured her that her way of dividing people up was a false one, learned from the way power was misused in her family, and that there were other alternatives.

When Kim met David at a party, she found him attractive, easygoing, and good humored. He took her phone number and said, "I may not call you for a little while because my schedule for the next week or two is incredibly busy, but I will call." She didn't know what to think about this—it sounded like the old elusiveness that had always hooked her addictive weak spot. As the days went by she found herself alternating between thinking about him in the old obsessive way ("Why doesn't he call?") and being turned off at the idea that he could be like Kevin. But then David did call, and they made a date for the following week. They had an enjoyable and easy time and began to see each other more often.

It became clear to Kim that David would neither treat her badly nor let her treat him badly. He did, however, have some qualities that although positive and healthy, struck the old insecurity button that had been installed in her by her father and which added a little kick without it being dangerous. For example, while he never played evasive games or trashed her needs and feelings, he did have a busy life and had good friends who he enjoyed, took seriously, and sometimes went away with on camping and climbing trips. Her inability to control these aspects of his life had a touch of the old insecurity that she felt as excitement. And while he wasn't judgmental and critical the way her father, Kevin, and others had been, he didn't respond to her actions with unconditional approval—he had definite standards and could become quite angry when she was inconsiderate of him or did not follow through on something she had agreed to do. It was important to her not to disappoint or anger him— important because she cared about him, not because she was afraid of being punished or rejected.

What had changed for Kim? Had she reached a point where her obsessive need to hold on to an elusive man by pursuing him in a humiliating way would never again be part of what attracted her to a man? Was this need to get involved in such demeaning relationships forever exorcised as the demonic trigger of her passionate feelings? To a great extent, the answer is yes. The growing love and mutual acceptance in her relationship with David reduced this need and, therefore, also reduced her underlying anger. That part of her that still could be turned on by an edge of insecurity was satisfied, as we have seen, by David's less than total availability and by his angry refusal to tolerate bad treatment from her.

In addition, Kim discovered another emotionally safe way for some of her old passions to be ignited. She found that as their lovemaking became freer and more uninhibited, they could act out in bed some mild fantasies of dominance and submission that were very exciting but were not destructive because they were clearly within the realm of play, were contained by their caring about each other, and did not spill over into their everyday way of relating. Many people with self-defeating or harmful scripts from the past—whether the scripts feature them in a role of dominance, subservience, self-effacement, combativeness, or whatever—can find mutually gratifying and innocuous ways of dealing with them through their sex lives or other forms of play. This solution is a lot better than weaving old destructive patterns into the very fabric of the relationship, and it can, for many couples, add an intensity that strengthens their bond.

SULKINESS IS NOT DESIRABILITY

After Warren broke off his frustrating relationship with Diane, he puzzled over why he had repeatedly been attracted to the same kind of self-centered and ungiving women. What was there about them?

He looked at the hundreds of photos he had taken of models in his studio and observed that the models he found most attractive, besides being generally beautiful, had certain characteristics in common. They all had high cheekbones, and they all had a certain energy in their eyes. But even more striking to Warren was that they all had a similar expression—sulky, sullen, and unfriendly. In fact, Warren had gained something of a reputation among ad agencies as being a master of the "drop dead" look—that glum, moping or petulant look that seemed to be saying "back off" or "I dare you."

Warren's fatal attraction was women similar to the depriving parents of his childhood. This was implicit in the rejection reflected in their expression and their personalties yet neither his insight into these origins nor his wish not to repeat the past, led him to reverse that tendency. He simply could not get excited about women who had the sunny look and disposition of a cheerleader. How was he to find a woman who would both appeal to him and be a good campanion? Was there nothing of what had always attracted him that was safe?

It was clear that there was no need for Warren to put aside his attraction to women with high cheekbones and energy in their eyes. There was nothing about these qualities in themselves that did him any harm. Perhaps, he hoped, there were women with enough of those special facial features that attracted him who would not be moody or mean. He also concluded that he had best pursue women who, although capable of being close and nurturing, would not seem too easy or too available.

Warren had met such a woman in Pamela, a former model who now ran a models' studio. Pamela could be hard edged but was also soft, caring, and very mature. At times she was petulant, but it was a passing mood, easily dispelled. Besides she had the high cheekbones that turned him on. Unlike his previous relationships, or theirs was not a battlefield. There were few scenes of screaming, door slamming, and tearful reconciliation. In fact, being with Pamela felt good most of the time. And, not unlike Kim with David, Warren was able to act out some of his remaining needs for the drama of combat, conflict, and jealousy in sexual fantasies shared with Pamela and in bouts of sarcastic repartee that were meant more to amuse than to hurt. In contrast to his concerns with Diane, Warren never worried that whatever disagreements they did have would lead to Pamela's throwing a tantrum or walking out on him. So with Pamela he could find the qualities that engaged his feelings and his passion, but without the pain that, until now, had always gone with it.

SPICING UP THE TOFU

When Laura moved from her position of "Don't give me that garbage about seeing what personal journey I am on" to a period of self-discovery and then to her statement that "I need someone whose journey goes well with mine," she had made an essential shift in her orientation to relationships. But she was still far from connecting with that new kind of love companion. In fact, it was at this point that Laura made the statement I quoted in Chapter 1: "I'm finally nauseated by the kind of self-centered charmer who used to turn me on, and I'm thankful for that. I wasted enough tears and years. But I still find a man who could offer me a good and solid relationship about as exciting as tofu."

I asked Laura to try to put her finger on just what traits she had found so attractive in Les and the other men with whom she had had intense but limited involvements. She answered, "They've all been power men, to some degree. Mostly, they conveyed a feeling of not really needing me or anyone. I always felt that if I disappeared off the earth they would hardly notice."

"And that was so appealing? Not to matter? Why?" I asked. As Laura explored this, she realized her answer had several dimensions. "First of all, it feels familiar. My father dominated me and the rest of the family as if we were his possessions, particularly when he got into his periodic drunken rages, which were terrifying. I can't recall a single conversation with my father in which he wasn't giving me an order or shredding me for doing something wrong. I cannot recall one conversation in which I showed him my feelings or asked his advice. He just didn't care what I or my brother or my mother felt. My mother was totally ineffectual, and the few times I went to her when I was upset, she acted helpless. So I plunged myself into my schoolwork and became a superachiever. I was the valedictorian of my high school class and all the time held a job after school to make my own money. I was not going to need anyone. As I got older I learned more and more to take charge of myself and the situations I was in."

As Laura looked at this, she could see that she chose men

like Les not only because they were familiar and allowed her to continue in the old task of trying to win the love of her difficult father, but also because these uninvolved and distancing men made her feel safe. I asked her, "Safe from what?" We discovered that Laura had chosen men who, because of their own well-defended boundaries and limited caring, never tempted her into letting her long-buried needs for closeness and intimacy emerge. She had never selected a man who made her feel it was okay for her to show her fears, her worries, her longings, her wish to have her feelings heard and to be reassured. Nor did she feel, with the men she chose, that she could express her anger at them for not being there for her. The kind of relationship she had with men like Les encouraged her to keep sitting on all these feelings that she had long ago concluded were shameful and unwelcome. With Les and others it was clear from the beginning that she had better keep her expectations and needs very much under wraps and this was safety. Cold, cold safety.

Laura could also see how her own actions and choices were continuing the deprivation she had suffered in her childhood. At this point she did what Kim, Warren, and many other people do when they discover their attraction has been to characteristics that are bad for them—she went to the other extreme. She began to date men who were in many ways the opposite of Les, men who were good guys but who tended to be insecure and socially uncertain and who seemed overeager to form an initimate bond. As hard as she tried, she could work up no excitement about these men. In fact, she felt choked and suffocated. There was nothing inherently unappealing about them; other women might be drawn to and feel comfortable with this more sensitive and relationship-hungry type. But for Laura they were indeed tofu. She was afraid that the combination of their neediness and her own underlying neediness would result in a sticky emotional dependency. She was also afraid that her own drive and her tendency to take charge could easily overwhelm some of these men. Seeing them this way, it was hard to feel much passion toward them.

During this period of not being able to go backward to men

like Les and feeling turned off by these other more emotionally available men, Laura was deeply discouraged about ever finding a love relationship. Slowly she began to realize that she had gone from one extreme to another, trying to force herself to get excited about men who clearly would not excite her. Then she began to notice that there were men who were self-contained without being afraid to show any neediness or vulnerability, who could set clear boundaries without walling themselves off, who could take care of themselves without being uncaring, and who could be separate without running away or disappearing. She realized there were men who could be open, loving, and intimate without drowning the relationship in mutual dependence. What she wanted was neither Les nor his opposite, but a man who was sufficiently self-assured that he could permit sustained intimacy without fear of either her very real strengths or her emerging neediness. That kind of man began to seem not only as "good for her" as tofu, but very interesting and spicy. With renewed optimism, Laura redirected her gaze to begin to notice men who were exciting and interesting despite their actual and emotional availability. And as so often happens when people let themselves notice those they had previously overlooked, more such men seemed to appear in Laura's life. One of them was Bob.

Laura and Bob were assigned by their respective companies to work on a proposal for a joint undertaking. They clearly enjoyed being together and laughed a great deal even though the enterprise was often difficult and trying. She liked the way he could work with creativity and dedication without taking himself or the project too seriously. She liked hearing him talk of his many interests and that he seemed genuinely tuned in to the things she revealed about herself. When the proposal was near completion Bob asked her out for lunch. "Thanks for making these past few weeks so much fun," he told her. "But I didn't ask you out to lunch just to thank you and to say good-bye. It's more to say hello. I'm very attracted to you. You must know that. But I didn't want to move things in that direction until the project ended. I think I worked particularly hard so we would finish it quickly and I could ask you out!" He was smiling broadly. "I left

144 GETTING IT RIGHT

the office every night thinking about how much fun you were to be with and how special you are. I have a feeling that you and I might be very good together. I like to think that you feel that, too. Or is that just my wishful thinking?''

Laura was taken aback by his directness. Was it just a line? If it was, she knew how to play that game very well. But looking at him she could have no doubt about his sincerity. She found that she was smiling as openly as he was. She also realized that she was feeling a familiar excitement in an emotionally unfamiliar interchange. "Good together? Well, I think it will be fun finding out.''

THE ANTIDOTE TO HIS ALLERGY

Daniel is the twenty-nine-year-old science teacher who I quoted in Chapter 2 as saying "I am now allergic to the kind of woman I used to be attracted to and who made my life a living hell, but now I am attracted to no one. I feel in limbo.'' He had had two serious involvements with women who were playful, seductive, and full of energy. "I love those qualities—they chase away what is drab and humdrum about life and make it a lot of fun. I was enormously turned on to each of them, and was darn near destroyed by discovering each of them being unfaithful after we had agreed to be monogamous.''

Daniel also went to the other extreme, dating subdued and serious women. He tried to work up enthusiasm about these women, but with no success. There were two changes Daniel had to make at this point. First, he had to work on making his life and his moods less "drab and humdrum'' so he wouldn't need such a flighty and "hyper'' woman to bring flash and color to it. Second, he had to realize that if he is especially drawn to women who are energetic, playful and sexual, he does not have to give that up in order to have a love relationship. Many women who are energetic and sexual are perfectly capable of being monogamously committed. Daniel had to learn to see the difference between a woman who enjoys being playfully flirtatious and a woman who is promiscuously seductive, between a woman who is fun loving and a woman who is irresponsible, between a woman who is carefree and a woman who is careless. He began to ask himself not why he had chosen women who are fun, but why he had chosen women who hurt him. This freed him to seek the traits that had always delighted him—but in a benign and positive form.

STONINESS IS NOT STEADINESS

Carla's loneliness in her marriage to Jack had led her to separate from him. To her surprise, she found that she often missed Jack, and it surprised her because she felt there had been so little emotional contact between them. She began to realize that it was to a great degree his reserved, taciturn, uncommunicative manner that had appealed to her right from the start. There seemed something rocklike and solid about it. And because Carla was brought up in a home where things were often chaotic and communication often invasive and disrespectful of privacy, and she often felt herself to be unsure and unsolid, Jack's seeming "quiet strength" was enormously attractive to her. However, as the years went by and her frustration deepened, she came to see it less as strength and more as the desperate defense of a man terrified of his own feelings and of intimacy. In one bitter fight with him after they split up she said, "I used to think you were strong, but you're just stony."

For a while Carla tried to feel attracted to Jack's opposite—men who were very emotional, who eagerly shared all the nuances of their feelings, and who wanted to know all the nuances of hers. She found these men interesting, but they made her uneasy and they elicited no excitement or passion. She saw that "quiet strength" was still something that turned her on in a man so, instead of pursuing Jack's opposite, she decided to concentrate on distinguishing between men who appeared strong because they were rigidly defending against emotions and those who felt sufficiently secure and at home with themselves to respond to her feelings and disclose their own.

During Carla's period of discovery and development, Jack

was also going through some drastic changes. His stony facade proved not to be of enduring granite. He was devastated by Carla's leaving him. Feelings of pain and rage and intense love for her came smashing to the surface from some underground reservoir so strongly that he was almost unable to function for a while. This man who had scoffed at psychotherapy and had looked down at people who "delved too much" began to see a psychologist for both individual and group psychotherapy. He faced feelings he had long repressed and experienced the agony and joy of being in touch with himself and of expressing himself to other people. He discovered he had probably chosen Carla because her need that he be detached and austere with his feelings meant that she would not threaten his defenses. Now he, too, began to need something different. In his contacts with Carla he was able to express his love for her and to tell her about the changes he was going through. He confronted her with the fact that she had colluded with him to keep him "stony" out of her need to have a rock to lean on. He told her that now he, too, wanted a fuller, deeper relationship. She found herself feeling attracted to him again and more open to giving the marriage a new chance.

RECEPTIVE IS NOT THE SAME AS NEEDY

When Peter, the medical biologist, had broken up with his last girlfriend, Elly, she had clung to him in tears and he had pushed her away screaming, "You're trying to strangle me. Get a life!" Peter soon recognized that Elly and the other women he was drawn to tended to be immature and dependent. He realized that his need for time alone to immerse himself in his research made their dependence an intolerable burden. He could also see that he was drawn to these women because doubts about his appeal and adequacy made him afraid that a more independent woman would not be interested in him or would eventually leave him. These insights led him to the statement, quoted in Chapter 6, "I'm not sure I can easily change who I'm attracted to. But at least I'm determined not to keep getting involved with the same kind of dependent woman who I will disappoint and be disappointed by."

Peter began going out with women closer to his age who were often fellow scientists or had other well-developed careers. But these women seemed so knowledgeable, experienced, and self-contained that he could not fathom what they could want from him. In therapy he could see that because of poor self-esteem he was underestimating his appeal to women. Once he could let himself see that many women were drawn to him, he began to feel more comfortable with women who had a lot on the ball. But he noticed that there was still, for him, a certain lack of excitement in these relationships. He missed the extra kick he got from women who showed that they admired him for all he knew and who enjoyed learning from him. He wondered whether he would have to give up that sort of turn-on if he was to have a relationship with someone who was not too dependent.

When he met Marilyn, a woman who had started a small advertising business ten years before and built it into a major agency, he for the first time became excited and passionate about someone who met both sets of his needs. She was a strong, successful and independent woman and he found that very attractive. Because she was so heavily involved in her own business and other activities it gave Peter lots of unpressured time to be buried in his own work. At the same time, Marilyn was somewhat awed by his medical research and she loved to go with him to museums and concerts and hear how knowledgeable and impassioned he could be. She told him, not with fluttering eyelashes but with genuine affection and appreciation, "When I go to a museum with you, I feel I have my own private guide." He said to me, "I never thought I could have my cake and eat it, too. But I guess by honoring both sets of needs, instead of trying to squelch the fact that I really do love to be in that teaching role with a woman I'm close to, I've found that they're not incompatible. Marilyn is a real grown-up and I love that. Yet in certain areas she looks up to me in a way that both she and I really enjoy."

HARD TO PLEASE BUT NOT IMPOSSIBLE
TO PLEASE

When Harry was finally finished with Ruth and determined not to get into any more relationships with women who treated him badly he began to consider what he needed at this point in his journey. His conclusion, quoted in Chapter 6, was: "I want my remaining years to be something they've never been before— mellow, fun filled, easy, and loving. I am not saying that I want to drift passively into old age—I want plenty of fun and adventures—but I don't want to struggle anymore to get someone to be nice to me." Harry found that there were many women who were quite willing to be nice to him, because he was an interesting and handsome man and because they were nice women. He enjoyed their attentions and affections but had difficulty responding to them romantically and sexually.

At times Harry would catch himself longing for Ruth, despite the demeaning way she had treated him, or perhaps because of that. "Maybe you just can't teach an old dog new tricks," he told me. "I won't go back to Ruth or anyone like her, because I would lose my self-respect and it would probably kill me. The woman I'm going out with now is as sweet and responsive as could be, but there's no fire, and I still want that. I may have to accept that I'll have to settle for companionship without any fire. I'm not sure I'm ready for that."

Then Harry met Elaine when she sued the dry cleaning chain he owned for damaging two of her dresses. He appeared in small claims court and quickly became aware of two things: Her claim was justified and he was very attracted to her. He instructed his lawyer to settle and asked if he could take her to dinner. "I liked the feisty way you stood up for yourself," he told her in the restaurant, and he wondered if he wasn't attracted to the same kind of aggressive and difficult woman who had bedeviled him all his life. But he sensed she was different. "She can be tough and stand up for herself. She can also be pretty demanding. But I don't think she's mean," he told me. I urged him to stay alert for any signs of meanness, but neither he nor I could find meanness in her. At times she could be difficult and insist on having her way, but she was straightforward about it and did not put Harry down. She could also be quite warm, affectionate, and protective with him.

Harry laughed when he told me, "I guess I could never be drawn to Little Mary Sunshine, but I've discovered something important. Being difficult is not the same as being impossible, and being demanding is not the same as being contemptuous. And I've made enough progress so that I can be turned on by a woman who is difficult and demanding without her having to be impossible and contemptuous!"

NARCISSISM IS NOT SELF-CONFIDENCE

In almost all the examples discussed here, the people who are the objects of the addictions have one major characteristic in common: They are unusually self-centered and narcissistic. Different love addicts may be attracted to different kinds of narcissists (some to a mean narcissist, others to an unavailable one, and so forth). But there is something about narcissism that is in itself appealing, at least initially, to many people—and not just love addicts. Long ago, Sigmund Freud, in his paper "On Narcissism" speculated that the appeal of self-centered people is that we take the self-promoting way in which they behave as a manifestation of an enviable self-confidence. To whatever degree our own self-confidence is less than we would wish, we may find their sense of entitlement admirable and feel drawn to connect with it.

This was illustrated in a comment of Laura's. I had remarked that the one common goal she and Les seemed to have was the satisfaction of his every need. She said, "Les and the others I have been obsessed with made themselves number one. They have no need to put themselves out to win my approval the way I always try to win theirs. They have no need to keep me happy the way I'm always trying to keep them happy. I admire it, even when it's at my expense. I wish I could be more like that." Then she added, "After all, it's a sign of strength, isn't it? Doesn't it reflect a healthy ego?"

What I would say to Laura and so many others who hold this misconception is "No, it does not—not for narcissists like Les, Kevin, Diane, Ruth, or countless others. You are mistaking a weakness for a strength." I say this because a close hard look at narcissistic people reveals that their self-involvement and their demands are a reaction to hidden feelings of shame, inadequacy, and worthlessness. Psychotherapists will often walk on eggs with narcissistic patients because they are so sensitive to anything they view as a criticism or a suggestion of imperfection. Even a hint that they may be at fault in some conflict can lead them to feel injured or enraged. People with true self-confidence are not that vulnerable. They can take criticism and can acknowledge imperfections. And they can form a relationship that is caring and reciprocal.

So if you find that you have been drawn to narcissistic people, challenge any assumptions you might be making that their behavior reflects healthy and enviable self-assertion. This change of perspective can prepare you for two changes you might be well advised to make. The first is to work on increasing your self-esteem rather than trying to get it from an attachment to someone else. Putting yourself in such a one-down position can only reduce and even shred your self-esteem. The second is to seek people whose self-esteem is anchored securely enough that they do not have to elevate themselves at your expense.

THE ART OF THE POSSIBLE

Politics has sometimes been called "the art of the possible." In some ways, this phrase could also be applied to the process of forming a love relationship. Some love addicts, it is true, free themselves so completely that they are able to become romantically involved with people who have no visible trace of the toxic quality that once was so compelling. But, as we have seen, many others can find contentment with people who have a touch of the old attractive venom, but in a form so mild and so diluted that there is little or no destructive potential. If you have been ad-dicted to bad relationships and simply cannot feel attracted to people who are diametrically different from those who used to attract you, try to identify which previously attracting traits have been dangerous to you and to think about what a less malignant form of those traits may be. For example:

- If you've been drawn to but hurt by people who "live dan-gerously,"
  look for someone who
  skydives rather than dives into promiscuous sex or some-one who makes ambitious career moves rather betting the rent money in blackjack.

- If you have been drawn to people who need more space than an astronaut because of their fears of closeness and intimacy,
  look for someone who
  is deeply involved in some activities and interests but can be close and intimate, not someone who fears closeness and intimacy. Look for just enough unavailability to turn you on without it being so much that you feel abandoned.

- If you are excited by people who intimidate and frighten you,
  look for someone who
  can get very angry when you have given him or her cause but who will not be sadistic, mean, or violent.

- If you have been attracted to relationships of dominance and submission,
  look for someone who
  can enter into those power ploys on a mild level in day-to-day life or who can satisfy this need in the "pretend" of sexual play or nonsexual play.

• If you have been turned on by those whose concern with their appearance has reflected a narcissistic obsession,
look for someone who
has good taste and enjoys dressing well but has not made a personal religion of it.

• If you have been excited by those whose seemingly unflappable self-assurance has turned out to be a grandiose self-centeredness, that has left little room for you and your needs, you can
look for someone who
has a healthy sense of self-worth as a solid base from which they can reach out to you.

• If you have been attracted to those who are unloving and ungiving (perhaps as part of your task of trying to get more warmth from an unnurturing parent) you can
look for someone who
is reserved, taciturn and perhaps has trouble verbalizing love but is clearly able to feel love and to be there for you.

• If you have been compassionately and passionately drawn to those who have a broken wing (for example, a substance addiction, behavioral addiction, depression, an unsuccessful work life, or some other major weakness) and have found that your efforts lead only to a debilitating, and unending rescue operation, you can
look for someone who
has a few appealing vulnerabilities and the capacity to admit weaknesses openly but who is basically able to deal with life adequately and does not seem hell bent to end up a loser.

• If you have been repeatedly captivated but let down by someone who is childlike, impulsive, and in constant pursuit of immediate gratification, you can

look for someone who
can be playful, fun loving, and spontaneous but in the context of being a responsible adult.

◆ If you have been drawn to arrogant and demanding types who must always have their own way, you can
look for someone who
is strong and decisive but who can be flexible, fair and respectful of your needs and views.

◆ If you have frequently let yourself be lured into relationships with people who have pushed you around and you have needed to be with someone who seems strong and forceful, you can
look for someone who
has no need to push you around but who definitely won't let you push him or her around.

◆ If you have been drawn to compulsive people, who are so intent on keeping their lives in perfect order that there is little room for flexibility, spontaneity, or you, you can
look for someone who
can live competently and effectively but without being so rigid that it narrows his or her life and yours.

You can become an artist of the possible. Your goal is to find someone who really appeals to you *and* who you can have a good relationship with, not simply to find someone good for you like some spiceless health food or boring exercise. The element of excitement and attraction may require a touch of something similar to the old destructive stuff but in a harmless and even beneficial form. This touch will not guarantee that you will feel an immediate strong sexual attraction. Switching to someone who has not been your "type" is not likely to be easy. Obviously, the more *benign* similarities there are to the old *malignant* objects of your sexual passion, the better. You may have to make a deliberate effort to focus on the most appealing attributes of your new partner. Warren, in his early days of dating Pamela, said, "I have to learn to feel passionate toward her even though she's nice and does not give me a hard time. She's certainly attractive, but to feel really stimulated by her I have to zoom in on those great cheekbones and on that pouty look she sometimes gets. Those are still the old aphrodisiacs." But as his feelings for Pamela deepened he could say, "It's not just those parts of her that turn me on. It's her! The excitement and appeal has spread to who she is. Now I can't wait to be with her, to touch her. She's so sexy."

In this way, passion initially triggered by one or two attributes eventually is triggered by the total person. The growing feelings of love and caring themselves become stimulating and eroticized. This does not mean that you can manufacture sexual passion out of nothing. But if there is someone who you care about and who is good for you, focus on those attributes they have that attract you and give your passion time to ignite.

10

GETTING YOURSELF READY FOR A REAL LOVE RELATIONSHIP

At one point in that hiatus between Kevin and David, Kim said, "I'm a very caring person, and I feel so ready to be in a good love relationship."

"You have certainly taken a big step in that direction by breaking off with Kevin," I responded. "But this would be a good time to look at whether you, too, have some deficits in your ability to form a good love relationship."

Kim was hurt and angry. "Are you telling me that I don't have what it takes to make a love relationship? I really was in love with Kevin. And even Kevin would admit that I was giving and thoughtful. There's nothing wrong with my ability to form a love relationship—it's Kevin who had the deficit."

Under similar circumstances, Harry also became defensive. He told me, "I was very loving to Ruth. If she had been anywhere near as considerate and affectionate with me as I was with her, we could be on cloud nine. The trouble is, I was too loving."

Kim and Harry's irritation at me is understandable. There was an obvious truth to what they said. They had each been deeply in love and put a great deal of time and effort into trying to make things work out. But, as we have seen over and over again, the feeling of being in love, though a vital ingredient in forming a love relationship, is not enough. Even putting a lot of time and effort into it may not be enough. Many other ingredients are necessary. And if you have been in love with an unsatisfactory partner, it is possible that the very intensity of your loving feelings (as well as your tendency to make bad choices) may have concealed impairments in your overall ability to form a love relationship.

What factors go into your ability to form a love relationship? We will explore eight crucial factors:

1. The capacity to be romantically in love
2. The ability to see who your partner really is
3. The ability to accept who your partner really is
4. The ability to be loving in words and actions
5. The capacity to receive love
6. The ability to create balance and reciprocity
7. The courage to take risks for love
8. The ongoing effort to expand your selfhood and your world

We will look at each factor in turn—at what it is, how it may have become weakened or impaired, and what you can do to strengthen and develop it. To get the most out of this exploration it is important not to concentrate on the shortcomings of your partner, which has often been a necessary part of our previous focus. Now, however, it is time to take an unflinching look at your own strengths and deficiencies as a love partner. This will not be easy or comfortable. Hermann Hesse says in his book *Demian*, "I realize today that nothing in the world is more distasteful to a man than to take the path that leads to himself." Even though honest self-appraisal isn't always pleasant, bear in mind that the path that leads to yourself is also the best path to a good love relationship.

1. THE CAPACITY TO BE ROMANTICALLY IN LOVE

What is this thing called romantic love? Clearly, emotional intensity, *excitement* and *passion* are central to the experience of romantic love. But as we have seen, these feelings, no matter how tumultuous, blissful and rapturous do not, in themselves, make for a fulfilling romantic love *relationship*—that requires many additional strands of caring, commonality and committed involvement. But a satisfying degree of passion and emotional intensity must be there or we do not experience it as romantic love. I subscribe to Nathaniel Branden's description of romantic love as "a passionate, spiritual-emotional-sexual attachment between two people that reflects a high regard for the value of each other's person." Branden goes on to say:

> I do not describe a relationship as romantic if the couple does not experience their attachment as passionate or intense . . . if there is not some sense of being "soulmates"; if there is

not a deep emotional involvement; if there is not a strong sexual attraction . . . and if there is not mutual admiration.

If your capacity to feel romantically in love has led you to painful experiences, you may well have concluded that the love-disabled Kevins of the world are the fortunate ones. One young man I worked with said, "The song has it wrong—people who do *not* need people are the luckiest people in the world."

But despite the fact that feeling romantically in love can bring to the fore the most irrational, needy and childlike aspects of us, despite the danger that it can render us vulnerable to hurt, disappointment and loss of autonomy, romantic love is essential to the formation of a love relationship and can help hold the relationship together through the trials, conflicts and hardships it will have to face. It can transform the ordinary into the exceptional and the plain into the beautiful, both in our own eyes and in the eyes of our beloved. And the beauty we then find in each other has its own reality.

A romantic love can bring out, not only the worst in us, but the best in us. It can impassion and elevate our sexual experience by adding an element of specialness and joy, intimacy, timelessness and even a temporary merging that is often extraordinarily

renewing. It can lead us beyond ourselves, in the concern and caring we feel for our beloved. It can propel us out of our self-absorption or, at the very least, it can induce us to include our beloved as part of our self. Ethel Person put it this way:

> Romantic love, subjectively experienced, is an emotion of extraordinary intensity. The experience of love can make time stop, therefore giving one the rare opportunity to live in the present. . . . Love may confer a sense of inner rightness, peace and richness, or it may be a mode of . . . enlarging and changing the self. Hence, it is a mode of transcendence.

The capacity to feel romantically in love can be contaminated by Attachment Hunger. When your romantic love feelings combine with Attachment Hunger, the love feelings take on an urgency and desperation and therefore, instead of leading to "enlarging and changing the self," lead to a distortion and narrowing of the self. *This difference—that a loving passion enlarges us while an addiction inevitably diminishes us—is a crucial distinction, even though both may be experienced as romantic love.* People in the throes of an addiction—that deadly amalgam of feelings of romantic love and Attachment Hunger— usually think of the actions that flow from these feelings as being extremely loving. That is why Kim and Harry were angry when I suggested that they had a defect in forming a love relationship. Yet their actions, characterized by subservience and lack of self-respect, were more masochistic than truly loving. Their capacity to feel romantic love, as we have defined it, was impaired, but because they equated their capacity to feel in love with the capacity to have a love relationship, they did not know it.

For most of you, increasing your capacity for being romantically in love will probably involve detaching that mature romantic capacity from the infantile Attachment Hunger that downgrades your love into something narrowing and masochistic. But some of you may have different problems caused by weaknesses in your capacity for romantic love being weak and fluctuating. You may find yourself easily discarding relationships that may have promise but that need persistence and work. Or you may find that your diminished capacity for feeling in love can leave you unhappily tied to your partner only by your Attachment Hunger with none of the elevating passion and transcending excitement that being romantically in love would bring to it.

The twin enemies of our ability to use feelings of romantic love in forming a love relationship are, then, the distortion and dilution of these feelings by Attachment Hunger and the diminished capacity to feel in love. Much of this book has focused on the first, on what you can do to recognize and control Attachment Hunger. As for the second, if you think there is a deficiency in your ability to feel romantic love, you need to look closely at your personal history, from your earliest years, to see what may have dulled your feelings. Here are some questions you would do well to explore:

- Did I ever feel romantically in love? As a child or adolescent did I ever have a crush on someone? What happened in that situation?
- Did I see any feelings of romantic love expressed in my home?
- Was there any inappropriate sexuality between me and any family member that made me fearful of feelings of passion? Or did I become afraid of my own taboo fantasies and longings for sexuality, passion, and love?
- Were my feelings of love subject to ridicule and shame?
- Do I try hard to purge myself of romantic love feelings or to repress them because they seem silly or dangerous or make me feel vulnerable?
- Do I have an underlying belief that romantic love is always irrational, immature, and neurotic?
- If I were to feel romantically in love with someone, what do I picture will happen?

In general we can speculate that two broad areas might account for your stunted capacity to feel in love: (1) there was a lack of models for this kind of feeling and behavior in your growing up; (2) you had and still have fears about some traumatic or shameful consequence of experiencing and expressing feelings of romantic love. This does not mean that you cannot have a caring and compassionate relationship without a strong feeling of being romantically in love. Many people are content with such a relationship. But if you want a more transcending experience or believe that without it you have not had enough incentive to build a satisfying relationship, then you will find this self-examination worthwhile. Undertake it with the goals of identifying and alleviating your fears, freeing yourself to notice new models for love, and becoming accepting of your own romantically loving thoughts and feelings.

2. THE ABILITY TO SEE WHO
YOUR PARTNER REALLY IS

Love addicts usually do not see their partners accurately. If you have been a love addict, then you may have glossed over or even blocked out your partner's negative traits, like Kim did when she saw Kevin as a nice guy who just happened to be afraid of commitment or like Harry did when he saw Ruth as proud rather than as hostile and unloving.

You may have even gone further than just blinding yourself to your partner's shortcomings. When your needy inner child takes over, it can shape your perception of your partner to fit your needs. In the film *The Gold Rush*, there is a hilarious but terrifying scene: Charlie Chaplin and another man have been trapped in their arctic cabin by a huge snowstorm and have run out of food. As they approach starvation, Charlie's companion suddenly perceives him as a giant chicken and pursues him with the intent of making a much-needed meal of him. Just as his companion's hunger for food has distorted Charlie into a clucking source of protein, your Attachment Hunger can distort your companion into a satisfier of such powerful needs that you fail to see your companion for who he or she really is.*

Such a distortion can threaten a love relationship in three ways. First, it can lead to repeated disappointments on your part. Some of your disappointments will be about small things. For example, you may take it for granted, that your partner will want to go to a concert that you got tickets for when, if you knew your partner better, you would know that that is not something he or she would want to do. Or it can be about big things, such as believing that your partner's deepest beliefs and wishes are really the same as yours, or that the kind of life he or she wants is the same as the kind of life you want or that you know what most

* Many centuries before Charlie Chaplin, Plato quoted Socrates as saying to Phaedrus that "in the friendship of the lover there is no real kindness, he has an appetite and wants to feed on you. *As wolves love lambs so lovers love their loves.*" [*Phaedrus*] Clearly implied here is not just distortion of the loved one in accordance with the lover's need, but also an attempt to devour him and obliterate his separate identity to satisfy that need. Such an attempt is, of course, the very opposite of seeing, accepting, and enjoying the loved person for who he is in his own right.

pleases him or her sexually. The second threat posed by distortions is that these inevitable disappointments are likely to lead to frequent anger and ongoing confrontation. The final threat is that your partner, feeling that you do not see him or her accurately, will do just what Charlie Chaplin does when he is seen as a giant chicken—he flees for his life. It is frustrating and even infuriating not to be seen truly. While we all take great care to conceal some of our inner life and our behavior, we also want to be known deeply by those with whom we are most intimate. When we or our partner feel that we are not clearly seen, the deprivation can seem so basic that the fabric of our love relationship can disintegrate.

How can you improve your capacity to understand your partner? You must begin by *taking seriously* any complaints by your partner that he or she feels unseen or misunderstood. Keep in mind that, although the discussion has focused on distortions that "improve" reality, your distortions can also paint a picture that is unrealistically bleak. You need to be aware of three mechanisms for distortion:

- Your Attachment Hunger may cause you to *attribute* to your partner all kinds of characteristics you feel you need him or her to have (e.g., you see your partner as strong and secure and overlook his or her feelings of vulnerability and insecurity) or to assume your partner shares positive characteristics of yours (e.g., you see your partner as giving when you are but he or she is not).
- You may *transfer* onto your partner negative aspects drawn from people and experiences in your past (e.g., you may inaccurately interpret certain actions as uncaring or mean, based on someone from your childhood).
- You might *project* onto your partner certain negative aspects of yourself that you may not want to own up to (e.g., inaccurately see your partner as controlling and manipulating rather than recognizing these tendencies in yourself).

Your inclinations to attribute, transfer, and project usually operate outside of your awareness. But, once you recognize that you may be looking through a distorting lens, you can begin efforts to sharpen the acuity of your perceptions. The key is to stop assuming that you know what your partner is thinking or feeling and to *check it out* instead. I recall a relevant example involving Laura and Bob, the man with whom she had begun to develop a promising relationship. Bob was obviously very fond of Laura but was getting annoyed at her tendency to be bossy and controlling. They decided to consult with me together. As they were taking their seats in my office, Laura said to Bob, "Before I forget, I want to tell you that Hal and Judy asked if we wanted to come up and help them open the summer house. They said it would be a lot of work, but I told them we'd love to." The expression on Bob's face was more than dismay—he looked as if someone had held a dirty diaper under his nose. Laura missed it completely and went on talking about what fun it would be. I asked her what she thought Bob was feeling about it. "Oh, he loves to do that kind of thing," she answered. "Ask him," I suggested. She did and Bob said, "To tell you the truth, after the workweek I've had, about the last thing I want to do is take down storm windows and sweep out somebody else's house." Laura was astonished. She had so completely assumed that Bob wanted to do what she wanted to do that she failed to recognize the blatant distaste on Bob's face. She had blurred the boundaries between her inner life and his. As we explored further, it became clear that most of their conflicts were not because Laura wished to control him, but simply because this tendency to attribute her own wishes and preferences to him blinded her to what he was really feeling. This made him feel disregarded and pushed around. And since Bob liked to avoid confrontations, he often did not speak up about his feelings until a great deal of anger had accumulated. We worked on getting Bob to speak up more readily and on getting Laura to check out with him what he was feeling. She became more and more familiar with how and why she distorts her perceptions, and better and better at seeing him correctly.

To increase your capacity to sustain a good love relationship be aware that your wishes, expectations, and past experiences can distort your vision of who your partner is. Make an effort to tune in to both the words and the music that your partner is broadcasting. Do not assume that because you are in love you instinctively know your partner's feelings and preferences. Encourage him or her to state what they are. And if there is any doubt about the messages you think you are receiving, ask for clarification.

3. THE ABILITY TO ACCEPT WHO YOUR PARTNER REALLY IS

Sometimes seeing your partner accurately can be a turnoff. It can even lead to the end of the relationship. That is understandable, if what you see is unappealing or distasteful or disturbing. But often what you will see is a mixture of characteristics, beliefs, goals, values, likes and dislikes, and ways of thinking and being, some of which you will find endearing and others of which you will find bothersome but probably not intolerable. No doubt, he or she would be different in some ways if you had drawn the original blueprint or if even now you could tamper with the programming. But your partner is who he or she is. If, seeing your partner clearly, you still want a love relationship, then you must work toward being able to lovingly accept the package as it is.

Many years ago I attended a banquet honoring the eminent psychologist Carl Rogers on his seventieth birthday. While I do not have the text of his after-dinner address, the gist of it has stayed with me. He stated that the ongoing central task of his own development was to increase his capacity to positively accept the other persons in his life as they were and that the more he succeeded at it, the more his life became interesting and exciting. Then he used an analogy I have never forgotten. He noted that sunsets are universally beloved and speculated about why this is so. He decided the reason was not simply that sunsets are brilliantly colorful but that each sunset unfolds completely uninfluenced by our wishes or control. If we could control sunsets, turning a knob that would add a little magenta here, a little indigo there, we would at some point become bored with them. They would be limited by our own limitations and would no longer have the power to make us respond with wonder and delight. So it is, Rogers believed, with the people around us. We need to increase our capacity to accept and enjoy their undirected unfolding.

It is a striking analogy, but it presents us with a difficult prescription. How hard it is for us not to want to influence, manipulate, and even coerce the other person to be who we wish him or her to be. And we have to be careful not to misunderstand the prescription. It is similar to the idea, advanced by writers such as Ken Keyes, that to be in love relationships we need to become *unconditionally loving*. But this concept, like many good concepts, can be misused. Kim at one point had just read Keyes's book called *The Power of Unconditional Love* and told me, "You see, there's nothing wrong with my loving Kevin. Maybe the difficulty was that I should have become more unconditionally loving despite his treating me badly and his seeing other women. That's who he is." This is a common misunderstanding of the idea of making ourselves unconditionally loving. I pointed out that Keyes makes it clear that even while he is loving a particular person he "can totally reject and even actively oppose what [that] person is saying and doing." While it is undoubtedly valuable to expand our capacity to be unconditionally loving, this does not mean we can have a love relationship with anyone, no matter what they are like or how they treat us. Keyes writes:

> If a loving person were to use *only* love as a basis for choosing a partner, it would be like using the existence of a steering wheel for deciding which car to buy. Since all cars have steering wheels, we need other criteria for deciding.

As valuable as the concepts of "loving acceptance" and "unconditional love" are, you must avoid misinterpreting and misusing them as justification for being in a relationship with someone who is abusive or ungiving. Such a misinterpretation, which Kim was making, distorts these constructive concepts into destructive rationalizations for you to behave even more masochistically. On the other hand, Kim later made good use of these concepts in her loving acceptance of David. Even when she felt most adoring of him, she was quite clearly aware that she did not like or accept everything he did. "I hate it when he goes through periods of insecurity about his work. He gets impossibly testy and brooding. But overall, I accept those moods as part of who he is, because he's not that way too often and I can usually live with it without getting too upset. Sometimes I stay out of his way, sometimes I pamper him, and sometimes I tell him I've had it with his moodiness and want him to cut it out. Sometimes we'll have a fight about it. But I never feel I'm 'settling' for something that's harmful to me, as I did with Kevin's abrasiveness. Nor am I 'settling' for something passionless as I did when I tried to force myself to feel involved with men I dated only because they were the opposite of Kevin. I accept who David is because I love him, because mostly I feel wonderful with him, and because the things I don't like are not that important to me."

Though there is danger of misusing your unconditional loving self destructively, developing that ability is still a crucial element in readying yourself for a love relationship. As you do, several positive things happen:

- The increase in your capacity to love will mean that there will be more people to whom you can be loving. This creates a greater "pool" of people with whom you might develop the intimacy and compatibility that make for good love relationship.
- When your feelings of love no longer are contingent on other people acting in accordance with your needs, there will be less of the anger, conflict, and disappointment that can cripple or kill a relationship. You and the other person are both freer to be yourselves.
- Your increased ability to love makes you more lovable. By being loving, you encourage other people's feelings of love

to emerge. (And, if instead, the other person responds with fear or by trying to manipulate or exploit you, you will know that person is not a candidate for a love relationship.)
◆ The capacity to love is a general and basic ability that can be directed not only outward toward others, but also inward in the form of a healthy regard for yourself. This allows you to love another person deeply without surrendering your right to look out for yourself in the relationship. As a result, it can increase your ability to take care that you are treated with respect and regard.
◆ Becoming more loving feels good. It makes you feel better about yourself and the world. Even your old addictive love had elements of caring and commitment, and you can build on those elements. In this way, your addictive loving can be a significant step in the evolution of your ability to love.

We deepen our ability to love each time we permit ourselves to see the other person clearly and accept who he or she is apart from our needs and demands. We can then decide if there are enough of the ingredients for a good relationship present to commit ourselves to work it out with this person.

4. THE ABILITY TO BE LOVING IN WORDS AND ACTION

It is not enough to *feel* loving toward another person. For a love relationship to take root and grow, the love must be expressed in some form that the other person can receive. As the song from *My Fair Lady* goes, "If you're in love, show me." Too often there is a dam between the feeling of love and its expression that can leave the object of that love feeling thirsty even though there is an unseen reservoir of caring right nearby.

If you have been in a relationship with someone who could not or would not express love in a way that felt meaningful to you, then you know how frustrating it can be. Perhaps you are among the many who felt as Carla did when she would ask Jack if he loved her and he would reply, "I'm here, aren't I?" If the speaker of such words does indeed feel love, then this inarticulate response is clearly an inadequate communication of those feelings. The hearer is left to wonder whether the problem is inadequate communication or lack of feeling. But, rather than simply blame your partner, you should examine whether you, too, may not have been communicating your loving feelings in a form that he or she can receive. We each have our own verbal and nonverbal love language—our own ways of sending and receiving love. When partners have a similar love language, there is an ease, a flow, and a deep gratification for both people. But when each speaks a very different love language, both can feel confused and deprived. In this period of developing your capacity to be in a good love relationship, it is important to become more attuned to what kind of love communications are important to your partner and more receptive to the ways he or she shows love.

Jack, for example, really loved Carla, but he had to grasp the fact that his not expressing it in ways Carla could receive was hurting her and was damaging the relationship. He had to work on becoming more articulate and feelingful in verbalizing that love. At the same time, Carla had to work on recognizing the many ways Jack did communicate his love. She had to recognize the caring he expressed by picking her up at work when she had a rough day, by making sure that they were seated at a restaurant table that was out of the way of drafts that he knew made her uncomfortable, by seeing to it that her car was well serviced, and a bit more romantically, by bringing her a gift at an unexpected time (even though he might forget her birthday). Carla also had to learn to let Jack know that these caring actions made her feel nice things about him.

And Jack then had to learn that if it felt good to hear Carla's words of appreciation, it might also feel good to Carla to hear his words of appreciation.

You also need to communicate your loving feelings not just in your words but also in your actions. After all, words will mean little if they are used to substitute for loving actions or gloss over unloving actions. As with words, you need to tune into what actions would make your partner feel cared about. These may be different actions than those you would need to receive to feel cared about or what your last lover or your parents needed to feel cared about.

I could make a long list of complaints I have heard in my consulting room from people who felt their partner's behavior was unloving, but it might be more useful to paraphrase some statements from people whose partner's actions made them feel they were loved:

"The last person I was involved with would have us on a busy social schedule every weekend despite my saying I needed some time for the two of us to be quietly together. It feels wonderful to be with someone now who understands my need and makes sure that we have that quiet time."

"When he knew I had a very hard work day he said, 'I'll cook you your favorite soup tonight'—and he did."

"He knows that sometimes I need a lot of holding and caressing before I can feel sexually relaxed, and he goes slowly and sensitively at those times."

"She helps me out around the apartment without my having to ask and nag about it as I've sometimes had to in the past."

"She knows that I hate to stand on long lines to see a movie, and she is perfectly willing to wait until the movie has been around for a while and the lines are short." Or, the opposite: "She knew I was dying to see that movie and suggested it even though she hates long lines."

"She knows there are certain things that really turn me on sexually, and she remembers and drives me wild. I don't have to remind her each time."

"He knows that I am likely to be uptight after spending a day with my mother. When I've been with her, he gives me hugs or leaves me alone, depending on what I seem to need. This makes me feel understood and cared about."

"She knows that sometimes I have a quick temper, but she lets it blow over instead of turning it into World War III. I feel she understands and cares." Or, the opposite: "He knows that when he gets so furious it shakes me up and so he tries real hard not to."

"He knows that I get insecure when he has to work real late and always calls me." Or, the opposite: "She knows I hate to feel I have to report in or be checked up on, so she doesn't demand that I call. I appreciate that."

If you have been told in previous relationships that your partner has not felt tuned into, understood, or loved, then take these statements seriously enough to do some honest self-exploration. And if you feel that you are unable to express love in the verbal and nonverbal language your partner understands, you can ask yourself what may be impairing that ability.

There are several factors that can interfere with your effectively expressing your love. The simplest of these factors is simply *not knowing how*, perhaps because you were brought up in a family where expressing love and the empathic attunement to feelings and needs was sorely deficient. In that case, you will in effect have to develop a new skill, to learn a new language. A second factor is that *you may not realize that your partner's language of love is different than yours.* You may make the false assumption that everyone speaks the same language that you do and therefore may not tune into the unique needs of your partner or to hear his or her expressions of caring. A third factor is that *you may be afraid that expressing your feelings of love in direct and easily understood words and actions will make you vulnerable.* There is a certain nakedness and vulnerability that can go with expressing love. You might feel especially vulnerable if childhood experiences with showing love led to embarrassment, rejection, or exploitation. But you and the relationship are much more endangered if you do *not* communicate your loving feelings openly and adequately. Finally, *you may hold the defensive and invalid belief that expressing your love is not necessary*, as illustrated by Jack's question "I'm here, aren't I?" or by the oft-heard "If you don't know, I'm not going to tell you." But it is necessary—and the more direct and attuned the expression, the better. So if you have any reason to believe that you may have some impairment in this expressive ability, practice your empathic attunement and your verbal and nonverbal expression of love with those you care about—your friends and your family as well as your romantic partner.

5. THE CAPACITY TO RECEIVE LOVE

Just as it is important to learn to express love in the other's language, so it is important to learn to recognize and receive love expressed in that language. Carla and Jack were able to rekindle the love and passion in their marriage not only because Jack was so shaken by Carla's leaving him that he made courageous efforts to become more in touch with and expressive of his feelings but also because Carla was able to let herself recognize and feel nurtured by the love expressed in his steadiness and reliability. Carla told me, "I began to see that his quietly 'taking care of business' and his dependability were not simply because he was 'emotionally constipated' or 'compulsive,' which is what I had always dismissed them as, but were his expressions of love. They were his way of caring about me and containing me when I would tend to go off on a hysterical tear. I began to feel the love in it, and I realized how important a part of my initial attraction to him those qualities were. I am not sure I could have fallen in love with him again if he didn't make efforts to loosen up and become more open and expressive, but I know it was just as important that I let myself be receptive and responsive to his characteristic ways of showing his love."

Sometimes the problem may be, not simply a matter of your being deaf to or out of tune with the other's love language, but an impairment in your ability to permit yourself to be loved. There are two broad reasons why some people cannot easily allow themselves to let love in: *They are afraid of it* or *they feel they don't deserve it.* Many of the specific fears are the same as those discussed in Chapter 8 as people's hidden reasons for avoiding a love relationship. Thus, if you fear intimacy, loss of selfhood, abandonment, rejection, or a forbidden victory, you may have erected barriers against your partner's love. If you feel unsafe, you deprive yourself of this gift. The feelings of not deserving love may relate to once having been made to feel ashamed about wanting love or to a general lack of self-esteem. But whatever the reason, not letting yourself receive love wholeheartedly is destructive to the relationship. At one point, Laura, when she was still rigidly defending against her desire for love, was told by a man who was ending a relationship with her, "Every time I showed my love to you, whether with a word, a gift, or a gesture, it left me feeling empty. It's not just that you didn't show me love back, but that my own love bounced off you or disappeared somewhere inside you without a trace." It took her a long time to even understand what he was talking about.

If you have a deficiency in your capacity to receive love, there are several questions you should ask yourself:

- ◆ Am I afraid to let love in? To acknowledge receiving it? Why? What is the danger?
- ◆ What happened in my childhood experiences with love that made it dangerous? Were my needs for love ignored? Were my efforts to get love somehow punished? Was I made to feel that I wanted too much? That I was too much? Were these needs beyond my parents' ability to fulfill?
- ◆ Have later experiences with romantic love been so disappointing or traumatic that I have shut down my receptors and responsiveness to another person's love?
- ◆ Have these childhood and adulthood experiences made me wary and cynical about the possibility of being genuinely loved?
- ◆ Am I ashamed to show another person that I would like his or her love? Am I ashamed to recognize that need in myself? Does it make me feel too needy? Too dependent? Too

demanding? Too vulnerable? Do I believe that it is a weakness that will lead to ridicule? To exploitation? To rejection? To painful disappointment?

◆ Do I feel undeserving? What makes me undeserving? Do I feel I am not good enough, attractive enough, or otherwise not worthy enough for someone to love me and want to make me feel loved?

It is also important for you to become aware of the particular ways you close off to love. And that means looking at another set of questions:

◆ Do I try to keep everything light and superficial? Do I use humor (or misuse humor) to make a joke of romantic or loving moments?

◆ Do I fail to let my needs for loving be known? Do I take a position of "if he (she) really loved me, he (she) would know what I want so if I have to tell him (her), it's no good anyhow?" (This childhood position derives from early experiences of having parents who were either so *tuned in* to your nonverbalized needs that you still expect others to know what you want or so *tuned out* that you are constantly recreating the frustration and disappointment. But a love partner is not a mommy or a daddy and you are not a nonverbal child. As an adult, you mostly have to let the other person know about your wishes to be treated in ways that make you feel loved.)

◆ Am I so afraid to let love in that I respond with coldness, anger or indifference to expressions of love? (Try to imagine what that feels like to the other person and ask yourself if you really want that result.)

◆ Do I devalue the other person's love with a stance that if he (she) loves me, his (her) love can't be worth much?

Try to catch on to your relationship-destroying ways of blocking the other person's love and to the reasons why you play such a dirty trick on yourself. To work on countering this tendency, try the following exercise. *Assume that you (including your inner child) want to and deserve to be loved.* Then, in writing:

- ◆ State what qualities you would like to be lovingly recognized and appreciated for.
- ◆ State how you would like that love to be shown.
- ◆ State what kind of expressions of love would make you feel happy, affirmed, and valued.
- ◆ Notice whatever feelings of fear, shame, or uneasiness you are experiencing and write those feelings down. Do not block your feelings or push them aside. In writing them down, try to understand their origins and thereby defuse them.
- ◆ When you have done this, move forward in declaring and owning, in writing, your wishes to be loved. State more and more specifically how you want that love to be shown.
- ◆ Finally, indicate the ways you will show the other person that his or her love has been received.

Why is it so important to work on your capacity to receive love? Bear in mind that while it is true that there is no one who can be so perfectly giving that he or she can cure or make up for all your old wounds and deprivations, it is also true that *letting love in, in the context of an adult love relationship, has enormous healing power.* If you expect love to be a cure-all, you will inevitably be disappointed. But if you are so afraid of potential disappointment that you do not let love in, you shut yourself off from the healing a love relationship could bring you. It can be helpful to view your receptiveness to the love of another person as something that you are actively giving to the child in yourself; you are taking care of this child rather than further depriving him or her, and that caretaking can heal at least some old wounds and bruises.

Also bear in mind that, while there is some truth to the saying that it is better to give than to receive, open and appreciative receiving is a generous form of giving.

6. THE ABILITY TO CREATE BALANCE
AND RECIPROCITY

A song called "Nature Boy," made famous years ago by Nat King Cole, ends with the line, "The greatest thing I've ever learned is just to love and be loved in return." This line suggests the important point that, if a love relationship is to bring mutual happiness and fulfillment, it must have some reasonable *balance* of loving input from each partner. This does not mean a perfect symmetry of loving. Rarely if ever is there an exact equality in the ongoing give and take or in the intensity and quality of loving feelings. Even in the best of relationships, one partner may love more, or differently, or with a different emphasis or mode of expression than the other. And at different points in time one partner may be more deeply involved in the relationship than the other.

Balance is not the same as tit for tat. It is not a matter of "I did this, so you must do that." It is not an outgrowth of your grade school years when you and a sibling or friend counted the french fries at McDonalds to be certain that you each had the same number. It is a matter of fostering a back-and-forth flow, a commonness of purpose, a substantial degree of fairness and reciprocity, and your mutual development as a couple and as individuals. This requires steering a course between the relationship-destroying extremes of fastidiously measuring who does more and passively permitting your contributions to the relationship to become dangerously out of balance.

This relationship balance can be upset when the partner who needs the other *less* tends to put in reduced effort, becomes less giving, and even exploits his or her partner, or when the partner who needs the other *more* tends to submit to and perhaps invite this unevenness and exploitation. It can also be upset when one partner is always in the role of the giving parent and the other the dependent child, or when one partner is always being the controlling parent and the other the compliant child. It is important to become aware of any ways in which you might be contributing to an imbalance. Do you tend to control, to withhold, or to be dependent? Do you fail to let your own needs be known? Do you take advantage of your partner's fear of your anger or of losing you? Or do you let your fear that your partner will be angry with you or leave you lead you to accept significant inequities? And, as always, where do these impairments in your capacity for reciprocity come from?

There is one other issue you have to come to terms with in regard to balance and reciprocity. If it is true that no relationship is a precisely even distribution of love and caretaking, you have to ask yourself the question, What degree of imbalance can I accept and genuinely feel all right about? When Carla decided to resume her marriage, she said, "Jack will never be as expressive as I am about his love or any other feelings, and I will usually be the one to initiate the little caretaking things that can nourish a marriage. But before our separation and his therapy, he was so emotionally withholding that it was intolerable. Now he's loosened up enough so that even though it is still out of balance as far as bringing feelings into the relationship, it is okay—particularly since I have come to appreciate that I really need his steadiness. So it works, and I'm more and more happy with it."

If past romantic relationships have been out of balance, and if this has been a reason why it did not work out, decide now that you will be alert to this issue of balance and reciprocity in your next relationship. The key will be paying attention to your feelings about the inevitable imbalances so that you neither get upset about every little inequity or tell yourself that the imbalance is okay with you while ignoring evidence that you are filled with hurt or resentment about it. If early in the relationship you are aware of uncomfortable imbalances, you are in a position to try to assess whether these really exist and to then, depending on the assessment, work on either reducing your overreaction or correcting the imbalance.

You can work on impairments that could lead you into destructive imbalances by looking closely at your past romantic relationships and at your current relationships, including those with friends, family, and coworkers. To what extent do mutuality and reciprocity exist? In what ways don't they exist? What patterns do you see? Making yourself ready for a good love relationship means making yourself ready for a mostly balanced and reciprocal relationship; that is where contentment lies.

7. THE COURAGE TO TAKE RISKS FOR LOVE

Downhill ski racing, playing the stock market, bungee jumping, starting a new business, betting on a horse, identifying the person who mugged you in a police lineup all have recognizable risks of different types and with different consequences. Establishing a love relationship also involves great risks. Although these risks may be less recognized, because coupling is a near universal enterprise, like any venture, establishing a relationship requires its own kind of courage. What are the risks and how can we increase our capacity to face them?

The Risk of Being Rejected

From the moment you meet someone you feel attracted to and interested in, you risk the possibility that he or she may not return those feelings. That rejection can lead to relatively minor disappointment if rejection of your interest is early or can cause profound feelings of pain and depression if you were deeply involved over a long period of time. For some, that risk of being rejected is so terrifying that skydiving seems like a piece of cake in comparison. This fear leads some people to avoid romantic relationships entirely. They always find excuses not to reach out or not to get involved or to disqualify people where there is a potential for involvement. It leads others to avoid reaching out to people they really want, only to people who reach out to them or give them so many green lights that they feel safe enough to take some cautious steps forward. Sometimes this works out well. Other times it leads people only to an unhappy awareness that they are involved with someone they would not have chosen had they not been limited by their fears.

Paradoxically, fear of being rejected can sometimes lead people to choose someone who is certain to reject them. Harry had always been drawn to critical and rejecting women like Ruth and was familiar with the misery and despair that come with such a relationship. But with Elaine, who was affectionate and accepting, he experienced feelings he had never had before in his romantic relationships—terror and panic. He was very perplexed and wondered what it could mean. Then, awakening one night in a state of anxiety, he had an insight. "With my wife and Ruth and all the Ruths in my life, I never had to worry that I would be rejected because I never felt accepted in the first place! With Elaine, I feel she really cares about me, and as I begin to relax and enjoy it—and I really do enjoy it—I suddenly become terrified that she will reject me. And that would be devastating."

As Harry and I talked, he was able to push his insight even further. "I thought the only reason I chose women like Ruth was because I was addicted to making my bitter and rejecting mother love me. That's certainly true. But now I see that when my mother went from being loving and affectionate before my father left her to being an angry witch after he left her, the pain of that rejection was so awful that I remained terrified of it ever happening again. So I chose women who were not loving and affectionate so that it couldn't happen to me again. What craziness! What a waste! It has governed my life, and I'm only seeing it now in my sixties."

The fear of rejection when one is in love is not unusual or in itself pathological. As Ethel Person put it, "The specter overshadowing love is the feeling that it will end." But Harry's story illustrates an important proposition: *When the fear of rejection produces attacks of panic or anxiety so unbearable that it causes the sufferer to avoid or sabotage a love relationship, it is always an indication that there was a previous traumatic rejection, usually in childhood, and that it is the fear of the repetition of that trauma that is causing the panic.* If a fear of rejection has haunted your love life, look for the early experiences of that rejection, so that you can limit its unwarranted intrusion into your present functioning. Harry was able to use his insight to confront his fear. Once he was aware that it was the little boy in him that was so frightened, he could soothe that little boy and simultaneously recognize that he was no longer a little boy and could now survive a rejection. As a result, he neither fled from nor undermined his relationship with Elaine.

While it is generally true that "it is better to have loved and lost than never to have loved at all," if you have reason to believe that a rejection could be so painful and depressing as to seriously impair your functioning or even make suicide a tempting option, then it is essential that you strengthen your vulnerability to rejection before taking such an enormous risk. You may need professional help. But even without professional help, you can work on preventing yourself from bringing the fears generated by past rejections into the present. This involves, first of all, recognizing that you are letting past events continue to label you as someone likely to be rejected. If the original traumatic rejection occurred in your childhood, you have to see this rejection as a statement about the person who did the rejecting—about that person's limitations, circumstances, and state of mind—rather than as a statement about your rejectability. If the traumatic rejection was in a later romantic relationship, you have to ask yourself several questions:

- Was I "softened up" by childhood rejections so that I reacted too intensely to the romantic rejection?
- Did I behave in a way to bring about the rejection or was it just one of those things that could happen to anyone?
- If I did do something that contributed to my getting rejected, either through my choosing badly or through negative or self-defeating behavior, how can I make changes to reduce the possibility of that happening again?

In his book *Risking*, David Viscott wrote, "People fear being rejected as unlovable, being revealed as powerless and being embarrassed as worthless. They avoid taking risks that might unmask them. Unfortunately, unless a person risks being rejected, he never finds a lover he can trust." So, if you want a love relationship you will have to take the same risks everyone else takes, but you shouldn't have to take the additional terrifying risk that rejection will overwhelm and crush you. That is why you must work, in the ways discussed here, to strengthen yourself so that if your next gamble for love does not succeed it will only be painful, not catastrophic. You can reframe the fact that you have survived the rejections of the past, even though with some scars, as manifesting your toughness rather than your weakness.

The Risk of Humiliation

Feeling rejected can be painful enough, but some people experience a particularly excruciating reaction to rejection and that is the feeling of *humiliation*. While the reaction to rejection is hurt, the reaction to humiliation is *shame*. It is the shame of being exposed as woefully immature, inadequate or lacking in important desirable qualities. The prospect of humiliation can be so terrifying for some people that it can keep them from reaching out at all, or make them so cautious that they permit themselves little involvement or intimacy, or they may get involved only with people who seem so dependent or lacking in appeal that the risk is minimized.

Peter, the biologist who repeatedly chose dependent women, discovered that he did so not only because he enjoyed being in the guru role in his choices, but because of a fear that more adequate women would leave him and this would trigger unbearable feelings of humiliation. What led us to this awareness was a session in which Peter reported that he had just been out with a group of friends and someone told a joke which made him uncomfortable. The joke was about a boy and a girl of kindergarten age. The boy was trying to impress the girl by telling her all the things he could do—throw a ball, ride a tricycle, and so on. The little girl responded to each by saying, "I can do that, too." Finally, in desperation, the little boy dropped his pants and said proudly, "I have one of these." The little girl dropped her pants and said, "Well, I have one of these, and with one of these I can get all of those I want."

Peter said that "Everyone laughed heartily, particularly the women, but my laugh was forced. I felt annoyed, and for some reason, a feeling of shame swept over me." As we traced the origins of Peter's feelings of humiliation, he recalled his first serious romance—with Wendy, a girl in his high school class who was beautiful and very intelligent. "We used to study together, and then we began to 'make out,' and then we fell in love with an intensity that I guess happens in a first love. But we never had intercourse, because I had this thing about respecting her virginity. Then she told me she wanted some time out from our relationship, which hurt and bewildered me. I found out from my best friend, who was dating her best friend, that Wendy was 'going all the way,' regularly, with this big, muscular jock in our class. It was like a punch in the stomach. I actually vomited. And I felt so humiliated, so small and inadequate."

Peter said that he then went through a period of social withdrawal. His face would burn with shame whenever he passed either of them in the corridors. "Before, I had felt that I was at least equal to Wendy, and suddenly I felt that she was all-powerful and I was nothing. It was as if she had acquired his strength and power. They became, in my eyes, this dynamite duo. I would picture that they were laughing at me together, talking about me as puny and inferior. I would picture them having wild sex and laughing hysterically at how I respected her virginity. Even now, so many years later, I still feel embarrassed when I think about it."

As Peter and I explored this feeling of humiliation we found that, as is often the case, it had antecedents. "I guess I was my mother's good little boy—that's how she treated me, and that's how I behaved. And my father used to ridicule me for it. He would call me a 'mama's boy,' would laugh at me for studying too much, and in general, would shame the hell out of me. I always felt inadequate around him."

While such dread of humiliation is more frequently expressed by men, women also often experience it. Laura once said, "I would go out with these emotionally unavailable powermen because I dreaded the humiliation of being dependent on a man and then having him leave. I tried to prevent that feeling by choosing to be with men who I knew wouldn't get involved, so that I could tell myself that it was under my control and therefore I wouldn't be humiliated by their leaving. But even so, I hated the feeling that I could be wanting more—more time, more closeness, more sex, more talking, more holding—and he could just zip up his pants and go home. And I always pictured that he was leaving me because he'd rather be with a tall, willowy blonde, not a short brunette like me." Laura's dread of humiliation also originated in her childhood—in the general lack of emotional warmth or affirmation in her home and in her father's relentlessly kidding her about being a "peanut."

From Peter and Laura's descriptions, it is evident that their feelings of shame are rooted in an early sense of sexual inadequacy and undesirability. This is not surprising, because when one risks a love relationship, there is usually a feeling of putting one's sexual attractiveness on the line. The Italian psychotherapist Giovanni Salonia put it this way:

> I desire the other, certainly, but above all I want to be desired by the other. Only in this way, only if the other desires me, do I feel my value is recognized and confirmed. In the end, this is the only thing the lover wants, his greatest expectation. "Only if she desires me, if I am the object of her sexual desire, do I feel alive and appreciated." "You can say you love me, that you are close to me, that you understand me, but . . . I want, I need, to be desired by you."

Our dread of humiliation comes, then, from this profound need to be desired by the one we love coupled with our early experiences of having our adequacy and attractiveness doubted or shamed. If fear of humiliation gets in the way of your freedom to love, you need to work on reducing it by seeing it as a vestige of childhood feelings. In the best of circumstances, childhood is filled with experiences of humiliation and shame. We have all known countless awful moments of losing control of our bodily functions, dropping things, spilling things, saying the wrong thing, being caught with our pants down, being ridiculed, and being too small and ineffectual to deal competently and to feel significant in a very big and complex world.

What can you do to reduce your being tyrannized by humiliation and the fear of it?

◆ You must make yourself aware that emotions from the past are distorting and trashing your current feelings about yourself and are twisting the meaning you give to other people's responses to you.
◆ You have to recognize that the child you once were experienced daily incidents of not being up to dealing effectively with many aspects of his or her world and that these awkward efforts were sometimes met by derision instead of bolstering and support.
◆ You have to look at that little child you once were in a sympathetic, loving way and at the same time recognize that you are no longer that little person.
◆ You have to recognize that it is neither inevitable nor logical for you to feel humiliated just because you are not someone's cup of tea.
◆ You have to recognize that, if you have chosen people who reject you in a demeaning way, it is you who made those choices. Such rejections reflect not on your adequacy or desirability but on your self-defeating need to put yourself in that position. You have to explore what that need is all about and resolve not to involve yourself with people who want to belittle or degrade you.

Taking these steps toward reducing your tendency to feel humiliated is a lot better than the alternatives of avoiding or limiting involvement or choosing people you may not love or may not even find very interesting just because they seem unlikely to humiliate you.

The Risk of Making a Mistake

In choosing a love partner, as in many choices in life, if you select A, then you can't have B. Or C or D, for that matter. Or any of the other letters of the alphabet that you have not even met yet. Fear of locking yourself into a mistaken choice can impair or even paralyze your efforts to form a love relationship.

People differ widely in their ability to risk mistakes. Some people make life-changing decisions impulsively and even blindly, while others are paralyzed by the fear that they will discover, after it is too late, that they have chosen badly.

The fear of making a mistake may be concealing other fears—for example, fears of intimacy, commitment, being dependent, or being rejected. But often it reflects a belief that there is a perfect decision, a perfect love partner. I remember Warren once telling me, "I've sometimes gotten close to making a commitment, to getting all excited about it, and then this awful feeling comes over me that the next day I'll meet this absolutely wonderful woman and it will be too late."

Some people have this anxiety about almost everything. It is as if there is a perfect job, a perfect apartment, a perfect choice of dessert, and they hesitate and ruminate about the possibilities. Others are very decisive in most areas of their life and become obsessively wavering only about risking full involvement in a love relationship. Either way, it can be self-defeating.

Overcoming your indecisiveness in a situation can be difficult. You can readily justify your hesitancy on the grounds that it makes sense to be cautious and use good judgment, particularly if you made some bad judgments in the past. But if you know that you have a tendency to vacillate unduly, you need to investigate whether you might not once again be on an obsessive seesaw. You have to ask yourself the following questions: Am I using my fear of making a mistake to hide other fears I have about being in a love relationship? If so, what are these fears? Am I caught up in the myth that there is a perfect person for me? If so, am I ready to challenge that belief? Can I, instead, be satisfied that this person excites and interests me a great deal? That I love him (her) a lot and he (she) loves me? That he's (she's) a mostly terrific person who makes me feel good? Can I let that be enough instead of dwelling on the possibility that there might be someone perfect (or much, much better) out there? And if I choose to fully involve myself in a love relationship with this person but later find I made a mistake, does that have to be the end of the world?

These are the questions you must deal with in an undertaking where there are no certainties, no guarantees, and no perfection. You need to recognize that if you make a bad choice there is no reason to be locked into one forever. You can always get out if you judge that is what is best. Admitting that you made a mistake, learning from it, and then taking the necessary steps to change it is an act of courage and wisdom, not weakness.

The Risk of Being Honest and Open

One of the greatest rewards we can derive from a love relationship is the possibility of being able to be especially honest and open with another human being. This possibility is, for most people, both inviting and threatening. For some, however, the threat is too great; they cannot allow themselves this kind of candor and openness. Yet, without honesty and openness, a love relationship may never take root or may not develop the staying power or the gratification that it could have.

At the beginning of Chapter 8, I discussed how many people avoid revealing much about themselves, usually because early attempts to do so led to bad experiences. If you know that you have been self-concealing and that this has deprived you of the sharing and authenticity that add so much to your life you need to work on overcoming your fears of being honest and open. The three areas in which many people find honesty most difficult are: admitting imperfections; admitting vulnerabilities and hurt; and expressing negative feelings and dissatisfaction with the relationship.

Many of us feel that any admissions to what we see as our *imperfections*—in our abilities, knowledge, habits, beliefs, fantasy life, sexual prowess, sexual interests or personal history, or whatever—will almost certainly be met with disgust and disdain. And when the person we believe will take such a dim view of what we reveal is someone we hope will admire and love us, it is understandable if we react by actively or passively covering up these "blemishes." Of course, there are no guarantees that another person will not have a negative reaction to some shortcoming you reveal. I am not saying that your relationship will always benefit from such revelations. In general, however, the more openness there is, the deeper and stronger the relationship becomes. But it requires sensitivity and a feeling for timing to know what your relationship can accept at any given moment. You have to navigate between the extremes of keeping your relationship shallow and thus minimally nurturing and overwhelming it with heavy and indigestible revelations that it is not yet strong enough to assimilate. Too often, however, people err on the side of concealment, plagued by the belief that they are expected to be a model of perfection—strong, uncomplaining, endlessly energetic, and always at their attractive best. This belief persists even though at a rational level they fully understand that nobody is perfect, that their partner is unlikely to really expect perfection, and that if their partner does, it is an inappropriate and immature expectation.

It is important to recognize the demands for perfection you are making on yourself and their unrealistic basis. You have to ask yourself what you picture will happen if you admit your imperfections. Who from your past would have been upset and disappointed about these imperfections? Who would be upset and disappointed now? Is your appraisal of this realistic? What is the price you pay for maintaining this cover-up?

Fears of risking the exposure of your *vulnerabilities* are similar to those about admitting imperfections but include the specific fear of being hurt. In revealing vulnerabilities related to your needs, your temperament, or painful episodes from your past, you could be giving someone ammunition to hurt you or take advantage of you. So it is understandable that you would employ some caution and prudence as to how and when to reveal what. Keep in mind that if someone deliberately uses such confidences against you, it is much more a negative statement about his or her character than about your vulnerabilities. If a person's reaction causes you pain, let this serve as an unplanned but excellent screening device. I would agree with David Viscott that "the risk of admitting hurt becomes the risk of testing the trust in a relationship, of discovering what two people feel about each other."

Some people have a particularly hard time revealing that they have been hurt by something their partner did or said. Sometimes you can resolve your hurt within yourself, for example, if you see that it was caused by an overreaction or distortion on your part. But if this was not the case and you do not openly admit your hurt, it will probably turn to anger. If you are someone who has too often swallowed your hurts and covered up your vulnerabilities, it can be helpful to practice risking such revelations in many of your relationships, not just romantic ones. Again, this does not mean throwing caution or your most intimate secrets to the wind; you have to use your best judgment taking into account the person, the information, and the timing. Being more relaxed about revealing your thoughts and feelings will help you to feel less shameful, less alone, and more connected.

Fears about expressing *negative feelings* about the other person and the relationship are understandable. Such dissatisfactions, which can be difficult to voice in any relationship, are particularly daunting in a love relationship. The bond may seem fragile, perhaps more fragile than it is, and the fear of distressing or angering your partner and disturbing the romance can make handling your dissatisfactions feel as hazardous as handling unstable explosives. How do you communicate with honesty and openness in these circumstances?

Feelings of anger can feel especially risky to express. Anger is almost always a response to feeling hurt, disappointed, exploited, insulted, frustrated, betrayed, or abused. In any love relationship there will be incidents that arouse such feelings. Expressing your anger and your feelings about the incidents that trigger it requires trust. You have to trust yourself not to engage in overkill, and you have to trust the other person not to react with overkill, or to collapse, or to withdraw their love. If the fear of these reactions makes you ineffectual in expressing your anger, you can put both yourself and the relationship in jeopardy.

Unexpressed anger is dangerous to you because you can convert it into physical symptoms, depression, or when the dam bursts, uncontrollable fury. And it is dangerous to the relationship because it can fester as impacted and toxic resentment that can poison your feelings of love.

There is no correct, prescribed way to manifest your anger. As in all the other arenas, you need not adhere to some rigid code of Boy Scout truthfulness nor should you aim to reveal your every thought and feeling without regard for the consequences. You have to take on the responsibility of expressing your dissatisfactions with as much tact, consideration, and maturity as you can. If, under the guise of "I'm only being honest," you give yourself license to provoke guilt, to induce shame, or otherwise to lacerate the personality and feelings of your love partner, the outcome is not likely to be a deepening of caring but the widening of a chasm. Nevertheless, even if your anger carries a strong wish to strike out and hurt the other person, it does not have to deal a fatal blow to the love feelings or the relationship. Instead, you can both take on the tasks of understanding the anger, owning the part you played, making repairs, and using the process of working it out to strengthen the relationship. Thus, even volatility is often better than if the dissatisfactions are not expressed at all. So if expressing anger has felt too risky to you, learn to understand why, to listen to what your anger is telling you, to evaluate when it is an overreaction, and to express it in ways that can help the relationship to grow. You can discover much about each other from the way you each express anger and react to the other's anger. Moreover, being able to together deal with anger is crucial to the success of your relationship.

In discussing these various kinds of risks, I have implied the need to develop a particular type of courage—not physical bravery but an emotional courage that you will need to navigate the unchartered and unpredictable waters of a new love relationship. It is important to accept the reality that there are risks, that the risks can be frightening and that you must embrace both the risks and the fear. Many years ago, when I gave my presidential address to a conference of the American Academy of Psychotherapists, I chose the topic of courage in psychotherapy. I quoted from a poem by James Stephens called "In Waste Places." In this poem a man is relentlessly pursued through the desert by a lion. He finally realizes who the lion is:

> I am the lion and his lair!
> I am the fear that frightens me!
> I am the desert of despair!
> And the night of agony
>
> Night or day, what e'er befall,
> I must walk the desert land,
> Until I dare my fear, and call
> The lion out to lick my hand!

Courage does not mean not being afraid; it means daring your fear rather than letting it pursue you. It means calling out your particular lion, which will be different from someone else's lion. If you have been terrified of revealing vulnerabilities, it will take courage to expose them, but if you have been someone who can overwhelm a relationship with tales of the "poor me" variety, it will take courage to stop making yourself appear victimized and helpless. If you have been afraid to speak up when something is bothering you, it will take courage to voice your dissatisfactions, but if you are often too critical and confronting, then remaining tolerantly quiet can be an act of valor for you. If you timidly squelch and suppress your anger, it can take considerable courage to risk expressing your anger, but if you blow up easily and permit the child in you to have tantrums, then it can take just as much courage to restrain that fury and look instead at why so much rage is being triggered. You will need to decide what type of courage you have to develop in order to risk honesty and openness. For, if you take this risk, the depth and authenticity your relationship will gain will be well worth it.

8. THE ONGOING EFFORT TO EXPAND YOUR SELFHOOD AND YOUR WORLD

In the beginning of this chapter, I indicated that there were eight crucial factors in your ability to develop a love relationship. I went on to discuss seven of these factors and show changes you could make in each. The eighth factor—making an ongoing effort to expand your selfhood and your world—is so crucial and complex that it deserves a chapter—Chapter 11—for itself.

11

EXPANDING
YOUR SELFHOOD
AND YOUR WORLD

"Little people are involved in little questions, and big people are involved in big questions." I heard these words many years ago in a paper presented by Dr. Sidney Jourard, a leader in the humanistic psychology movement. A love relationship carries enormous potential for enlarging us, for taking us out of ourselves, and by stimulating our capacity to love, for leading us to care both more deeply and with a wider scope. But, paradoxically, there is something about being in or seeking romantic love that also tends to make us lose touch with our own bigness. We can become so preoccupied with the ups and downs of a romantic relationship that our world shrinks—other relationships, issues of great moment, actions of everyday necessity, even our recognition of the wider sorrow or beauty that surrounds us can all be lost to our attention. Even in the most satisfying and fulfilling love relationships, at times of conflict or doubt or insecurity, the questions "Does he (she) love me?" and "Do I love him (her)?" can seem like the only important questions in the world. In a bad or addictive relationship, even smaller questions can become the entire focus of one's existence: "Will he (she) call?" "Why can't he (she) ever be on time when he/she knows that it means so much to me?" "Does he (she) find me desirable?" "Does he (she) like my hair this way?"

The most dramatic example I can recall of how the big questions can be dislodged by the small ones involves a woman I saw for psychotherapy who was a widely respected cancer researcher. She was to give a groundbreaking paper at a medical conference. It represented the culmination of years of work and was a big step toward a cure for a cancer particularly affecting children. But all she could think of was that Stanley, the man she had been seeing for the past two years, had not called that morning to wish her a happy birthday. All day, worried and angry questions ran through her mind: "Why didn't he call? Does he still love me? Is he so self-involved that he doesn't realize how much it would mean to me? How can he do this to me when he knows how important the paper I am giving is? Has he found someone else?" She presented her paper through the thick fog of these dark, intruding thoughts. Her work was enthusiastically received and highly praised, but her satisfaction was muted. When she got back to her apartment, she found festive balloons on her door and Stanley waiting inside with champagne in an ice bucket. They had a giddy double celebration of her birthday and her triumph. Later she was able to say: "Once I was relieved of my worry and anger about Stan, I could look back and see that it was all pretty crazy. My work means so much to me and I had found a tiny but important piece of a puzzle that could lead to saving countless children, but for a while it was totally eclipsed by my upset at thinking that Stan had forgotten my birthday. What a loss of perspective!"

It is not so much a loss of perspective as an intense shift of perspective. In his book *The Panda's Thumb*, Stephen J. Gould notes that the earth is an incomprehensible 4.5 billion years old, that "the standard metaphor for earth history is a 24 hour clock with human civilization occupying the last few seconds," and that our personal lives account for only a "cosmic millimicrosecond of that time." From this vantage point it is easy to feel that nothing we think, feel, or do has any significance. Yet, as we also know, the very transience and tininess of our brief, mayfly lives necessitates that we give significance to what we think, feel, and do. What we elevate as the important questions and commitments defines us, if only for the moment. And, at moments, the smallest questions can become the biggest questions. Just as a raging toothache can make one oblivious of the next person's tumor, the emotional investment we make in a love relationship can change our perspective markedly: When we love someone the relationship with them *is* the most important thing in the world to us. At the same time, we can be rationally aware that our life and what is going on in the world is bigger than our relationship. Paradoxically, as we will see, these diametrically opposed perspectives are both true. But if you know that when you have been in romantic relationships your perspective has become too constricted and one-sided, then you need to work on widening and deepening your capacity to be a bigger you living in a bigger world. When you have done this work, your larger perspective will not be lost to either the glories or tribulations of love.

There are several paths that you can take toward expanding your selfhood and your world:

1. The path of psychological insight
2. The spiritual path: connecting to the timeless
3. The path of essential self-love
4. The path of active commitment

Let us explore each of these.

THE PATH OF PSYCHOLOGICAL INSIGHT

Deepening our self-knowledge, particularly about aspects that we have repressed or denied, has been the major path explored in this book. We have especially tried to understand how self-defeating patterns in our relationships are based on early experiences and feelings. The unrecognized influence of our past on our current feelings about ourselves and others insidiously narrows our perceptions, our interests, the kinds of people we are attracted to, and the kinds of relationships we form. It can be enormously helpful to you to explore, with as clear sight as you can manage, how you have been programmed by childhood urges, fears, inner conflicts, and family relationships.

In Anita Brookner's novel *Latecomers,* one of the characters, a middle-aged man named Fibich, has a revelation about himself and the people in his life:

> Ah, he thought, the truth bursting on him suddenly, nobody grows up. Everyone carries around all the selves that they have ever been, intact, waiting to be reactivated in moments of pain, of fear, of danger. Everything is retrievable, every shock, every hurt. But perhaps it becomes a duty to abandon the stock of time that one carries within one's self, to discard it in favor of the present, so that one's embrace may be turned outwards to the world in which one has made one's home.

This eloquently points to how transforming it can be if we let ourselves fully grasp how our past lives on in us and then take on the task of discarding (or at least overriding) its unseen images and unbidden feelings so that our "embrace may be turned outwards to the world." We have, then, another paradox: The more we know and come to terms with our *inner* life from our past, the freer we are to interact authentically, effectively, and lovingly with the *outer* life of our present.

One of the main things we need to know about the impact of our past on our present is how it predisposes us to choose particular love relationships. Harville Hendrix, a renowned couples' therapist, said of our search for love partners, "What we are doing, I have discovered from years of theoretical research and clinical observation, is looking for someone who has the predominant character traits of the people who raised us." This is an expansion of Freud's observation in 1905 that the child at the mother's breast was "the prototype of every relation of love." Freud went on to note that "*the finding of a (love) object is, in fact, a refinding of it.*"

Obviously, if the traits you are seeking to "refind" are positive ones, you are on a happier expedition than if you are looking for negative traits. But if your infant and childhood experiences with love predisposed you to seek relationships with people who have serious or even destructive drawbacks as love partners, then the insights you gain into this connection will give you powerful tools to counter and change that original programming. You can get in touch with what you now want and need from a relationship and can decide to seek it from a more likely source. And even if your childhood experiences were heavily negative, one or both parents may have had positive aspects that you might want to try to "refind" in seeking new love relationships.

Even though you may be programmed to refind, your awareness of that influence can help you to put your own twist on it. This is what Ethel Person was implying when she wrote: "Love is in some sense a refinding. But it is also—and this is love's ultimate triumph—the creation of a new experience. . . . Love may be regressive but it is also progressive, giving direction and content to the maturation of the self." The chances of your finding love to be such a catalyst for change is greatly increased by your insight into your own developmental history of love.

Insight into your early programming and how it still operates in you may not lead to immediate changes. In fact, I could probably count on the fingers of one hand the people I have worked with, in my four decades as a psychotherapist, who had the capacity for almost instant change through insight. One was Rachel, a thirty-year-old woman who was in an unhappy and subservient relationship with Sid. After only a few sessions in psychotherapy she said, based on our discussions, "I can now see how I feel the same desperate feelings and make the same desperate efforts to win Sid's love that I did with my mother. But he is not my mother, and I am no longer a needy little girl. I'll have to change that." By the *next session*, only a week later, she had firmly and clearly redefined the relationship in line with her insights! (Although this generated considerable initial conflict, mutual respect took root and the relationship was still growing the last I heard.)

I was astonished by the swiftness of Rachel's shift—I always am when I encounter the rare person who can use insight so quickly and dramatically. For most of us, the ability to utilize even our keenest insights evolves slowly, sometimes very slowly. But whether your pace is "fast forward" or "slow motion," the process of gaining and applying insights involves the same elements:

1. Permitting yourself to see and feel your connections to your past, including your very early past and more recent experiences

2. Seeing how your actions and options have been limited and shaped by your past

3. Opening your eyes to fresh new possibilities for thinking, feeling, and creating your life

4. Deciding to stop behaving in accord with the old self-defeating and limiting programming and to take the risk of trying the new and more fulfilling courses of action that have become open to you.

There are many vehicles you can take to travel the path toward increased psychological insight—among them, reading books like this, undergoing psychotherapy or psychoanalysis, attending self-help groups, having candid discussions with trusted and perceptive friends, and keeping a journal of your thoughts and feelings, and dreams. The important thing is that you commit yourself to understand the way your innate temperament and basic needs have interacted with the environment created by your family, society, and the defining events of your life to make you who you are. This requires that, instead of focusing on bad luck or on a particular other person as the source of your problems, you see yourself as the main author of your evolving autobiography. I am not suggesting that you shift to self-blame—that would be equally unproductive and would only cause you to misdirect the energy and perspective you will need in order to write new and more fulfilling chapters. What I *am* suggesting is that you take on the task of deepening your self-knowledge by repeatedly asking yourself, not with a prosecutor's zeal but with an explorer's curiosity and a friend's caring, how did I get myself here, and how can I move on? This exploration will enable you to take responsibility for creating your life, rather than blindly allowing your past to be a blueprint for your present and future.

THE SPIRITUAL PATH: CONNECTING TO THE TIMELESS

Another inner path toward expanding your selfhood and your world is the spiritual path. This will mean different things to different people and will mean nothing at all to some people. In the present context, I would say that we are on a spiritual path when we are feeling or pursuing our connection to the timeless.

Romantic love, even though it narrows our love to a specific person, can make us bigger by stimulating us to feel our connection with that which is more enduring—even with the timeless and infinite. One way it does this is by releasing a feeling of unbounded love. A second way is by leading us to find in and through our beloved a greater wonder and purpose. Whether a love relationship will inspire this expansion in you, or whether it will shrink your scope to the minute details of that one relationship, will largely be a function of the nature of that relationship. But it will also greatly depend on how connected you as an individual already feel with the immense and timeless scale of the world around you.

There are many ways of feeling an attachment to the timeless. Some experience it in beholding a breathtaking landscape or contemplating the wonder of the numerous suns and vast spaces of the universe. Others feel it in the exalting aesthetic experience of contemplating or creating a painting, a symphony, a poem. For others the attachment resides in their sense of connection to other living things or their kinship with all mankind. For some it is their attachment to the traditions of their heritage or their family. For many it takes the form of communing with a Supreme Being, either through formal religious doctrine, ritual, and prayer or through their vision of a personal higher power.

What makes these experiences *spiritual* is the direct experience of *something more*—something more than yourself, than this moment, than your current attachments and preoccupations.

These approaches to the timeless usually also entail getting in touch with a core self, a self that is not time bound or finite and that exists apart from one's psychodynamics, history, or current events and attachments.

Yogi Amrit Desai (Gurudev), the inspiring teacher of the Kripalu Ashram in Massachusetts, speaks of the importance of being in touch with that core if we are to expand our ability to love:

> We are always searching for the powerful experience of unity and integration. What we do not realize is that we have within us the inborn potential to manifest that unity. . . . We believe we must look outside of us. But whenever we look outside of us for the many forms of love—romantic love, recognition, approval and rewards—we create dependency. Dependency immediately creates fear, a fear of loss or of not getting what we long for. Instead of making us whole, such love reinforces our sense of incompleteness, creating an internal division or split. True love is self-sufficient, self-fulfilling . . . comes from our inner source.

This is a very Eastern perspective, and I would not agree with Amrit Desai that all attachment is negative. It is clear to me that romantic love can be a powerful catalyst for intimacy, growth, and a sense of purpose. But his admonition reminds us that if we use our romantic attachment to neglect or bypass that sense of loving that "comes from an inner source," we create a dependency that once again, makes us smaller rather than bigger.

So you may find it of great value to turn inward not only to gain psychological self-knowledge but also to be in touch with a unity that underlies and at the same time transcends your psychological self. In that endeavor, many individuals—whether or not they practice a formal religion—have found meditation an extremely effective approach. The kinds of meditation vary enormously and are too numerous to list here. If you start with a basic primer, such as Lawrence LeShan's *How to Meditate*, you will find not only instruction but also a guide to further exploration. To the introductory question "Why meditate?" LeShan writes:

> We meditate to find, to recover, to come back to something of ourselves we once thinly and unknowingly had and have lost without knowing what it was or where or when we lost it. We may call it access to more of our human potential or being close to ourselves and to reality, or to more of our capacity for love and zest and enthusiasm, or our knowledge that we are part of the universe and can never be alienated or separated from it, or our ability to see and function in reality more effectively.

He describes asking a group of scientists who practiced meditation daily to say why they did. None of the answers given quite met with everyone's satisfaction until one man said, "It's like coming home." LeShan comments: "There was silence after this, and one by one all nodded their heads in agreement."

Dr. Marlin Brenner, a psychoanalyst who also explores the usefulness and insights gained from Eastern meditation, told me:

> Meditation provides the opportunity for a person to get a broader perspective on his life. While he may feel himself to be trapped by forces he cannot control and driven by urges that remain unfulfilled, meditation permits him to get an overview of his situation. This leads him to the insight that he is not trapped but free and to the discovery that he does not need what he believed he needed as much as he thought he did. In this way, meditation can provide an almost miraculous and beneficial shift in perspective concerning one's place in the world.

I asked Dr. Brenner how this specifically applied to love relationships. "In love relationships we can be trapped in the belief that we need the other to avoid terrible pain. A shift of viewpoint through meditation can show us that in place of need we can substitute appreciation, mutuality, fulfillment, generosity and creativity." And what about sexual desire? I asked. "Sexual desire, like love itself, also changes as we change perspective. We can come to express the fulfillment of our sexual desire as an act of mutuality, sharing, respect, and a deep penetration into understanding ourselves and the other, rather than feeling the object of our sexual desire as food and the absence of sex as tantamount to starving to death."

The spiritual path, then, can bring you homeward through a transforming self-awareness and, at the same time, can deepen and expand your connection and sense of unity with what lies outside you. The result is to lessen the narrowing effect of your Attachment Hunger on your romantic relationships and thus to enlarge your capacity to love, including your capacity to love yourself.

THE PATH OF ESSENTIAL SELF-LOVE

The term "self-love" is often misunderstood as having the same meaning as selfishness or narcissism. So defined it would connote the very opposite of love for others. A healthy self-love, however, is part of our general capacity for loving and can free up and nourish our ability to love others. In *The Art of Loving*, Erich Fromm noted:

> If it is a virtue to love my neighbor as a human being, it must be a virtue—and not a vice—to love my self, since I am a human being, too. . . . The idea expressed in the Biblical 'Love thy neighbor as thyself' implies that respect for one's own integrity and uniqueness, love for and understanding of one's self, cannot be separated from respect and love and understanding for another individual. The love for my own self is inseparably connected with love for any other being.

This type of "love for my own self" is what I have come to call "essential self-love." The word "essential" here has a double meaning: First, it refers to a self-love that is of critical importance, to one's well-being, in the same way that essential vitamins or minerals are. This meaning refers to a basic concern for our own survival and well-being. But the word "essential" also refers to valuing our core *essence* both as unique individuals and as members of the human family. This expands our self-love beyond narrow self interest. Without this essential self-love, our ability to love others is greatly limited; we are left with our narcissistic and survival concerns, valuing others only as potential satisfiers of our needs. From that position we are likely to experience the other person's needs as inconvenient or even outrageous demands, which we then ignore, resent, or manipulate for our own ends. Without essential self-love we may easily become codependent, attaching to others to deal with our emptiness, self-loathing, or feelings of unworthiness. In the novel *The Company She Keeps*, Mary McCarthy's love-addicted heroine makes a chilling discovery:

> Now for the first time she saw her own extremity, saw that it was some failure in self-love that obliged to snatch blindly at the love of others, hoping to love herself through them, borrowing their feelings, as the moon borrowed light. She herself was a dead planet.

If you are between relationships it is an excellent time to look at your deficiencies in self-loving. This exploration must begin with the recognition that in *not* loving yourself something is drastically wrong. Some people, having lived a lifetime clothed in shabby self-esteem, so totally accept their unworthiness and inadequacy as indisputable givens, that they do not realize the malignant nature of what they are perpetrating on themselves. But this lack of essential self-love is destructive, and it enormously overburdens a love relationship with its negativism and its silent or vocal demands for rescue and reassurance.

A second vital recognition is that your lack of essential self-love almost certainly has its origins in distorted programming from your past. It is etched in your neurons from too many put-downs, from too many times of being made to feel shame, guilt, or inadequacy, and from too many times of not receiving needed encouragement, recognition, and support. And your lack of essential self-love was further programmed by the way your child self—and every child self tends to do this—exaggerated your weaknesses, failures, and embarrassments. When you have really grasped that it is that demoralized child part of you that makes you feel unworthy, you will be in a position to respond to that internal child with the compassion, support, and love that a child needs. When Harry, for example, could feel the connection between his self-loathing and the abasing ways his mother treated him, and when he could clearly see her rejection of him as a reflection of her state of mind rather than a measure of his value, he could begin to question his long-standing view of himself. This gradually led him to feel that he not only deserved but required better treatment from his romantic partners.

Early programming may not be the only contributor to your lack of essential self-love. Your essential self-love can be damaged when you engage in current patterns of being and behaving that you truly disapprove of and dislike. Ultimately, the antidote lies in trying to change those patterns. It is a hallmark of maturity that part of your self-esteem rests on how you behave in areas that really matter to you. But, while confronting and working on problems, don't let go of your unconditional love for the essential person that you are.

There were times when Kim would cringe when she thought of some of her self-debasing behavior with Kevin—the way his cruel criticism made her strive even harder to please him or the way she would self-respectfully break it off only to find herself soon begging him to come back, almost on any terms. "There are moments," she confessed, "when I suddenly flash back to things that make me want to crawl under a rock, like the night when he came over very late and I made love to him even though I could smell the scent of another woman still on his body. Remembering it makes me ask myself, what kind of lowly creature are you?"

At other times, Kim would recall that pained and angry period after her final break with Kevin when she found herself abusing men just the way Kevin abused her. "It was so mean of me to slam the door in the face of that perfectly nice guy just because he brought me flowers, and to stand men up on dates and to disparage their sexual performance. Thinking about these things makes me hate myself."

Kim slowly came to terms with her feelings of shame and guilt about these past actions. "I really despise that kind of behavior, in me or anybody. All I can do about it now is to make a commitment to try never to treat myself or anyone else so cruelly." Kim was candidly acknowledging that her actions did not meet her own standards for self-approval and was pledging her efforts not to violate those standards in the future. At the same time she was able to say, "While there are really no excuses for what I did, I can see explanations in my past history and in what I was going through at the time. That lets me forgive myself. Basically I'm a good person." In this way, Kim's *unconditional essential self-love* combined with her *conditional self-approval* to give her a complex, balanced, compassionate, and mostly positive sense of herself.

It might be helpful for you, too, to recognize that *you need your conditional self-approval to motivate you to be the person you want to be and you need your essential self-love to value yourself even when you are not pleased with some aspect of yourself or are being rejected and even scorned by others.* Developing your essential self-love as well as your conditional self-approval not only feels good, but it increases your capacity to form a good love relationship and widens the compass of your loving attention to the world you live in.

THE PATH OF ACTIVE COMMITMENT

Warren, as part of his growing freedom from his obsessive and narrowing pursuit of unloving women like Diane, extended his range from fashion photography to art photography, an earlier interest. In that pursuit, and almost by chance, he photographed some homeless families in his neighborhood. Soon Warren became deeply invested in exposing the plight of the homeless. In addition to taking photos that depicted their lives with dignity and compassion, he became their spokesman with the media and before legislative committees. "When I was a kid and all through my teens I really believed in things. Phrases like

'due process of the law' and 'equal opportunity' and 'brother-
hood' were sacred to me, like religious doctrine. In fact, I really
got interested in photography when I saw the 'Family of Man'
photo exhibit. Then I lost my 'religion' to this compulsion to win
women like Diane. In fact, I lost a sense of who I was in my total
obsession with making such women love me. Now I feel I've gotten my religion back. I've taken my self back. And I feel such a
bigger capacity to love that I wonder if what I felt for Diane was
love at all."

Freeing yourself from addictive love can widen the scope of
your interests and involvement and widening the scope of your
interest and involvements can help to immunize you against falling into another addictive relationship. It can also make you
more available to a gratifying nonaddictive love relationship.
When Kim's magazine did a series of articles on some abuses of
the foster home system, she became very involved in supporting
efforts to help troubled families stay together. Neither she nor I
think it was a coincidence that it was while she was dedicated to
this cause that she began a satisfying relationship with David.
Her horizons had become wider and her heart had become more
open than ever before.

Involvement in caring for others is a way we exercise our
ability to behave lovingly and stretch our capacity to love. It is the
active and outreaching counterpart of the spiritual connection
with the timeless or the "something more". After all, *values* are
also "something more" and commitment to these values enlarges us. We nurture ourselves when we care for others. I recall
Virginia Satir, the inspired family therapist, saying, "For people
to nurture themselves means being in contact, loving and valuing. It means each being able to stand in his own little puddle
and connect."

Standing, each of us, in our "own little puddle" is essential
if we are to develop the autonomy and selfhood we need in order
to avoid the addictive attachments that can cripple our loving.
But we will never know love unless we can reach out from our
puddle to touch and embrace the larger world. And that is something you can do even if there is no specific romantic love relationship in your life right now.

12

NAVIGATING LOVE'S PARADOXES

The road to a love relationship is replete with contradictions. Both ends of these contradictions can seem like truths. What is even more confusing is that both ends of these are true! These are paradoxes, assertions that in themselves are true and yet are contrary to other truths. The world of proverbs are filled with such paradoxical contradictions, such as "Look before you leap." vs. "He who hesitates is lost." I have already pointed to some of these paradoxes in loving. Now I will take a closer look at a "daunting dozen" that you will have to come to terms with in the course of navigating a love relationship.

On the one hand . . .	On the other hand . . .
1. I want to be generously loving to my partner and others.	I want to be generously loving to myself.
2. I want to be independent and self-reliant.	I want to be lovingly and dependably connected in a love relationship.

On the one hand . . .	On the other hand . . .
3. I want to increase my capacity to love unconditionally and without strings.	I want my partner to attend to and meet many of my needs.
4. I want, more than anything, to be loved and desired by the one I love.	I want to be mindful of and involved in bigger questions than whether he or she loves and desires me.
5. I want to be happy in myself.	I want a good love relationship because it would make me happy.
6. I want to be able to respond to and take care of the little child inside me.	I want the one I love to hear, respond to, and take care of the little child inside me.
7. I want to become better and better at healing my own wounds and repairing my dysfunctions.	I want to enjoy the healing and growth-promoting power of a good love relationship.
8. I want to become a more loving person through the pursuit of insight and self-knowledge.	I want to become a more loving person through active and caring involvement in the world.
9. I want to be able to live fully in the moment with my partner.	I want to be able to plan and actualize a satisfying future with my partner.
10. I want to be able to love a wide range of people.	I want to be totally devoted to the one person I romantically love.
11. I believe that you have to work hard to make a love relationship successful.	I believe that if you have to work hard to make a love relationship successful then there is something basically wrong with it.
12. I want, above all, to feel passion and excitement in my love relationship.	I want, above all, to have friendship, sharing, and reliability in my love relationship.

Life and love would be so much easier if just one side of these contradictions were true. Then our yearning to have The Answer could so easily be met. We would know what to do, or at least at what goal we should aim. Instead, we must face that the answer lies in recognizing the simultaneous validity of contrary truths. This recognition, while frustrating and far from satisfying, will enable you to see that in pursuing a love relationship you need to steer a course between the two sides of the contradictions. If you veer too far toward either side, you can smash against the rocks. So you must be guided by your most insightful and most loving judgment.

PARADOX #1

I want to be generously loving:
(a) to my partner and others.
(b) to myself.

As we have seen, love for others and self-love (as distinguished from narcissism) do not oppose each other but nurture each other. In his book *What Love Asks of Us*, Nathaniel Branden writes:

> If I enjoy a fundamental sense of efficacy and worth, and if, as a consequence I feel lovable as a human being, then I have a basis, or precedent, for appreciating or loving others. I am not trapped in feelings of deficiency. I have a surplus of life within me, an emotional 'wealth' that I can channel into loving.

The opposite is also true. I can reverse Branden's statement and say with equal validity that when I appreciate and love another, it makes me feel that I am a good and giving person—and that gives me further impetus to appreciate and love myself. Warren discovered this in his loving involvement with Pamela. He said, "Now I can see that my love for Diane was so twisted by my insecurity and by my incessant efforts to get her to love me that it made me feel bad about myself. Loving Pamela makes me so generous and caring that I can't help but feel good about myself. I know I had to learn to like myself before I could love someone like Pamela, but I like even more the person I am with her."

The ability to love is a human capacity that is within our power to develop and strengthen. It can be directed inwardly toward yourself and outwardly toward others. The greater your ability to direct it both ways, the more you will be able to be in a good love relationship. Nobody has described the need for both self-love and loving others better then Hillel, the first-century rabbi and philosopher who taught, "If I am not for myself, who will be; but if I am for myself alone, then what am I?"

PARADOX #2

I want to be:
(a) independent and self-reliant.
(b) lovingly and dependably connected.

If you maintain a position of total independence and self-reliance, you rule out any chance of making a loving connection; if you form an altogether dependent connection, you leave yourself no room for independence and self-reliance. (One woman said of her mutually suffocating relationship with her husband, "It's awful. We're like two soggy spaghettis trying to lean on each other.") But it is only in these extreme forms that one position rules out another. They can go hand in hand when you recognize the importance of creating an ongoing balance between the pulls of these two human needs.

Dr. Althea Horner once pointed out to me that her book on achieving independence and intimacy was called *Being and Loving*, not *Being or Loving*. She wrote that "[*loving*] entails an emotional attachment to another human being, one predicated not only on one's dependency needs, but also upon cherishing the other as the real person he or she is. . . . *Being* refers to that clear and uninterrupted sense of 'I am. I exist. I go on.' It is the capacity to experience oneself as a separate, real and whole human being." These two states can facilitate each other, because a "separate, real and whole human being" can have the security and courage to reach out and make a strong connection with another separate individual, and can have his or her separateness and realness confirmed by the loving response of the other. Many people have told me that when they developed a great sense of their own independence and self-sufficiency they were more easily able to develop a love relationship, and that when they had a happy and affirming love relationship their feelings of empowerment and independence were strengthened.

Laura had striven hard all her life not to need anyone. When she began to recognize her repressed longings to be in a relationship where she could depend on someone, she had to face her belief that if she gave in to those longings she would become needy and powerless. Laura struggled with the question of whether it was possible to trust a man to be there for her and still maintain her independence. That struggle became intense when she fell in love with Bob. She told me, "I can't believe that I am really allowing Bob to take care of me in many little ways and that I am trusting that he won't disappear. And even though I depend on him, I still have control over my decisions and my life."

A description I once wrote of what makes for a good love relationship between a parent and grown-up child could just as well apply to a romantic love relationship: "We are attached by caring, not strings. We stand in a loving relationship at enough distance so that each can see the other clearly in the spankingly crisp space between us and around us, yet close enough to reach out and touch each other with our fingertips or our eyes, close enough to offer a hand in support when it is needed, close enough so that with a single step we can embrace each other when our feelings call us to it. A loving separateness. It is what a relationship . . . can be."

PARADOX #3

I want:
(a) to increase my capacity to love unconditionally and without strings.

(b) my love partner to attend to and meet many of my needs.

Why should you want to increase your capacity to love unconditionally? Dr. Judy Kuriansky gives this answer:

> That an unconditional love is a state worth aspiring to is abundantly clear to people who experience it. . . . It is a transcendent state where you give and receive love without thought of gain or loss. This is truly the highest state of love— where love is most healing and nurturing. It enables you to rise above so much of the "warfare" you may now think is inevitable between the sexes. It is the state where you *accept* your lover and feel accepted by him . . . where you experience loving without being concerned about whether, or how, the other person responds.

Unconditionality is a powerful, basic, and even spiritual way of loving.

As we saw earlier, unconditional love does not mean accepting any kind of treatment or behavior from one's lover. You can love a person deeply and fully without feeling that you have to like everything he or she does, says, or thinks and certainly without feeling that you have to ignore your own needs in service to his or her needs. You enter a love relationship not just because you love someone, but also because you have many fundamental wants that you hope to gratify—for emotional intimacy, sexual pleasure, emotional and practical support, affection, companionship, and so on. Even if your love is deep and unconditional, you are not likely to be content if the love relationship does not provide some substantial satisfaction of these basic and legitimate wants.

Kim faced this dilemma with Mel, one of the men she became involved with in the interim between Kevin and David. Unlike Kevin, he was considerate, clearly liked her and enjoyed being with her. And he had another attribute that was very appealing to Kim—he was handy with cars, electronic appliances and home repairs. Besides the obvious benefits of this handiness, it was particularly attractive to Kim because it was the trait she most admired in her father. She used to say, "My dad may give me a hard time but he can fix anything." Later she said, "I have fun with Mel and I'm really getting to love him." She was delighted that she could have love feelings toward a man who was good to her. But Kim felt one major dissatisfaction with Mel—his lukewarn interest in sex. "If I don't take the initiative, weeks could go by without sex. And when we do have it I don't see much earthy passion in him." Because Kim had loving feelings for Mel and because she was trying to set fewer conditions on her loving, she kept dating him. She talked to Mel about needing more sexually from him, and he tried to be responsive to her need, but nothing changed very much. Finally Kim ended the relationship. "I feel lonely," she said, "not just because I'm losing a great guy but because I wasn't big enough to love him if he didn't give me what I want sexually." I responded, "You did love him but sex is so important to you that you couldn't sustain a *love relationship* unless sex was a much bigger part of it." Kim said, "Some other woman may feel very satisfied with Mel sexually." "Sure," I answered, "but they might find some other shortcoming to be non-negotiable—one that is perfectly acceptable to you."

Kim met David soon after she stopped seeing Mel. She found David passionate and sexually fulfilling. But he didn't come close to meeting her wish for a man as handy as her father. "I asked David to put up a hook on the bedroom door. I ended up with a big hole in the door, and he ended up with a bashed finger. I decided that I can't have everything. At least he's great at the essentials."

In general, if you care about someone, the caring should be basic and deep and should have enough unconditional acceptance so that you can live with the needs that are unmet. Unless your unfulfilled needs feel essential or major, keep in mind that stretching yourself to accept some frustrations and disappointments is in great measure what love is about.

Also bear in mind that having feelings of unconditional love and getting your basic relationship needs gratified often go together because unconditional love, unless directed toward an impossible source, generally leads to a loving response.

PARADOX #4

I want:

(a) more than anything, to be loved and desired by the one I love.

(b) to be mindful of and involved in bigger questions than whether he or she loves and desires me.

I do not believe it is possible to be in a love relationship without the question of whether you are loved and desired by the one you love being a central (though not always burning) concern. If you tend to be inordinately jealous, insecure, or possessive, this question may well take up too much time and space, leaving little for questions such as: Will I get the promotion I have worked so hard for? Will my friend's biopsy results be negative? Is the ozone depletion going to fry us? Am I a good person? Is there a Higher Power? If you are in a panic of doubt about being loved and desired, your answer to such questions, if you think about them at all, may well be, Who cares? But if your partner's affection is clear and steady, you should be able to turn from your concerns about the relationship back toward the larger world—whether this means your work, other people you care about, issues that concern you, creative efforts, or personal and spiritual growth.

There are extreme situations when people feel they can attend only to their relationship or only to bigger questions. When you have reason to feel the relationship is being jeopardized by a lessening in the caring and commitment of your partner, no question will feel more important than whether he or she loves and desires you. In such a case, you will need to immediately focus on whether your preoccupation reflects some basic insecurity or jealousy that has been characteristic of you or whether the danger signals you are picking up are real. It would be a mistake to let your involvement in other areas of your life, no matter how important and compelling, to unduly distract you from giving caring attention to your love relationship. When, however, there is an overarching crisis in the bigger world, your relationship might seem quite secondary. You may feel, painfully, what Rick felt in the airport scene of *Casablanca* when he encourages his beloved to go off with her freedom-fighter husband because it's quite clear to him that their love affair doesn't amount to "a hill of beans" in the context of the tryanny and slaughter enveloping the globe.

Most of the time, however, we do not have to choose between our concern with the relationship and our larger concerns. In fact, the two usually support and quicken each other. You can find in the mutual affection and desire of a love relationship the inspiration that can motivate you to actively participate in other areas of your life and to experience the love bond as a glimpse of "something bigger" than yourself or the moment. Then, flowing back the other way, your greater caring involvement with the larger world can deepen your love for your partner and may also make you more lovable and desirable.

PARADOX #5

I want:
(a) to be happy in myself.
(b) a good love relationship because it would make me happy.

PARADOX #6

I want:
(a) to be able to respond to and take care of the little child inside me.
(b) the one I love to hear, respond to, and take care of the little child inside me.

PARADOX #7

I want:
(a) to become better and better at healing my own wounds and repairing my dysfunctions.

(b) to enjoy the healing and growth-promoting power of a good love relationship.

I grouped these three paradoxes together because they all relate to the question of whether a love relationship is important to and even necessary for our happiness, growth, and healing, or whether our pursuit of happiness, growth, and healing is independent of a love relationship. Perhaps the writer who comes down hardest on the side of the necessity of love relationships is Harville Hendrix, a couples therapist, who in his book *Keeping the Love You Find* argues that finding and keeping love is essential to our intact survival and forms "the context in which to explore our true nature." He writes:

> Relationships pave the way for us to recapture our wholeness by correcting the distortions of caretaking and socialization that distanced us from our original selves. It is in unconditionally loving our partner, making it safe for them to open to love, letting that love sink in over time so that trust can build, that allows their fullness to come back into being. . . . The radical position I'm taking is that *love is the answer*. It is the love we give that heals our partner, and the love we receive that heals us. But it is only in loving that we truly change the rigid parts of ourselves. . . . a committed partnership (far more effectively than the traditional paths of religion or psychotherapy) can bring us back to our original connectedness. . . . It is nature's repair process.

What a persuasive and beautiful statement of the crucial role a love relationship can play in our growth and healing processes! And there is evident truth in it to which I wholeheartedly subscribe. But in these three paradoxes, as in the others, the other side also contains much truth. First of all, as I have discussed at length in this book, we can achieve major growth and healing on our own and by putting ourselves into situations that can make us more ready for and available to a love relationship. Second, I have known people who seem to flourish and grow well outside of a love relationship but seem to wither and become more limited within one. While we can then say that they were not yet ready for a love relationship, that they made bad choices, or that they unremittingly repeated past destructive patterns, I nevertheless have to join them in concluding that, unless or until they wish to and are able to be in a relationship in an entirely different way, their greater contentment and development may well lie outside a committed relationship. Hendrix would probably disagree. He states that "people disappointed in love don't want to hear that they *need* a relationship to heal. They want to feel they can be autonomous and restore their spiritual wholeness on their own. . . . But this is a delusion. While there is much you can accomplish on your own . . . you can't go the whole way to healing without a partner."

How do you deal with these contradictions? As usual, by recognizing the truths inherent in both positions and then trying to steer the course that is best for you. Hendrix's statement supports that part of you that is seeking a love relationship because you feel it will be a vital source of happiness, flowering, and restoration. You can also take it as an important warning that you do yourself a terrible disservice if you let past hurts or disappointments in love discourage you from seeking what a good love relationship has to offer. But if you choose to live and grow without a committed relationship, then your truth is that this is what you find works best for you.

For most people, however, the two poles of these paradoxes are not mutually exclusive. Both are necessary components of a full and satisfying life. Most people would agree that they want to find happiness both within themselves *and* in a love relationship; they want to be able to take care of the needs of their own inner child *and* would want their love partner to be responsive to those needs; they want to become better at healing their own emotional wounds *and* want their lives to be graced by the healing power of a good love relationship. It is a matter of finding your right balance.

PARADOX #8

I want to become a more loving person:
(a) through the pursuit of insight and self-knowledge.
(b) through active and caring involvement in the world.

You can so single-mindedly turn inward on a psychological or spiritual path that you become too disengaged to be lovingly involved with people in general or with a particular person. Conversely, you can get so engaged with the outside world, through work, activities, courses, or intense romantic and sexual encounters, you are distracted from pursuing self-knowledge and self-development. It is important to be sure you are not using your quest for insight to keep you from dealing with a world that frightens and frustrates you, or are not using external involvements to keep you from traveling the painful and arduous path of self-knowledge.

If you are not using one end of the polarity as a defense against the other, then you can exchange and integrate the knowledge and energy you derive from each. This integration will increase your ability to deal with yourself and others in an increasingly effective, nourishing, and loving way. "The more we succeed in putting love and harmony into our outer world," Susan Jeffers writes, "the more we will succeed in putting love and harmony into our inner world. Our life has to be about creating a context for love which touches everything and everyone that comes into our sphere of being."

The pursuit of psychological self-knowledge can help you to see and correct many of the ways your past is distorting your present, can reduce some of your fears and anxieties, and can modify defenses that stand as a real barrier to a real love relationship in that real world out there. The pursuit of spiritual self-knowledge can help you to reduce your feelings of separation from the world by focusing you on the underlying unity, can put your fears and preoccupations in a much larger perspective, and can reduce your need for addictive attachments so that love can flow more easily and freely. Energetic and effective engagement with the outside world can manifest that love in action; when you feel the impact of your caring involvement, you can be led to deeper levels of both psychological and spiritual insight.

It is often true that in the early, limerant, head-over-heels obsessive focus on that particular piece of the outside world, the beloved, everything else fades into the background. Your interest in pursuing self-knowledge and in dealing with issues outside of the love affair may evaporate in the sun of that limerence. As the headiness of the limerence fades and a loving relationship remains, the intense feelings of love that have been discovered and released can make you more generally and generously loving. You will have gone from finding the wonder and beauty of the world in the being of your beloved, to finding the wonder and beauty of your beloved in many places in the world.

PARADOX #9

I want to be able to
(a) live fully in the moment with my partner.
(b) plan and actualize a satisfying future with my partner.

"When I used to go with those distant, slippery and usually married power men," Laura recalled, "many of my friends would berate me because there was no future in it. I used to tell them, smugly, 'the present is all we can be sure of, and in the present I'm having a ball.' But now that I'm in love with someone who is available, someone who loves me back and who enjoys being with me as much as I enjoy being with him, the future can be a wonderful part of the present."

I asked Laura what she meant. "Take tonight," she said, excitement in her eyes. "Bob and I have decided to take our vacation together, and though it is months away, we are meeting to go through travel brochures and make some decisions. We're planning it together. Planning! I never knew that planning for tomorrow could be so much fun today!"

Laura's words underscore the value and pleasure of being able, with some degree of confidence, to look forward to doing things with a person you care about. At the same time, it is important to be aware that if your love relationship is too future oriented—if your only concern is Where is this headed? and How do we get there?—you can cheat yourself of a lot of fun in the present. In such a relationship, you can easily lose the spontaneity of the unplanned, the often delightful unpredictability of the impulsive, and the intensity of full involvement in the mo-

ment. If you put so much value on the future that you walk
around with it gripped tightly in both your hands, how can you
touch or hug the person you are with?

To reconcile these extremes, you have to recognize that you
can have intense *love feelings* and romantic encounters while living totally in the here and now, but it is not possible to have a
good *love relationship* without there also being a mutual wish to
have some meaningful degree of a shared future. If you recognize that, it will bring the future (or at least your speculating
about it and planning for it) into the present where you can look
at it, help to shape it, see if it is what you want and hopefully to
enjoy it.

For women who want to have children, finding the right balance between present and future fulfillment can have a particular urgency, because of the stark biological fact of a time limit
on fertility. There are three categories of women for whom this
is especially relevant: women who are in love with a man who

does not want children (or with whom they would not want to have children); women who are involved with a man they are not in love with but who wants to marry them and have children with them; and women who are not currently involved with a man. All are aware that the clock is ticking. All are facing difficult decisions.

A woman who is in love with a man who does not want to have children wrestles with questions like these:

- Should I settle for being in a good love relationship and give up on my wish to have children?
- Will my being childless poison my love feelings with resentment?
- Should I try to talk him into having a child?
- If he agrees to have a child because he doesn't want to lose me, will his love be poisoned with resentment?
- Should I tell him that if there will be no children in our future I will have to end it?
- Can I take the chance that I will find another love relationship soon enough to have one?
- If I do not find a love relationship, would I dare to be a single mother? Will that be more fulfilling than having this good but childless love relationship I have now?

A woman involved with a man who would have a child with her but who she does not love faces other questions:

- Should I marry someone I am not in love with in order to conceive?
- Will having a child with this man deepen my love feelings toward him?
- Is having a child so essential to my happiness and fulfillment that I ought to grab this chance while I have it? Or will finding someone I can have a romantic love relationship with hold enough fulfillment even if I do not have a child?
- How long should I hold out in order to seek both love and motherhood?

♦ If I do not find a love relationship that will include having a child, would I be willing to become a single mother? Could I handle that? How do I feel about it?

Women who want to have a child but are not currently involved with a man face similar questions about how long to wait and whether they would consider single motherhood. And women in all three categories would find it useful to try to understand why they reached this point without having the marriage and children they would like to have. If you are in this position, you might ask yourself: Have I only recently decided that a relationship and children is what I want? Have I not been ready before? Am I now? Have I had difficulties falling in love or maintaining a love relationship? If so, what can I do to make myself more able to be in a love relationship that can lead to motherhood?

I have worked with women who confronted these questions and who arrived at very different decisions. While each woman must make her own choices, there are some useful guidelines.

First, calculate, as well as you can, the emotional weight you give to your different needs and goals. Do not let the time pressure cause you to fool yourself about what you feel. (For example, I have seen women deceive themselves about loving a man because they are afraid that this will be their last chance for motherhood.) Sometimes women put time pressure on themselves even when they have many years of fertility ahead. Other women handle their conflict the opposite way—they keep themselves from being aware that time is running out. So use your best and most careful judgment.

Second, no matter what you decide, it has the best chance of working for you if you are able to accept the emotional task of sacrificing one goal for another. For example, I have seen a woman's decision to forego having children in order to marry a man she loves have very happy or unhappy consequences. Some women found they were delighted to have the time and energy to focus on their couplehood, as well as on their work and other interests. When their husband had children from a previous marriage, they often became involved in being a stepparent and experienced the joys and problems of parenthood in this way. But others became flooded with feelings of chronic regret, deprivation, and anger. They were not able to stop thinking, "If he really loved me, he would want to give me a child," even when there is ample evidence of their husband's love. Such continued feelings of unfulfillment can capsize and sink a love relationship.

Third, it is almost always an invitation to conflict and unhappiness to marry someone expecting or even seriously hoping that he (or she) will come to feel differently about something so central and crucial.

Men can be faced with similar choices related to having children. For example, a man may have to decide whether to father a baby he does not want in order to hold on to the woman he loves or to make her happy. As with women, the same decision can have happy or unhappy outcomes. A happy outcome is most likely when the man has strong loving feelings toward the woman, cares about her desire to be a mother, feels committed to be an involved father, and maturely accepts that his needs will not have the same priority with her as in their unencumbered preparenthood days.

The need to choose between present and future fulfillment, and among various possibilities for future fulfillment, is a factor in many decisions about love—for example, about whether or not to make a commitment, whether to stay in or end a relationship that is wonderful in the present but a poor risk for the future, whether to put career development ahead of a love commitment or vice versa, and whether to give precedence to the goal of parenthood or that of a fulfilling romantic relationship. How is one to find the right balance?

What is essential is that you attempt to deeply and honestly know your own feelings and priorities. In your imagination, stand at a crossroads where you can choose one or the other path you are considering. First go down one path trying to see as clearly as you can the most likely consequences of that choice. Ask yourself, where will that path lead? How will I feel about taking this road just after I choose it? How will I feel the next day? In a month? A year? Five years? Then do the same with the other path. You cannot foresee all the consequences. But in undertaking this investigation you are acknowledging that you must seek fulfillment in both the present and the future. And that often involves the disappointments and satisfactions of compromise.

PARADOX #10

I want to be:
(a) able to love a wide range of people.
(b) totally devoted to the one person I romantically love.

When you develop your capacity to be a loving person, you are able to love not only more deeply but also more widely. It is possible to have strong feelings of caring and affection toward many others without these feelings conflicting in any substantial way with a primary love involvement. But if those feelings of caring and affection combine with romantic and passionate feelings, you will face a conflict between wanting to be romantically devoted to one person and wanting to be romantically involved with more than one person. That is why one of the questions most frequently asked by readers of my syndicated column "On Your Own" was, in essence, "Can you love two people at the same time?"

The answer is, sure you can. To say otherwise I would have to deny the experience of many people I have consulted with who have convinced me that they felt themselves to be quite romantically in love with two (or more!) people at the same time. However, they were often consulting me because this state of affairs provoked an internal crisis of conflicting feelings and loyalties, practical dilemmas involving time and commitment, and hurt and rage in the people who knowingly or unknowingly shared their love. *The important question, then, is not whether you can romantically love more than one person at a time but whether you can have a full love relationship with more than one person at a time. The answer to this question is no.*

A love relationship requires commitment, availability, and a good chunk of devotion. It requires the courage and persistence to resolve the inevitable disagreements without having the escape hatches provided by another ongoing love relationship. Being in more than one love relationship can hold forth many "double delights," offering the stimulation of variety and the thrill of intrigue, adventure, and danger. It can spark a heady feeling of being adored by more than one desirable partner. It can also grant you the freedom of not feeling tied to any one person and the safety of having a "spare tire" if you are rejected or fall out of love with either one. I have seen instances where people became simultaneously romantically involved with more than one person and where it was, at least for a while, a growth and esteem-building experience. Yet most people in this situation sooner or later find it unsatisfying and choose to give it up. How come?

Those who decide to give up being in multiple involvements usually do so not only because it becomes too nerve-wracking and confusing a balancing act and not only because it usually engenders hurt and angry feelings in their partners and moral dilemmas in themselves, but also because they sense that there is something incomparably valuable in building a love relationship that carries the commitment to become more and more intimate, honest, and trusting. They understand the value of a relationship that permits them to know and be profoundly known by another person and that satisfies many desires of their inner child while, at the same time, bringing forward their most mature and giving self.

Ted, a forty-five-year-old stockbroker, had been for most of his adult life simultaneously involved with two or more women. In addition to finding these multiple involvements exciting, Ted cared for the women and couldn't face dropping any of them. Over time, however, Kathy, one of the women, became very special to him. Ted came to the decision that he wanted a full relationship with her. But he also wanted to meet his need for a wider range of involvements. So he continued his friendships with the other women but on a nonsexual basis. He also strengthened his bonds with several men friends. "These friendships may not have the same kind of excitement that the affairs had, but Kathy and I are creating our own excitement. And I am learning a lot about the pleasures and struggles that come with commitment. . . . I find that I am more open in my friendships and my friendships keep me from feeling suffocated by the commitment to Kathy. My life has become narrower and wider at the same time.''

So how are the contradictions of this paradox resolved? The desire to love a wide range of people and the desire to be devoted to the one person you romantically love are not mutually exclusive. *These desires become opposed only if:*

* you become so addictively involved with one person that you are unable to love others.
* you are so involved with so many people that you lack the focus, time, energy, and commitment to be fully in a love relationship.
* your desire to love a wide range of people includes romantic and sexual love with people other than the one to whom you wish to be "totally devoted."

Moving in the direction of either pole of the paradox should not be at the expense of ignoring, impairing or damaging its counterpart. The goals of being devotedly involved with one person and loving a wider range of people should reciprocally nourish each other, raising your overall capacity to be a loving person. Within this context, the specialness and unique place of the romantic love relationship can and should be maintained.

PARADOX #11

I believe that:
(a) you have to work hard to make a love relationship successful.
(b) if you have to work hard at a love relationship, then there is something basically wrong with it.

At first Kim thought that there must be something wrong with her relationship with David because it moved along so smoothly, with little of the conflict and stress that had marked her relationships with Kevin and others. "It's too easy," she would say, trying to convince me that the lack of tension meant that there was a lack of intensity or passion. But she could not deny that she often felt wonderful being with David or that she always looked forward to the next time she would see him. When I asked, "What makes you think you have to work so hard?" she replied, "But aren't relationships supposed to take a lot of work? Every book and magazine article says so."

Nobody can deny that a love relationship, particularly after the early stage of limerence and idealization, requires a good deal of work to survive and flourish. It is unrealistic and Pollyannaish to believe that you can remain indefinitely on a cloud, mesh frictionlessly and simply live happily ever after. Even Kim and David will have much to work out. But there is productive and gratifying work, and there is unproductive and demoralizing work. How can you distinguish between the two?

You can be pretty sure that your work is of the unproductive and demoralizing kind if:

- You are doing all or most of it by yourself.
- The other person is not committed to the improvement and continuity of the relationship.
- You find yourself trying to make the other person love you.
- You are forever trying to win the other person's approval and twisting yourself out of shape to please him or her.
- You are giving much more than you are getting in terms of emotional support, affection, practical support, and degree of involvement.
- You are struggling to make your partner stop abusing you. (Nonabuse is an absolute prerequisite, not something you work on.)
- You are struggling to have a reliable and loving relationship with someone who is addicted to a substance or to a destructive pattern of behavior.

- You are trying to get a very narcissistic person to empathize with and caringly respond to your needs.
- You are working hard to get the other person to leave another relationship and be fully with you.

If you are involved in any of these exhausting and unproductive projects, then for you I would agree with the pole of the paradox that says that if you have to work hard on a love relationship, it indicates there is something basically wrong with it.

On the other hand, even when there are substantial and mutual feelings of love, reasonable give and take, and emotional availability of both partners—even then, a relationship still takes work! After all, each of you has a different history of hurts and a different set of needs and fears. Each of you has different preferences, ideas, and goals in love and life. Each of you is seeking, consciously or not, for the other person to make up for or heal the wounds created by previous deprivations, rejections, and traumas. Each of you may distort the other by overlooking or exaggerating shortcomings and imperfections. Differences will arise over how to spend time and how to spend money. Conflicts may arise about how sex should go and how often. Simple communication can get exasperatingly mixed up and frustrating. Each may feel unheard or misunderstood. There may be attempts at control and feelings of rage. Impulses to trash the relationship can feel overwhelming. *And all of this can occur in a relationship that has an abundance of loving feelings and many very fine things going for it!*

Negotiating and attempting to resolve these differences, finding out what each of you is willing and able to change, dealing with your own and the other person's self-centered and self-righteous demands, learning to say what you need and want, and learning to listen respectfully to the other person's needs and wants—all of this takes work. But it doesn't have to be bitter work; you don't have to feel lashed to an oar on the Love Boat. This work can bring you the deep satisfaction of seeing yourself and your partner become more intimate and trusting in your shared search for resolution.

Dr. Don Lathrop, in his work with couples at the Relationship Center in Boise, Idaho, advocates the following principles:

1. Each person is 100 percent responsible for their own unconscious, their own dark side, their own behavior, and 50 percent responsible for the relationship.

2. Assertive communication is a must. Ask for what you want. Accept no for an answer. Be scrupulously honest about what you are willing and able to give as well as what you want.

3. Conflict resolution means developing an ability to fight without killing the other, to back away when out of control, to commit to coming back when back in control, to learning from what the other is saying—which is learning to feel (empathize with) what the other is feeling. Apology is not a substitute for a change in consciousness and behavior.

These principles—and, more generally, the kind of work that must go on in a relationship—are illustrated by an episode between Carla and Jack that took place before their reconciliation. Carla and Jack had both learned a lot during the separation, and their contacts with each other began to reflect their new recognitions.

On a sparkling spring Sunday, Jack invited Carla to go for a drive into the countryside to celebrate her birthday. That in itself was new, because Jack had rarely proposed outings and had often forgotten Carla's birthday. They had a delightful day and a festive dinner at a picturesque inn. On the drive back, Carla said, "This has been a wonderful day. Thank you."

"I wish that I could have let us have more such days," answered Jack.

"Could you now?"

"I don't know. I want to. I'm working on it."

"That's honest," Carla said. After a pause she asked, "What are you up against?" Jack talked about the home he grew up in. Most of it Carla knew about, some of it she did not. What was new was Jack's clear awareness of how he had become detached and granitelike to protect himself from the terrible fear, insecurity, and deprivation he had felt as a child in an unstable family. Also new were Jack's awareness of how much he had been cheated of and his angry determination to break out of his prison.

Carla told him that she saw these new developments and liked them. She added, "Things would really have to be different if we ever got together again. I couldn't stand living with you the way you were. Not ever again."

Jack got angry. "Don't be so damn self-righteous. There's a part of you that needed me to be that way and that may still try to keep me from changing. I might have a better chance of making those changes with someone else."

Carla was stunned at his anger. "Well, I certainly liked your being Mr. Reliable, but I felt I was dying of malnutrition."

"It's not just my reliability that you liked. Maybe you chose someone like me to keep you away from recognizing your own needs and feelings. Or to end up feeling deprived. Or to feel like a victim. I'll only take half the blame for what happened with us. There were lots of instances where my feelings would start coming out and they made you so uncomfortable that I would back off."

"That is self-serving bull," Carla fumed.

They were suddenly in a heated argument that caused them each to wonder what in the world was the sense of trying to get this impossible person to see anything. Both proclaimed that if they were not in the car they would just leave. But the trip was long and they were able to get beyond the anger. Carla admitted that there was uncomfortable truth in the accusation that she felt safer with his detachment, and Jack acknowledged that he chose Carla in part because he believed she would let him remain detached. "Then you had to go spoil it and want more out of life," he joked candidly. Both could own up to their roles in keeping the other at a distance and in recreating a familiar childhood structure of emotional barrenness. Carla later told me, "It was the best fight we ever had."

Fighting, expressing feelings and needs, understanding where these feelings and needs are coming from, listening, acknowledging, appreciating, taking responsibility for your (and only your) contribution to problems, and making efforts to change old destructive patterns—these are the work of a relationship. You must do your half, while recognizing the disappointing possibility that the other person may not do his or her half and that in this case the relationship will probably not get better. But, even if the relationship doesn't, you will.

So how can we resolve the contradiction between the necessity for hard work versus the belief that a good relationship should not need hard work? We can realize that it is a false issue. Every relationship must involve work if it is to grow but when the effort is productive, mutual, and loving, it doesn't seem much like work. At times, as Kim discovered, it can even seem easy.

PARADOX #12

> I want, above all:
> (a) to feel passion and excitement in my love relationship.
> (b) to have friendship, sharing, and reliability in my love relationship.

Most people would not consider that they are in a romantic love relationship unless they feel some intense and passionate involvement, including a considerable amount of sexual attraction and sexual excitement. This sexual intensity need not be there all the time and need not remain at the same level over time, but the fact that it has been there and can come back makes for a powerful and special bond.

As important as sexual attraction is to passionate love, the two cannot be equated. Lusty sex can certainly occur in a relationship that does not have the strong emotional bonding and longing for fusion that mark passionate love. We know that lusty sex can occur with strangers. Kim's obsession with Kevin was both lustful and passionate. When they were together sexually, she could hardly get enough of touching him, kissing him, biting him, and wanting him to caress her and be inside her. When they were not together, she would often daydream about his body and imagine the magical feel of his skin. But her sexual feeling were only a part of her greater passion to ecstatically merge their lives forever. She longed to be the center of his existence the way he was the center of hers. Kim's passion was amplified by her Attachment Hunger, which was itself stimulated by Kevin's meanness and unavailability.

Kim's subsequent relationships, with men whom she chose for being the exact opposite of Kevin, were at best friendly and companionable but lacking in passion. Then Kim began to see David, who was emotionally present, available, and affectionate with her and whose feelings she reciprocated. She found, primarily because she had worked hard to make herself ready for it, that she became deeply and passionately responsive to him.

In one therapy session I asked Kim to put into words the difference in the passionate feelings she experienced with David and Kevin. "The passion I feel for David is very different than what I felt for Kevin. For example, when I would expect Kevin to come over I was so hyper that I could hardly sit still. My excitement had a nervousness in it, an unbearable tension. For one thing, I always had some doubts as to whether he'd show up. Sometimes I would change my clothes and makeup a dozen times to try to please him or to avoid his being critical. When we got together sexually it was fiery and intense, but there always seemed something sick about it, as if it wasn't just about sex and pleasuring but about doubts and insecurity and power and frustrated expectations."

"And with David?" I asked.

"When I am expecting David to come over, the passion I feel is less complicated. It has lightness and joy in it. I know it will be wonderful to see him and that he will be very happy to see me. I know there will be warmth and playfulness and sensuality that will drive me crazy because he loves to drive me crazy that way. I guess if you could measure the degree of passionate intensity and forget the quality of it, you would have to say that what I felt with Kevin was more intense. But the passion I feel with David is so much better! It leaves me feeling glowing and wonderful about myself, and it extends into all areas of our relationship."

This is a vivid statement of the power of *mutual passion* to bind and transform each of the lovers and the relationship. If the passion is not mutual, as with Kim's one-way passion for Kevin, it can be extraordinarily heated and yet more a basis for torment than for a gratifying love relationship. If the relationship is companionable and friendly but without much passion, it can be serviceable and in many ways satisfying, but it may carry less potential for transcending the ordinary and for provoking growth and intimacy.

Again, both poles of the paradox contain truth, and yet each pole without the other does not contain the whole truth. There is no question of the importance of passion in giving a love relationship vitality, but passion without friendship, sharing, and responsibility can be disastrous. If your passion has usually been tied to someone who, for whatever reason, is bad for you, I cannot guarantee that you will experience the same kind of inflamed excitement with someone who is good for you. A certain element of that old passion may be inextricably tied to the kind of person who provokes the old, self-destructive Attachment Hunger yearnings. But neither could I guarantee anyone who gives up cocaine that they will experience the same ecstatic high from jogging or meditating or loving that they experienced from coke. I could assure them, however, that these pursuits would provide them with a wonderful, more deeply satisfying high than a toxic mind-altering chemical. In like manner I can assure you that you can find passion in the caring, sharing, and reliability of a good and mutual love relationship. And while it may not have the same crazy intensity of your old destructive fix, it can be the most deeply satisfying high of your life. It may even turn out to be, as many people have discovered, even more exciting.

13

QUESTIONS AND
ANSWERS

During the seven years that my syndicated column "On Your Own" appeared in newspapers in the United States and Canada, many readers wrote with deeply personal and troubled questions about their romantic relationships. I have selected a number of their questions and the answers I gave. Together, these questions and answers cover all aspects of relationships—how to find them, evaluate them, keep them, nurture them, end them, live with them, and live without them. While the questions reflect the unique concerns of the individuals who asked them, I often used their queries as a springboard to dive into the broader underlying issues. This should make these questions and answers generally relevant to anyone who is seeking to finally get it right.

◆

Q I know that being open is an important part of intimacy, but I often wonder when I'm on a date how open to be about my insecurities. I'm torn between wanting to reveal feeling insecure or having self-doubts at times and fearing that I'll turn the other person off. How open should I be about revealing my insecurities?

A Revealing vulnerabilities and sharing doubts about oneself is just as important a part of intimacy as sharing hopes and dreams. Bonds of compassion and involvement can develop more easily when you do not put on a false front for someone.

In addition, there is something wonderful about finding out that even though we reveal our self-doubts and our greatest faults and vulnerabilities, others could like us. It nourishes us when we find that others would accept us with our insecurities and not cringe or dismiss us as weak.

But with all the positives that can come from self-revelation, it's still a very bad idea to advertise our feelings of self-dislike or lack of confidence early in a relationship. And there is no reason to highlight or dwell on past problems that you've had with work, with the opposite sex, or just with yourself. The relationship has to develop a foundation of fun, sharing, caring, and trust. And this has to be done slowly, so the foundation can support the revealing of the negatives. Then, the self-revelation will help build the caring and trust, rather than overwhelm the relationship.

While this kind of openness enhances intimacy by gradually letting the other person glimpse the real you, making a first or second date a confessional can have the effect of trying to force intimacy. Also, confessionals are sometimes used to test the other person's intentions and interests. They can be a way of saying, "Here's everything you could possibly find fault with in me—now can you deal with me? Are you going to reject me?" This type of communication has more to do with insecurity and defensiveness than it does with openness. It places an undue burden of responsibility on your date to reassure you and is more likely to push him or her away.

Openness entails a wish to reveal ourselves to another and contains within it an invitation for the other to get close. But forming a relationship also means tuning in to the other person and requires sensitivity to the pace of self-revelation he or she is comfortable with. So let the self-revelation flow gradually, naturally, and with good judgment as you get to know the other person.

◆

Q I have been seeing this man for a number of years, and I love him very much. During our entire relationship he's been trying to obtain his divorce, and it often seemed as if it would never come through. But last week, it finally did. When he told me, I was thrilled, but immediately after I got a migraine headache and I have felt sick ever since. Sick and shaky. I don't understand it. Do you?

A It quite often happens that when a person wants (or thinks he wants) something that is out of reach, suddenly getting it is surprisingly upsetting.

There is such a wide range of possible reasons for this that you will have to look very carefully into your own thoughts and feelings to figure out why you have reacted so strongly. But here are some possibilities that you can check out.

1. Possibly you were drawn not so much to this particular man as to the challenge of winning him. His belonging to someone else may have given him an exciting aura that he has now lost.

Even if you find this to be true, that doesn't mean he's not for you. It means that you have to distinguish between that part of your attraction that was to him as an unattainable man and that part that is to qualities and attributes that he has. You may still love him for these even if the old challenge isn't there.

2. His availability means that certain dreams can come true—dreams of being together, perhaps even being married. And with that, lots of fears may enter—fears of the unknown ahead, of commitment, of growing up, of having a man of your own, of whether he will continue to love you now that you can be together more, etc.

Your body is giving you a message that there are other feelings you are having besides pure joy that he is free. In time you will see what those feelings are if you get yourself to look at them.

◆

Q For the past four years I have been very involved with a man I love. We have broken up and come back together several times. The problem—and I know it must sound trite—is that he says he loves me but doesn't want a commitment. I do. How can I know that while he doesn't want a commitment now, he won't change his mind in a year or so?

A The fact is, you can't know. All you can know is that he clearly states he doesn't want a commitment now and that he has given you no reason to expect that he will change his mind. Ask yourself: If I felt the chances were very, very small that he would want a committed relationship with me at any time in the future, would I still want to stay with him for the enjoyment and good feelings I get out of it? What if I knew the chances of commitment were zero? How important is commitment to me? If I continue to see him, how much does it interfere with my meeting others? How long am I willing to give it?

There are no right or wrong answers to these questions. But it is very important not to fool yourself with false beliefs such as: (1) He is the one and only man in the world who I could love, be happy with, feel fulfilled with, enjoy sex with, etc.; (2) No other man will ever love me; or (3) He's bound to change his mind since it's so good between us.

A caring and enjoyable relationship is precious, and you seem to have that with him. If commitment is important to you, then look at the facts coldly to estimate what you think the chances are of also having that with him. Then you have to decide how much more time you're willing to give it and set a limit, at least in your own head, and not let the relationship go on endlessly as it is.

◆

Q I am a forty-year-old fairly successful businessman. I was married at twenty-four, divorced at twenty-six, and have been single ever since. I find that I am just not the type for long relationships. I've been in a number of close, intense relationships with women, including periods of living together, and none of them seems to last more than two years. After the first year or so, my interest tapers off and I want to move on. I am not particularly bothered by this. In fact, this pattern seems to suit me well. But I wonder if there is something wrong with me for not liking to have longer relationships.

A Whether or not there's "something wrong" with you depends on whether your pattern is truly a preference or is based on unconscious fears and needs.

For example, I have known men (and women) who get a tremendous high out of the seduction and conquest of someone new. It makes them feel alive, attractive, worthwhile, and very good about themselves when they make someone "crazy about them." But soon after they are assured of the other person's love, the high wears off and they must find somebody else. They have become conquest junkies.

I have known other men and women who are so afraid of being trapped and losing their independence and selfhood that soon after they get into a relationship they are looking for the exit door. Often these people have strong, hidden dependency needs and are afraid these needs will give the other person too much power.

Others have patterns similar to yours because they are so afraid of being rejected or abandoned by the other person that they have to quit before they may be fired.

Others are just incapable of relating on a deep level or caring about the other person, being mainly interested in getting their own needs met. As the relationship continues and the other person's needs require attention, they feel burdened and want out.

So you have to check your own motivations, as honestly as you can, to see if there are unknown fears and needs moving you or if this pattern is simply a preference and best meets your lifestyle, rhythms, and goals.

Why bother to check it out? Because there is much that you

give up in not having a sustained intimate relationship (just as there is much that people give up if they do). You give up the opportunity to grow through knowing and caring for another person, to risk being known and cared about, to share burdens and joys, to build a common history, and possibly, to create a family. So take a long look at what your pattern is all about.

◆

Q I'm fifty-three, and in the ten years since my husband died I have had several exciting and tumultuous affairs. For the past three years I have been going with a wonderful man. We have a close, warm monogamous relationship, but it does not have the excitement of previous affairs. At times I miss that, but mostly I'm very content and satisfied. Am I "settling" for something I should not be settling for?

A People find different types of relationships attractive at different times in their lives for the simple reason that their needs change. When you were younger, your need for passion and dramatic tension may have been much stronger than your need for emotional compatibility or for stable caring and commitment. Neither type of need or relationship is right or wrong. What is important is that you know your current preferences and that you feel free to choose what meets your needs at this point in your life.

Passion and some excitement are precious to a romantic relationship at any age. For many people it is essential. Only you can decide if there is enough excitment in the relationship to keep you feeling emotionally connected and involved with this man. If it seems there is not, you may have to let the relationship go, but it may be worth your while first to explore what the missing element is for you, whether it is missing because you are still looking for the kind of triggers of excitement that are no longer as appropriate or available. Earlier in life, your excitement may have been based on trying to overcome barriers between you and the man you were excited about, such as being attracted to his being unattainable, unreliable, self-centered, or withdrawn. The challenge of winning him and the anxiety of never feeling sure of him may have created a mixture of turbulence and passion that made you feel very alive. Certain specific physical attributes may have been all important. Perhaps now you can find excitement by concentrating on the positive aspects of this man, such as his being "close, warm and monogamous." Can you let those "close, warm" feelings add to the sensuality and intimacy of your relationship? Can you find in him any of the old elements that have previously been turn-ons?

While you can't force yourself to feel passion, you can give yourself the time to see if more excitement and intensity can grow on a different basis than in your previous affairs.

◆

Q I am involved with a sweet, bright, pretty woman who openly expresses her love for me. I can feel there's love in me for her that wants to come out, but it's behind an iron wall. Letting myself feel it has only led to horror before. I was married to a woman I met when we were both in law school. We were very in love and it was the happiest time of my life. Then she got her first job as a lawyer and the next thing I knew she left me for one of the senior partners. I was a basket case for a long time.

After several years I met another woman and my feelings began to thaw out. Everything began to go well and I began to feel happy again. Then she was in a terrible accident. After two months in a coma, she died. The woman I see now knows all this and reassures me, "I'm not going anywhere, and I will take very good care of myself." I can't help holding back. Sometimes I want to end it just to stop my conflict, and I may have to if I can't let myself love her. What can I do?

A There are many walking wounded who have suffered the loss of relationships although they may not have had experiences as dramatic as yours. They want love but are afraid of getting hurt again. What can be done to restore the courage to love? Here are some guidelines:

1. Don't pretend that you don't want a love relationship when you really do. Keep yourself aware that it has much to offer you and that the issue is not that you don't want it but that you are afraid.

2. Go slowly. Give yourself enough time to heal but not so much time that the scab hardens into a shell.

3. Recognize that the casualties of your losses include not only your trust in other people but also your trust in your own judgment about people and whether they are good for you. Going slowly and keeping your eyes open can help you restore trust in your own judgment.

4. If you are getting involved with someone but are hesitant, explain your fears to him or her and ask for the patience, understanding, and time you will need.

5. Be alert to any tendencies to develop a theory that you are doomed to be unlucky—that it's not in your stars to have a love relationship and that, if you try to, something bad will always happen. It is an understandable but false belief that is dangerous to your well-being and undermines your motivation to reach out again.

6. Get involved in activities, courses, and friendships. Increase your capacity to be alone and feel OK about it. These things will not give you what a loving hug can give, but it can make it feel less risky when you let that hug happen.

7. If you accomplish these things, and still are unable to risk feeling real love, then get yourself into psychotherapy to help you deal with and decrease the roots of your fear. Don't let your past experiences cripple your future.

◆

Q I always seem to get attracted to women who are of another color or another religion. I don't think I can marry someone where the difference is so great, so the relationship soon hits a wall, but I'm much more intensely attracted to these women than to women who are similar to me in background. I am worried about it because I am in my mid-thirties and I am looking to settle down but this problem stands in the way. Have you heard about this? What can I do?

A First, let's make it clear that the main issue you present is not that you are *sometimes* attracted to people of a different race or religion. That's true for most people. The issue is that you are intensely attracted *only* to people of different back-grounds and are not turned on by people whose background is more like yours. You have restricted your capacity to be attracted to members of a whole group. What makes it a problem is that you have taken away your own freedom to be drawn to certain women on the basis of whether they, as individuals, appeal to you.

What may go into it? If you were attracted to women of only a single different religion or race, we might speculate that you had some childhood experiences with someone from that group that felt so warm, exciting, and enjoyable that they shaped your taste in women. But for you, the appealing factor is mainly that they be in a group other than your own.

This can suggest two possibilities. First, you may have had some early experiences with some woman or women of your own background that were particularly distasteful or even frightening and you carry those feelings with you. For example, I know a man whose mother was so harsh, punitive, and controlling that he just couldn't be attracted to anyone remotely like her. Second, and seemingly almost the opposite, you may have been initially attracted to women of your own racial and religious group and this attraction felt taboo because it was toward "forbidden" peo-ple. For example, I know a woman whose father was so seductive and aroused such a mixture of sexual feelings and fear in her that she could only be attracted to men as different from him as possible. Exploring your own background and feelings with these possibilities in mind may help you to find out how your choices got narrowed. What you learn may free you from some of the restrictions the past has put on your feelings and thereby enable you to feel attraction where you haven't before.

While you're exploring, try on one more idea. Since you are only attracted to those you consider not marriageable and you are not attracted to those you consider marriageable, is it possi-ble that it's a way of avoiding the "settling down" you say you want?

And if you do want to settle down, there is another direction you could consider. Unless it's against your religious values or your very strong preferences, perhaps you ought to think over whether you really want to exclude as potential marriage partners the women who you currently find so attractive. Attraction is not enough to make a good relationship, but it's nothing to be sneezed at.

◆

Q I am one miserable guy because my girlfriend, Marilyn, just broke up with me after two years. It was like a bolt out of the blue. I never loved anyone so much. She had always said that she hated my temper and that it scared her, but after my explosions I would always apologize and buy her a present or flowers and we would make up, so I thought everything was all right. Could she really have been that turned off by my temper?

A Unfortunately, you refused to take seriously the many warnings she gave you that your temper not only upset and frightened her but was making her lose respect and love for you. You are not alone in facing such a rude awakening because of a failure to take a partner's complaints seriously.

Joan, a thirty-one-year-old interior decorator was devastated and furious when Paul told her he wanted to end it. He had been complaining throughout the two years they lived together that he didn't want her to schedule so many social appointments for them, that he would like more quiet evenings alone with her. When he ended it, she called him and promised to listen to his requests if he would come back, but he had met someone new who liked quiet evenings at home. Later, she said, "I never took him seriously because when we went out with other people he seemed to have a good time. But I have to admit he kept telling me he couldn't stand it."

Ted, a twenty-nine-year-old crane operator said, "She used to tell me that she wanted me to be more affectionate and to pay more attention to what she needed sexually. But I used to say, 'If you don't like it, get out.' And now she has and I'd do anything to take back those words." Later, Ted added, "She also used to plead with me to go to a therapist with her to work on our relationship, and I would tell her that she was the one who wasn't happy with things, so why should I go? Now I've told her I was wrong and I'd go with her and I'd work hard on it, but she says it's too late."

Margaret, a fifty-five-year-old widow and retired school-teacher, said, "I started going out with Mack about two years after my husband died. I was glad to have a man in my life again and I loved him, but it would make me furious when he told me that I was drinking too much. I would scream at him and tell him he was crazy. One night he came to pick me up to go to his daughter's house for dinner and I had been drinking before he came. He wouldn't take me. He said that I was in no shape to go and that I would never embarrass him again. He left, and it was over. I cried for days, but it led to my getting into a program and really quitting alcohol. I think of calling him, but I don't know if he could ever trust me again."

The message in all this is clear. If your partner in a love relationship is consistently complaining about some aspect of your behavior, even if it seems minor to you ("She said it was turning her off that I was getting fat, but—"), you ignore the complaint at your own peril. Just about everyone has a saturation point—a point at which feelings of dissatisfaction can wash away feelings of liking and loving. And once those positive feelings are gone, they may not be able to be restored.

Does that mean you should modify your every behavior in accordance with the other person's complaint for fear of losing him or her? Of course not. The important thing is that you hear the complaint, that you let yourself understand that your partner really feels that way. Then you can decide what to do about it. You may decide it is something about yourself that you feel you can't or don't want to change even if not changing means risking the relationship. You may decide to try to negotiate some compromises. But at least you wouldn't be in the awful position of feeling, I should have listened.

◆

Q I've been going with Dana for over a year, and we spend most weekends and usually one night during the week together. It seems that about four out of five times we stay at her place, though I often ask her to stay at mine. We live fairly close to each other, and we each have fairly comfortable apartments. But she always has some reason why it would be better to stay at her place. I think it's just a matter of her convenience, and I'm tired of being the displaced one. What can I do?

A Unless there is some overriding reason that Dana hasn't told you about for her always wanting to stay at her place, it may simply be self-serving for her not to have divided visits more equally. While some people prefer, for one reason or another, to stay over at the residence of the other, most like the comfort of being in their own home where all their things are, rather than having to lug clothes, toiletries, the book they are reading, etc. So Dana may be putting her convenience over her sense of fairness to you. But what's more important, you may be, too.

If your requests have not changed anything, it may be time for you to take a clear stand. Ask her to sit down with you and divide it out more equally. All it may require is your taking the initiative firmly. If she still avoids going along with this, next time you go out and she insists on returning to her place, say good night. It wouldn't feel good to spend the night with her under such conditions.

More importantly, if she isn't responsive to your request, you should question if this self-centeredness is limited to this one isolated area or is characteristic of Dana in the relationship with you. And it would be a good idea to question yourself about the extent of this imbalance and about why you let it go on for so long. Does this imbalance occur in other areas of the relationship? Are you afraid of Dana? Do you fear her anger or rejection if you stand up for your needs and wants?

If the answer to these questions is yes, then you have not been self-respecting and have to focus on changing the balance in the relationship. If the answer is no, then it is an isolated issue but still needs addressing.

◆

Q My boyfriend and I have been together for two years. One
night a few months ago we both had too much to drink
and got into a big fight. He said he was finished with me. A week
later, he called me and we spent the day together. After this he
slowly came back. Now I see him every day, we're always together, and our relationship has grown stronger in many ways.
Sometimes he openly points out that he is my boyfriend but at
other times he says he isn't. I am very puzzled. I know that in his
mind I am his girlfriend. His actions tell me this. He tells me
that he loves me and that he does not go out with other girls. I
don't know what to think. Is he afraid of commitment because
of our fight? Or is it something else?

A I can't know what's in your boyfriend's mind but here are
some possibilities:
   1. Something that you said in that fight may have upset him
and made him very cautious about you. That's the possibility you
can most easily check out with him.
   2. The fight only brought to the surface underlying negative
feelings he has about being close to you (there are always underlying negative feelings) and he has not yet come to terms with
them and decided whether his positive feelings outweigh them
enough to go further with the relationship.
   3. It may be that he is afraid of commitment and vacillates
between his caring for you and his fear. Perhaps his anger in the
big fight was a product of his fear of commitment and he was
finding reasons to angrily end the relationship.
   4. Some people have almost split personalities, with a part of
them that can be loving, giving, and intimate, and another part
that is antagonistic, ungiving, and distant. Sometimes alcohol
triggers their going from one personality to the other. Maybe that
happened to him that night.
   Those are some possibilities. But now that you've asked me,
why not ask him? Tell him you're puzzled. Ask him if he is aware
of the double messages he is sending you. Ask him what he understands about why he does that. Ask him if he's in conflict
about you and about commitments. Ask these questions in a way

that brings things, not to a showdown, but out into the open, where the two of you can look at them and deal with them. Your current lack of good communication could imperil any relationship. Take this situation as a crucial opportunity to get the necessary communication on track.

♦

Q My girlfriend and I frequently go away weekends and she, more often than not, falls asleep on the drive home. She says I should take it as a sign of her trust. However, I feel abandoned and I think she's inconsiderate. When I say that, she feels I am being ridiculous and selfish. Who is right?

A The chances are you are overreacting. Your girlfriend may simply be feeling relaxed in the aftermath of a romantic weekend; hers may be the comfortable sleep of someone who feels cozy and satisfied. If you did not feel so abandoned by it, you might be able to take pleasure in her enjoyment of that kind of delicious nap.

But it may not be so simple. You may be picking up something that does require your notice. For example, does her sleeping reflect unspoken depressed and negative feelings about the weekend or the relationship? Does it reflect a need to withdraw from you? You can investigate these questions by reviewing in your mind how the weekend and the relationship have been going. Does it seem to you that she has been happy, feeling close to you and enjoying being with you? If so, her sleeping doesn't carry a message of abandonment. If you have any doubts, discussing your observations and concerns with her can help clear them up.

It also can be annoying that, since you have told her you are unhappy about her falling asleep, she doesn't seem to make any effort not to do it. Again, look into the larger context. Is it typical of her not to respond to your requests? You may be reacting so strongly because you feel it's one more example of her lack of consideration. But if it's not typical of her, then you have to ask yourself why you respond with such feelings of abandonment. Is that an old, repeated feeling? Does it grow out of earlier relationships in your life? Do you get too uneasy if you are "alone" for a while? Do you need her to pay attention to you every minute? Are you centering on your needs and not respecting that her needs may at times be different?

If your reviewing the relationship and your self-exploration help you feel more accepting of her sleep, fine. If not, perhaps you can work out a compromise where she satisfies some of her wish to nap and you satisfy more of your wish for her company.

◆

Q I know I am not that attractive to men on the first meeting. Please don't tell me it's all in my head, because I've had more experiences than I'd care to remember of being at singles events and bars where nobody approached me. The few good relationships I've had were with men I met at work where, over a period of time, my personality could shine through. I'm not likely to meet anyone new at my current job, and I don't want to keep changing jobs. So now what?

A No, I won't tell you it's all in your head. There is no question that some people are better than others at initially attracting the opposite sex. It's unfair, but it's true. But there are things you can do to increase your chances of getting relationships started. They fall into two broad categories: finding the best situations for your most appealing self to emerge, and making the most of any opportunity to meet a man. As for the first, you already know when your most appealing self comes through—in situations where you and a man are engaged in a common interest or project. Depending on your interest, it could be a class, a political campaign, a cause, a sport, or an activity. I know a woman who felt like a disaster area at a bar but dated many men she met at a weekend hiking club, finally marrying one. As for making the most of every opportunity to meet a man, this involves several factors: (1) getting good advice on enhancing your appearance through clothing, makeup, diet, etc.; (2) daring to make friendly eye contact with a man you'd like to know; and (3) daring to approach a man you want to meet and engaging in the type of conversation that would let your personality *shine through*. It is important not to let your past rejections make you so afraid of further ones that you avoid reaching out.

◆

Q My closest friend is very attractive to men, and whenever we go to a singles function together the men gather around her like flies and totally ignore me. I like being with her, but it's murder to my morale. Do I have to stop going places with her in order to meet a guy? I hate going to these things alone.

A The attractiveness of your friend is obviously sufficiently magnetic that, on first meeting, you might suffer in comparison. So why consistently put yourself in that situation? Occasionally, it may be okay, but not with great frequency. Besides being damaging to your morale, it may really keep you from connecting with some men who are bedazzled by your friend's looks.

There are many ways you and your friend can keep the friendship strong and many places to go together that do not involve a competitive singles scene. You could meet to go to dinner, the movies, the theater, or museums or just visit each other.

As for hating to go to singles functions alone, you sound as if that particular friend is the only one you can go with. If that's true, one of your goals should be to make other friends that you can buddy with in braving the adventures of single places and events.

It is also important to recognize that the fears and anxieties that cause you to avoid going by yourself are hangovers of old feelings of inadequacy and self-doubt that almost everyone has to some degree. They are not based on realistic assessment of your value, attractiveness, or ability to handle social situations. Once you recognize this, you will be able to venture out to singles functions on your own.

◆

Q In some of your columns you wrote that personal ads can be a sensible way to meet people I am thirty-five and have been getting discouraged about how few compatible men I've been meeting in other ways, so I recently decided both to answer and place ads. So far I've had dates with two men, and I have a few more arranged. That part is great. But I find meeting with these men very awkward and unnatural. It's just too clear that we are there to look each other over. When I'm awkward I don't come across at my best. Am I unusual this way? What can I do to relax?

A   No, you're not unusual in feeling this way. It is a contrived situation. Certainly, it's different than getting to know someone at work or in a class. A letter from two researchers at the Department of Communications at Illinois State University in Normal, Illinois, made this preliminary observation: "In our inquiries we have found that the flirtation step of ordinary courtship is omitted by the very form of the personal ad and, more importantly, that the people who reply to personal ads move directly from greetings to self-disclosure, omitting the common step of small talk. It is very frank, almost a sort of 'I've told you what I am, now here I am: Take it or leave it' attitude. One must be ready to commence the relationship on a dead run!"

Since it can be difficult to meet new people, do not rule out ads because of this drawback. The question is, how can you make the situation more comfortable for yourself? Try talking to your date about your feelings that the situation is contrived and that it makes you feel a bit awkward, and ask him if he feels the same way. Or perhaps you can try what one man I know did when he met his "personal ad" date at a restaurant. He said, "This feels very unnatural. Let's make believe I just saw you at the bar over there and decided it would be nice to get to know you." She laughed and said, "Come here often?"

Don't get discouraged. The letter from the same Illinois State University Researchers adds, "Still, a number of people seem to find partners and mates by this means." I know of several good marriages of people who met through personal ads, as well as many relationships that did not lead to marriage but were significant and enjoyable. While sensible judgment should be used in screening who you agree to meet, initially getting together in a public place, and in pacing the relationship, these ads satisfy a real need for many.

◆

Q My last boyfriend, Fred, was someone I could really show off. He was good looking, outgoing, and a successful TV newscaster. I liked the way my friends and family responded to him. They seemed to look up to me because of Fred. But we had little in common, and I felt lonely with him most of the time. Last year I stopped seeing him and soon after I began dating Larry, a pharmacist who owns his own drugstore. Larry is quiet, introverted, and not as good looking as Fred. We get along very beautifully, but other people don't respond to him as enthusiastically as they did to Fred. I feel frustrated and uneasy that I can't show him off. Even though I want to keep liking him, my feelings are beginning to change. Maybe I'm just someone who needs a man people can look up to. Is that possible?

A Most of us feel good when others respond favorably to the person we are dating. It can make us feel a touch of pride that someone who others value has chosen to be with us. We might even enjoy some reflected glory and perhaps get a kick out of being an object of envy. But, as you discovered with Fred, and as countless others have unhappily found, other people's favorable responses are not nearly enough to make a relationship satisfying.

To be solid, a relationship must be based on the one-to-one interactions between the partners. This involves feeling good with each other, mutual caring, and being on each other's wavelength. You seem to have a solid relationship with Larry, and it would be too bad if you wreck it by overemphasizing how others respond to him.

The enjoyment you get out of other people's positive reactions to your partner should be the icing that tops the relationship. Thinking of it as the cake—as you are in danger of doing when you say, "Maybe I'm someone who needs a man other people can look up to"—can lead to some regrettable choices.

What you have to look at is the apparent shakiness of your self-esteem. You have to ask yourself, "What in my life history has made me so dependent on what others think?" Do you want to continue having others' opinions (or what you think are their opinions) determine who you will be with? Or can you muster the courage to believe that you know better than anyone else who is right for you?

Your best bet would be to work on these issues, rather than moving to end your relationship with Larry.

◆

Q I'm a thirty-three-year-old, single genetics researcher, and I am very respected in my field. Everyone says I am successful and mature. What people don't know is that most nights, particularly when I'm feeling tense or lonely, I sleep with a stuffed animal. It's a panda that I've had since childhood. I can sleep without him if I have to, like when I'm traveling or trying to prove that I can be without him. And I have no interest in sleeping with him when there's a man in my life I feel close to. But there are nights I find it difficult to fall asleep without my panda. I never told anyone this because I'm ashamed of it. And I'm too ashamed to sign this letter. Is my "relationship" with my panda sick?

A There is nothing sick or shameful about an attachment to a stuffed animal. Objects such as a teddy bear, a security blanket, or your panda help people bridge the transition from one stage in our development to another.

Why, for example, does Linus, the little boy in the "Peanuts" comic strip, always carry his security blanket? It stands for the comfort and warmth of mother. The blanket is an object that Linus can carry with him as he goes out into the world to meet its stresses and challenges. With it he can become more independent from his mother and yet carry around this symbolic representation of her to give him a sense of security. It helps him to go from the early stage of being attached to her to later stages of separateness.

Adults, too, sometimes need what we call "transitional objects" when they go from one stage of development to another. It's not uncommon for students going off to college to take along something they don't need—like a candle from their collection, a particular pillow, or a tattered poster—that makes them feel connected to home just when they are taking a giant step away. Sometimes, too, when older adults make moves toward greater autonomy or success, they deal with their anxieties by clinging to something from the past. Many times, when we keep something for *sentimental reasons*—an old address book, a certain piece of clothing that we wouldn't dare wear anymore, a present we got on a birthday long ago—we are really holding them as transitional objects.

Single people, because they are more likely to spend time alone, are often in greater need of attachment to some kind of security blanket. In a marriage, the spouse can provide the needed security, as can a home and child. A husband or wife may go out each day to slay dragons, but the connection to the spouse still serves as a basis for security. (Even so, transitional objects, such as a family photograph kept at work, can help when things get rough.)

Some widowed or divorced people find that by keeping objects from their old relationship around, they feel less alone and less vulnerable. These objects are a source of comfort as the individuals go forward to new experiences.

Can our use of transitional objects ever become unhealthy? Yes. It can be unhealthy if the attachment to the object is so great that separation from it is traumatic and unbearable, as sometimes happens with Linus when he loses touch with his blanket. It can be unhealthy if the attachment keeps the person from moving forward. Such was the case with one woman, an unmarried college professor I know, who made her apartment a kind of transitional object. The apartment was a tiny efficiency in a rundown, unsafe building. Although this woman claimed she wanted to move to a larger, better place and could certainly afford to do so, she was unable to break her attachment. It was not until she was nearly raped by an intruder that she could look for another apartment.

Transitional objects can also be unhealthy when the object itself is harmful. A cigarette can be a transitional object. As something we put in our mouths and draw on, a cigarette can stand for our early attachment to mother. (Perhaps that's why smokers smoke more when they are nervous and need comfort.) But here the object itself is destructive.

Your attachment to your panda, however, is not hazardous to your health. In your letter you indicate that you can live without it, and it seems that you are living a mature, independent life on your own. Perhaps your panda is helping you do so.

◆

Q I can get very turned on sexually with a man I like and find attractive until he shows that he's beginning to be in love with me. Then I just shut down and become physically unresponsive. This is crazy and frustrating. I'm thirty years old, and I want a close love relationship. What's wrong with me?

A The reasons behind this problem differ from person to person, but there are some reasons that can serve as guidelines for honest self-exploration.

1. For some people the turn-on may be to someone who is not emotionally available. They get very aroused by the challenge of making a person become responsive to them. But when the person does respond, the challenge is over and so is the excitement. When people have this problem, there was often someone important in their early life—usually one parent or both— who was emotionally unavailable. This caused them to be programmed into a pattern of trying over and over again to win a loving response. They need to change that programming so the excitement can be in giving, getting, and maintaining love, not in winning it. To do this, they have to understand how they got destructively programmed and to make up their mind to stay with a good loving relationship and to work on bringing their sexual feelings to it.

2. Some people are afraid of being exploited or engulfed by another person. They feel vulnerable because they are aware of their own neediness and wishes to be dependent. They therefore avoid total involvement by being in relationships that are primarily sexual, with no strong feelings of closeness and loving, or close and loving but without sexual passion.

3. Some people see sex and love almost as opposite experi-

ences. Gail, a thirty-two-year-old ballet dancer said of the problem she was having with her boyfriend, "When I'm close to Evan and feel his loving feelings toward me, I just want to be held and cuddled. All is calm and beautiful. Then, when he moves toward sex, I tighten up because it feels like the sex is something tumultuous and violent that upsets the calm feeling. It's like a cyclone coming on a beautiful and serene summer day and I become afraid." Very often people for whom there is such a sharp break between love and sex had early traumatic sexual experiences. Perhaps they were molested as children. Perhaps there were some incestuous overtones or acts on the part of someone in the family. Perhaps they were severely punished for sexual play. Some people react as Gail does. Others can enjoy their sexuality but only as a dissociated act.

4. Some people feel, usually unconsciously, that they are forbidden to have a good love relationship with someone all their own. Often this arises out of early feelings of rivalry that seem wrong and unacceptable. A little girl who feels her father is more drawn to her than to her mother or who is always in rivalry with her sister for her father's love may as an adult feel inhibitions about winning a love relationship. A little boy who feels in competition with his father or brother for his mother's love may also later be afraid of the triumph of having a good love and sex relationship. By splitting love from sex, these people sabotage the relationship and sooner or later destroy it.

5. There are people whose self-esteem is so low that they believe that they must have someone particularly worthy, even "perfect," to make them feel they are worthwhile. But since they themselves feel so unworthy, anyone who would love them can't be a worthy enough person to feel excited about.

People who separate love from sex have to work on understanding the fears, taboos, and inhibitions that are involved and to feel entitled to have the priceless experience of combining caring and passion.

LOVE NOTES
Aphorisms & Affirmations to Guide You to The Real Thing

A love relationship should make you feel better about yourself and your life—not worse.

◆

You deserve to be the number one person in the life of the number one person in your life.

◆

To have a satisfying love relationship, you must give up your lifelong task of trying to make someone unavailable available, someone ungiving giving and someone unloving loving.

◆

To feel in love in a bad love relationship is not romantic but painful and depressing; to feel in love within a good relationship is joyful, energizing—and romantic.

◆

Figure out what is so appealing about those who are bad for you, and then avoid them like the plague.

◆

Be alert to the distortions of Addiction Amnesia: remembering only what was good in a bad relationship and forgetting what was awful.

Maintaining the false belief that your last love was the "one and only" person for you can keep you from a new love.

◆

"Because I love him (or her)" may sound romantic but is simply not a good enough reason to stay in an unhappy relationship.

◆

Having shared memories is not enough reason to stay in a bad relationship; you will take your story with you, and add to it, and share it anew.

◆

Know what you want in your life journey, and choose a love that will support rather than impede that journey.

◆

Figure out what has been so irresistibly appealing about the kind of person who has been bad for you and look for these traits in a non-toxic form in someone who would be good for you.

◆

Owning up to the possibility that you may be unconsciously avoiding a good love relationship and questioning why this may be so will give you some tools for changing your "bad luck."

◆

If the kind of person you know would be right for you never seems to turn you on, it is probably not because he or she is inherently unappealing but because you have a problem that causes you to make self-defeating choices.

◆

Don't ignore the imperfections of someone bad for you or magnify the imperfections of someone good for you.

◆

Understanding how your choices have been shaped and limited by your *past* can free you to see and choose a more fulfilling love relationship in the *present*.

◆

Increasing your ability to be loving makes you more attractive and appealing—particularly to those who are able to have a good love relationship.

Once you see and accept the other person for who he or she is, you can decide if there are enough ingredients for a good relationship for you to try to work it out.

◆

Your increased capacity to love can be directed outward and inward, so you can love someone deeply and still lovingly take good care of yourself.

◆

Tune in as attentively to your partner's needs and wants as you want your partner to tune into yours.

◆

Passion can lift a love relationship above the ordinary, particularly when it is accompanied by mutual caring.

◆

It may be better to give than receive, but appreciatively receiving the loving words and actions of your partner is a generous form of giving.

◆

You deepen your ability to love each time you see the other person clearly and accept who he is apart from your needs and demands.

◆

When you give up your demand that other people be and act according to your blueprint, you automatically reduce the anger, conflict, and disappointment that can destroy a relationship.

◆

You may be able to feel romantically in love with more than one person at a time but you cannot have a full love relationship with more than one person at a time.

◆

True intimacy requires that you risk letting the other person see your imperfections and vulnerabilities, and that takes a special kind of courage.

◆

Awareness of your connection to things timeless and bigger than yourself counters the narrowing effect of your Attachment Hunger and enlarges your capacity to love both others and yourself.

Accepting the person you love for who he or she is does not mean you must go along with all of his or her behavior, particularly if it is detrimental or offensive to you and others.

◆

Developing your independence does not mean that you are giving up on finding a love relationship—it will make you more ready and able to have one.

◆

A love relationship may progress from your seeing the wonder and beauty of the world in your beloved to finding the wonder and beauty of your beloved in many places in the world.

◆

A good love relationship can help heal many wounds of your childhood, but you must do considerable self-healing to be capable of a good love relationship.

◆

In developing intimacy, navigate between the dangers of keeping a relationship shallow versus prematurely overwhelming it with heavy self-revelations.

◆

You cannot force passionate feelings, but you can strive for the patience, openmindedness and openheartedness that might enable you to develop passion toward someone who is better for you than your previous choices.

◆

Let lovingness rather than unlovingness be your aphrodisiac.

◆

Tune in to what makes your partner feel loved and cared about and, unless it goes against your grain, do it!

◆

It is enriching to develop your capacity to be unconditionally loving, but never let your unconditional loving become unconditional masochism or self-disregard.

◆

It is as easy to love someone good for you as someone bad for you—but for some people it takes more work.

If you let yourself get close to good people who do not fit your usual checklist, you may open yourself to a love relationship with someone who has not been your "type."

◆

One commitment is essential—that you will each do all you can to make the relationship as loving and fulfilling as it can get.

◆

Keep growing as if you will be alone forever, but keep yourself open for friendship and love as if you will meet someone wonderful today.

◆

Use the painful and hard-won wisdom gained in failed loves to *finally get it right.*

BIBLIOGRAPHY

Brookner, Anita. *Latecomers*. New York: Vintage, 1990.

Branden, Nathaniel. *What Love Asks of Us*. New York: Bantam, 1983.

Freud, Sigmund. *Three Essays on the Theory of Sexuality*. S.E., 1905.

Fromm, Erich. *The Art of Loving*. New York: Harper and Row Perennial, 1974.

Gould, Steven J. *The Panda's Thumb*. New York: W. W. Norton, 1980.

Gurudev, Amrit Desai. "The True Experience of Love" in *The Kripalu Experience*. Lenox, Massachusetts: Kripalu Center, 1991.

Halpern, Howard. *You and Your Grownup Child*. New York: Simon & Schuster Fireside, 1992.

Hendrix, Harville. *Getting the Love You Want*. New York: Harper Perennial, 1990.

————. *Keeping the Love You Find*. New York: Pocket Books, 1992.

Horner, Althea. *Being and Loving*. Northvale, NJ: Jason Aronson, 1990.

Jeffers, Susan. *Opening Our Hearts to Men*. New York: Fawcett, 1989.

Kuriansky, Judith. *How to Love a Nice Guy*. New York: Pocket Books, 1991.

Lathrop, Don. "Date Rape" in *Voices: The Art and Science of Psychotherapy*. Volume 28, No. 1, 1992, p. 51.

LeShan, Lawrence. *How to Meditate*. New York: Bantam, 1975.

McCarthy, Mary. *The Company She Keeps*. New York: Avon, 1981.

Person, Ethel. *Dreams of Love and Fateful Encounters*. New York: Penguin, 1989.

Satir, Virginia. *Tape Cassette #18*. Crested Butte, Colorado: Blue Moon Cassettes, 1986.